TRANSFORMING TECHNOLOGY

TRANSFORMING TECHNOLOGY

A Critical Theory Revisited

ANDREW FEENBERG

OXFORD
UNIVERSITY PRESS

2002

OXFORD

UNIVERSITY PRESS

Oxford   New York

Athens   Auckland   Bangkok   Bogotá   Buenos Aires   Cape Town
Chennai   Dar es Salaam   Delhi   Florence   Hong Kong   Istanbul   Karachi
Kolkata   Kuala Lumpur   Madrid   Melbourne   Mexico City   Mumbai   Nairobi
Paris   São Paulo   Shanghai   Singapore   Taipei   Tokyo   Toronto   Warsaw

and associated companies in
Berlin   Ibadan

Copyright © 2002 by Oxford University Press

Published by Oxford University Press, Inc.
198 Madison Avenue, New York, New York 10016

Oxford is a registered trademark of Oxford University Press

This volume is a revised edition of *Critical Theory of Technology,*
published 1991 by Oxford University Press.

Library of Congress Cataloging-in-Publication Data
Feenberg, Andrew
Transforming technology : a critical theory revisited / Andrew Feenberg.—2nd ed.
p. cm.
Rev. ed. of: Critical theory of technology, 1991.
Includes bibliographical references and index.
ISBN 0-19-514615-8 (pbk.)
1. Technology—Philosophy.
2. Technology—Social aspects.
3. Critical theory.
I. Feenberg, Andrew. Critical theory of technology.
II. Title.
T14 .F43   2001
601—dc21   2001021399

1 3 5 7 9 8 6 4 2

Printed in the United States of America
on acid-free paper

Preface

Must human beings submit to the harsh logic of machinery, or can technology be fundamentally redesigned to better serve its creators? This is the ultimate question on which the future of industrial civilization depends. It is not primarily a technical question but concerns a fundamental issue in social philosophy, the neutrality of technology and the related theory of technological determinism. If technology is neutral, then its immense and often disturbing social and environmental impacts are accidental side effects of progress. Much current debate polarizes around the question of whether these side effects outweigh the benefits. The advocates of further progress claim "reason" as their ally, while the adversaries defend "humanity" against machines and mechanistic social organizations. The stage is set for a struggle for and against technology.

This book rejects this dilemma and argues that the real issue is not technology or progress per se but the variety of possible technologies and paths of progress among which we must choose. Determinists claim that there are no such alternatives, that technological advance always and everywhere leads to the same result. This view is increasingly contested by students of technology. But if alternatives do exist, the choice between them will have political implications.

Modern technology as we know it is no more neutral than medieval cathedrals or the Great Wall of China; it embodies the values of a particular industrial civilization and especially those of elites that rest their claims to hegemony on technical mastery. We must articulate and judge these values in a cultural critique of technology. By so doing, we can begin to grasp the outlines of another possible industrial civilization based on other values. This project requires a different sort of thinking from the dominant technological rationality, a critical rationality capable of reflecting on the larger context of technology.

These remarks, adapted from the preface to the previous edition, *Critical Theory of Technology*, were written ten years ago. It was easier then than now to make a case for radical change. The defeat of communism followed by ten years of economic growth has discredited social criticism. The power of positive thinking has never been more in evidence. But despite the remarkable achievements of these last ten years, it is reasonable to entertain doubts about the ability of this society to realize our ideals. Surely it is not necessary to list the many discouraging events and trends that justify these doubts. To give an example, a society that imprisons nearly 1 percent of its population is deeply flawed. And it is still the case that most work is unfulfilling, if not actually painful and dangerous. Nor have we found a general solution to the environmental problems caused by the technologies on which we rely for our vaunted "way of life." While we are more than ever aware of both the promise and the threat of technological advance, we still lack the intellectual means and the political tools for managing progress.

Critical Theory of Technology addressed these problems by reconstructing the idea of socialism on the basis of a radical philosophy of technology. The central concern of the book was the growing conflict between democracy and capitalist and technocratic forms of organization. This conflict is still with us, registered not only in the ever narrower scope of democratic political debate but also in the social sciences, which confidently predict the coming reign of expertise. The alternative proposed here is the democratization of the many technically mediated institutions of our society. That proposal had a favorable historical context when the book was originally conceived. It was easier then to imagine a utopian political discourse tested in practice in the turmoil of disintegrating communism. Now that context has disappeared, and it is necessary to rethink the rationale for continuing to discuss utopian political ideas.

In this new context, radical politics has a somewhat different character than it did a decade ago. We have learned the negative lessons of the fall of communism but have not yet devised positive aspirations that respond to new trends toward globalization and computerization. Indeed, one is struck by the generally negative tone of contemporary social democratic and left discourse. One focuses on defending the welfare state against corporate attacks, while the other spends far more time criticizing capitalism than explaining what will replace it.

This book, with its utopian revision of the idea of socialism, still has something to offer. Consider it a provocation to rethink fundamental modern institutions in the light of the aspirations that have driven modernity for the last few centuries. Socialism is the name for one influential movement inspired by these aspirations. For long periods socialists interpreted the limitations of capitalism economically and their main concern was therefore with economic justice and growth. In the 1960s socialism was recast as a radical democratic ideology in opposition to capitalist technocracy and communist bureaucracy. Since then it has been associated with a broad conception of human liberation that includes gender and racial equality, environmental reform, and the humanization of the labor process.

These issues have not been superannuated by successful reforms. On the contrary, the struggles continue under changed conditions. But today the link forged at the origin between these struggles and the demand for a socialist economic system seems strange. It is widely assumed that capitalism is simply an efficient way of organizing production and distribution. The old socialist arguments about obstacles to human fulfillment under capitalism seem to have been refuted, at least insofar as economic growth is concerned. *Critical Theory of Technology* responded to this objection by developing an entirely different interpretation of the structural problems of capitalism centered not on obstacles to growth but on the nature of capitalist technology and management. Critique of this sort originates with Marx. As I will show in later chapters, his understanding of the social nature of technology was far in advance of his time. We are still able to learn from this aspect of Marx's theory, even if many others are long since discredited.

The reader will have to judge the argument on its merits as I defend it in later chapters. However, I do want to emphasize at the outset that the collapse of the Soviet Union does not refute it. The conception of socialism sketched in this book was not modeled on Soviet practice, but it was influenced by a generation of popular reform movements in Eastern Europe that were suppressed by Soviet invasions and threats of invasion. Finally, under Gorbachev it seemed as though fresh ideas would get a chance in Russia itself. That hope was not unreasonable, however illusory it may seem in hindsight.

Earlier Eastern European protests could have inspired a transformation of the Soviet regime. Workers' councils in Hungary in 1956 and Yugoslav self-management suggested a radical power shift in industry, from the bureaucracy to workers. Independent unions in Poland and market and democratic reforms proposed during the Prague Spring of 1968 promised a revived economy and civil society. One could hope that these and other innovations would be introduced in the Soviet Union, combining elements of public ownership with worker-controlled cooperatives, some private enterprise, particularly in agriculture, and much-needed political democracy. Such an outcome might have shown the way beyond the sterile dilemma of capitalism versus communism. It is likely that the Russian people would be better off had they tried this approach.

Would this still have been "socialism"? Not in the eyes of the communist bureaucrats who overthrew Gorbachev and discredited the regime so thoroughly that communism and the Soviet Union disappeared with the failure of their brief coup. But when one compares orthodox communism with the idea of socialism as it was first formulated in Marx and Engels, one discovers more differences than similarities. The Soviets could reasonably claim Marxist sanction for industrial planning, security of employment, and low-cost basic necessities. But state ownership of the entire economy, even where technical conditions were unsuitable as in agriculture, the bureaucratization of every aspect of social life, political and police dictatorship, slave labor and mass murder, the reduction of art to propaganda, none of this has its source in Marx. Much of what passed for communism in the Soviet Union contradicted what socialism has meant historically outside the range of Stalin's police.

The fall of the Soviet Union was disappointing to anyone who hoped to see the development there of an original society building on the accomplishments of the past. On the other hand, most observers expected that Russia would be enriched by participation in the world market. The actual outcome has been catastrophic economic and social collapse under a system so corrupt and incompetent it beggars the imagination. But the failure of Russian capitalism has not rebounded to the credit of a socialist alternative embodying the hopes of the 1980s. It is as though socialism could still make a claim on our attention only so long as it had the power to shape an actual society in however perverted a form. Having lost that power, it has all but disappeared from public awareness except as a vague memory of an unsuccessful historical experiment.

Since then we have been living in a very strange time. The end of the Russian adventure justifies skepticism about any and all significant historical change. There is an iron law of history; it is just not the one Marx promulgated, but the one effectively realized in the triumph of capitalism. For a decade now, disillusionment with high ideals has cohabited with optimism on the stock market. Unbounded confidence in the future is fashionable so long as it is confined to quarterly reports. What is naive in the social critic counts as shrewdness in the investor. No one can predict how long this peculiar constellation will last. If a book like this one can still be of interest, it is because we are all more or less aware that it cannot last forever. To dismiss radical critique out of hand testifies to an unfortunate susceptibility to the "irrational exuberance" induced by an economic boom. The fact that intellectual complacency, even arrogance, is respectable today is hardly a reason to condone it. The inevitable bust that follows every boom can be counted on to teach humility in the face of the immense problems of even the most advanced of capitalist societies. Someday, probably sooner rather than later, we will want to rethink the plan of our social life. For that purpose we will need imaginative social criticism, and that is what I hope readers will find here.

The text of this new edition has been heavily revised to bring it up to date. In addition, I have added a chapter on online education, an application of ideas presented in chapter 4 (chapter 5 of the original edition). The introduction defines critical theory of technology and situates it in relation to other approaches.

Part I argues that for all its insight Marx's critique of industrialism lacks a plausible strategy of change. The historical experience of communism shows that Marx was wrong to believe that states could be the primary agents of radical technological transformation. Later attempts by Marcuse and Foucault to take into account the role of technology in modern societies offer promising starting points for a new formulation of radical theory.

Part II addresses the relationship of human initiative to technical systems in the field of computers. Since modern hegemonies are increasingly organized around technology, this relationship has become central to the exercise of political power. Computer design is now political design. The specific example of the debate over online education is discussed at length.

Part III considers the larger cultural context of technological change. Too often technology and culture are reified and opposed to each other in arguments about the "trade-offs" between efficiency and substantive goals such as participation or environmental compatibility. A better understanding of the relation of technology and culture dissolves these apparent contradictions. These considerations open the way to a discussion of a socialist alternative to the existing industrial society. The conclusion develops this argument further through a holistic critique of technology and a theory of its democratic potentialities. Although suppressed today, in the future these potentialities may become the basis for a society that reconciles wider freedoms with more meaningful forms of material well-being.

This new edition of *Critical Theory of Technology* can now be read alongside my two other books on philosophy of technology, *Alternative Modernity* (University of California Press) and *Questioning Technology* (Routledge). The first of these books explores the implications of technological struggles in a number of domains, including medicine and national identity. The second develops the implications of constructivism for philosophy of technology. Together, these books present a common position on the nature of technology and its relation to society. I hope that the argument will become clear considered from the different angles of approach each book offers to the central theme they share, the radical democratization of technological societies.

Portions of this book are adapted from the following articles with the permission of the publishers: "Transition or Convergence: Communism and the Paradox of Development," in Frederick Fleron, ed., *Technology and Communist Culture*, Praeger Publishers, 1977; "Technology Transfer and Cultural Change in Communist Societies," *Technology and Culture*, April 1979; "The Bias of Technology," in R. Pippin, A. Feenberg, and C. Webel, eds., *Marcuse: Critical Theory and the Promise of Utopia*, Bergin and Garvey Press, 1987; "The Ambivalence of Technology," *Sociological Perspectives*, Spring 1990; "The Critical Theory of Technology," *Capitalism, Nature, Socialism*, Fall 1990; "Democratic Socialism and Technological Change," in P. Durbin, ed., *Philosophy of Technology: Broad and Narrow Interpretations* (*Philosophy and Technology*, vol. 7), Kluwer, 1990; "Post-Industrial Discourses," *Theory and Society*, December 1990; "Distance Learning: Promise or Threat?" *Crosstalk*, Winter 1999; "Whither Educational Technology?" *Peer Review*, Summer 1999; "Will the Real Posthuman Please Stand Up! A Response to Fernando Elichirigoity," *Social Studies of Science*, vol. 30, no. 1 (February 2000). Reviewers for these journals gave me much good advice. Chapter 3 is based on a paper written with Andreas Huyssen and presented in 1980 to the conference titled "Rhetorics of Technology," Center for the Study of Linguistics and Semiotics, University of Urbino. We received precious help from Michel de Certeau in the preparation of that paper. I wish to also thank Rafael Heller and Todd Sallo for editorial help with the articles on which chapter 5 is based.

The first essays on which this work is based were written at the suggestion of Frederick Fleron Jr. I am grateful to him for introducing me to the problems treated here. Gerald Doppelt read through so much of the background material to this book over the years that it is impossible to thank him enough for his many contributions. Without his frequently sharp criticism, many of my ideas would never have developed and matured. The complete manuscript was read by Robert Pippin, Marc Guillaume, Douglas Kellner, and Mark Poster. Their comments, especially those of Pippin and Guillaume, who discussed their impressions with me at length, have made a great difference in the final result. My wife, Anne-Marie Feenberg, also read everything and helped me to better formulate my ideas. Matthew Robbins's editorial advice was invaluable. I am more grateful than I can say to my assistant throughout this project, Yoko Arisaka. Individual chapters, in various stages of disarray, were read by many colleagues over the years. I want especially to thank Maria Bakardjieva, Ellen Comisso, Frank Cunningham, Jean-Pierre Dupuy, Henry Ehrmann, Linda Harasim, David Harvey, Sharon Helsel, Martin Jay, Kathleen Jones, Michael Levin, Edward Lindblom, Robert Marotto, James O'Connor, Thomas Rockmore, and Langdon Winner. Thanks are also due to Ruth Heifetz, Paul Thomas, and Sandra Djikstra.

This book was written at the Western Behavioral Sciences Institute, where I have enjoyed the encouragement and support of the staff with whom I have worked on many projects that brought me a practical understanding of the nature of technology. The patience of my colleagues in the philosophy department at San Diego State University is once again warmly acknowledged.

La Jolla, California
December 2000   A. F.

Contents

TRANSFORMING TECHNOLOGY

1

Introduction
The Varieties of Theory

Technology and the End of History

It is widely believed that technological society is condemned to authoritarian management, mindless work, and equally mindless consumption. Social critics claim that technical rationality and human values contend for the soul of modern man. This book challenges such clichés by reconceptualizing the relation of technology, rationality, and democracy. My theme is the possibility of a truly radical reform of industrial society.

I argue that the degradation of labor, education, and the environment is rooted not in technology per se but in the antidemocratic values that govern technological development. Reforms that ignore this fact will fail, including such popular notions as a simplified lifestyle or spiritual renewal. Desirable as these goals may be, no fundamental progress can occur in a society that sacrifices millions of individuals to production and disempowers its members in every aspect of social life, from leisure to education to medical care to urban planning.

A good society should enlarge the personal freedom of its members while enabling them to participate effectively in a widening range of public activities. At the highest level, public life involves choices about what it means to be human. Today these choices are increasingly mediated by technical decisions. *What human beings are and will become is decided in the shape of our tools no less than in the action of statesmen and political movements.* The design of technology is thus an ontological decision fraught with political consequences. The exclusion of the vast majority from participation in this decision is profoundly undemocratic.

3

Fundamental change requires a democratic transformation of technology. Historically, such a transformation has been called "socialism," but ever since the Russian Revolution that term has described a particularly undemocratic version of a society very much like our own in such essential respects as the organization of education, work, and the media. The differences, significant though they were, hardly constituted the basis of a divergent civilizational model. The recent breakdown of these communist regimes and their Marxist orthodoxy creates an opportunity to revive interest in democratic socialist theory and politics. Yet this opportunity may be missed by many who, regardless of their evaluation of communism, interpreted its stubborn resistance to capitalism as the chief symbol of an open-ended future. Today, as that resistance fades, the "postmodern" decades of the 1980s and '90s reach a fitting climax in the millennial "end" of history.

The end of history: the radical critique of modern societies is mere speculation; progressive development is a narrative myth; alienation is an outmoded literary conceit. Salvation is to be found in irony, not revolution; the fashionable politics, even on the Left, is privatization, not self-management.

This mood is shaped by the consensus that links much of the Left with the establishment in celebration of technological advance. Indeed, technology has become so pervasive that the consensus leaves little of practical import to disagree about. The struggle over a few emotionally charged issues of human rights, such as abortion, disguises the hollowness of public debate, the lack of historical perspective and utopian alternatives. There seems to be room only for marginal tinkering with an ever diminishing range of problems not inextricably bound up with technique. This outcome was anticipated more than a generation ago by Karl Mannheim:

> The complete elimination of reality-transcending elements from our world would . . . bring about a static state of affairs in which man himself becomes no more than a thing. . . . Thus, after a long tortuous, but heroic development, just at the highest stage of awareness, when history is ceasing to be blind fate, and is becoming more and more man's own creation, with the relinquishment of utopias, man would lose his will to shape history and therewith his ability to understand it. (Mannheim, 1936: 262)

In Mannheim's terms, the problem we confront today is how to sustain a faith in historical possibility without messianic hopes. Can a sober reflection on the future find anything more than a mirror of the present? I believe it can and have done my best to awaken a sense of the choices that lie before us through a critique of the largely fulfilled promise of technology. To this end I reopen the debate over socialism in confrontation with various technical and practical objections, and suggest a coherent alternative that would preserve and advance our threatened democratic heritage.

That heritage is endangered today by the growing gap between the intellectual requirements of citizenship and work. The frozen opposition of market and bureaucracy blocks the path to a solution. Can we conceive an industrial society based on democratic participation in which individual freedom is not market freedom, and in which social responsibility is not exercised through coercive regulation? I will argue that a democratic politics of technology offers an alternative that could overcome the destructive relation of modern industrialism to nature, both in human beings and the environment.

Instrumental and Substantive Theories of Technology

In the pages that follow I present this position as an alternative to several established theories of technology. These fall into two major types: *instrumental theory*, the dominant view of modern governments and the policy sciences on which they rely; and *substantive theory*, such as that of Jacques Ellul (Borgmann, 1984: 9). The former treats technology as subservient to values established in other social spheres (e.g., politics or culture), while the latter attributes an autonomous cultural force to technology that overrides all traditional or competing values. Substantive theory claims that what the very employment of technology does to humanity and nature is more consequential than its ostensible goals. I will review these theories briefly before introducing a *critical theory of technology* that, I believe, preserves the best in both while opening the prospect of fundamental change.

Instrumental Theory

Instrumental theory offers the most widely accepted view of technology. It is based on the commonsense idea that technologies are "tools" standing ready to serve the purposes of their users. Technology is deemed "neutral," without valuative content of its own. But what does the "neutrality" of technology actually mean? The concept usually implies at least four points:

1. The neutrality of technology is merely a special case of the neutrality of instrumental means, which are only contingently related to the substantive values they serve. Technology, as pure instrumentality, is indifferent to the variety of ends it can be employed to achieve. This conception of neutrality is familiar and self-evident.

2. Technology also appears to be indifferent with respect to politics, at least in the modern world, and especially with respect to capitalism and socialism. A hammer is a hammer, a steam turbine is a steam turbine, and such tools are useful in any social context. In this respect, technology appears to be quite different from legal or religious institutions, which cannot be readily transferred to new social contexts because they are so intertwined with other aspects of the societies in which they originate. The transfer of technology, on the contrary, seems to be inhibited only by its cost.

3. The sociopolitical neutrality of technology is usually attributed to its "rational" character, the universality of the truth it embodies. The verifiable causal propositions on which it is based are not socially and politically relative but, like scientific ideas, maintain their cognitive status in every conceivable social context. Hence, what works in one society can be expected to work just as well in another.

4. Technology is neutral because it stands essentially under the very same norm of efficiency in any and every context. Its universality thus also means that the same standards of measurement can be applied to it in different settings. For example, technology is routinely said to increase the productivity of labor in different countries, different eras, and different civilizations.

This instrumentalist approach places "trade-offs" at the center of the discussion. "You cannot optimize two variables," a truism of economics, appears to apply to technology, too, where efficiency is considered as one such variable. There is a price for the achievement of other variables, such as environmental, ethical, or religious goals, and that price must be paid in reduced efficiency. On this account, the technical sphere can be limited by nontechnical values, but not transformed by them.[1]

The instrumentalist understanding of technology is especially prominent in the social sciences. It appears to account for the tensions between tradition, ideology, and efficiency that arise from sociotechnical change. Modernization theory, for example, studies how elites use technology to promote social change in the course of industrialization. And public policy analysis worries about the costs and consequences of automation and environmental pollution. Instrumentalism provides the framework for such research.

Substantive Theory

Despite the commonsense appeal of instrumental theory, a minority view denies the neutrality of technology. Substantive theory, best known through the writings of Jacques Ellul and Martin Heidegger, argues that technology constitutes a new cultural system that restructures the entire social world as an object of control.[2] This system is characterized by an expansive dynamic that ultimately overtakes every pretechnological enclave and shapes the whole of social life. Total instrumentalization is thus a destiny from which there is no escape other than retreat. Only a return to tradition or simplicity offers an alternative to the juggernaut of progress.

Something like this view is implied in Max Weber's pessimistic conception of an "iron cage" of rationalization, although he did not specifically connect this projection to technology or suggest a solution. Equally pessimistic, Ellul does make that link explicit, arguing that the "technical phenomenon" has become the defining characteristic of all modern societies regardless of political ideology. "Technique," he asserts, "has become autonomous" (Ellul, 1964: 14). Heidegger agrees that technology is relentlessly overtaking us. We are engaged, he claims, in the transformation of the entire world, ourselves included, into "standing reserves," raw materials to be mobilized in technical processes (Heidegger, 1977a: 17). Heidegger asserts that the technical restructuring of modern societies is rooted in a nihilistic will to power, a degradation of man and Being to the level of mere objects.

This apocalyptic vision is often dismissed for attributing absurd, quasi-magical powers to technology. In fact, its basic claims are all too believable. The substitution of "fast food" for the traditional family dinner can serve as a humble illustration of the unintended cultural consequences of technology. The unity of the family, ritually reaffirmed each evening, no longer has a comparable locus of expression. No one claims that the rise of fast food actually *causes* the decline of the traditional family, but the correlation signifies the emergence of a new technology-based way of life.

An instrumentalist might reply that well-prepared fast food supplies a nourishing meal without needless social complications. At bottom, eating is merely a matter of ingesting calories, while all the ritualistic aspects of food consumption are secondary to this biological process. This response is blind to the cultural implications of technology. In adopting a strictly functional point of view, we have determined that eating is a technical operation that may be carried out more or less efficiently, and that in itself is a valuative choice.

This example can stand for a host of others in which the transition from tradition to modernity is judged to be a progress by a standard of efficiency intrinsic to modernity and alien to tradition. The substantive theory of technology attempts to make us aware of the arbitrariness of this construction, or rather, its cultural character. The issue is not that machines have "taken over," but that in choosing to use them we make many unwitting commitments. Technology is not simply a means but has become an environment and a way of life. This is its "substantive" impact (Borgmann, 1984: 204ff.).

It seems that substantive theory could hardly be farther from the instrumentalist view of technology as a sum of neutral tools. Yet I will show in the next section that these two theories share many characteristics that distinguish them from a third approach, the critical theory of technology.

Technology Bound and Unbound

Despite their differences, instrumental and substantive theories share a "take it or leave it" attitude toward technology. On the one hand, if technology is a mere instrumentality, indifferent to values, then its design is not at issue in political debate, only the range and efficiency of its application. On the other hand, if technology is the vehicle for a culture of domination, then we are condemned either to pursue its advance toward dystopia or to regress to a more primitive way of life. In neither case can we change it: in both theories, *technology is destiny*. Reason, in its technological form, is beyond human intervention or repair.[3]

This is why most proposals for the reform of technology seek only to place a boundary around it, not to transform it. We are told, for example, that the harm we do the environment can be reduced by returning to a more natural way of life, without cars, trash compactors, and nuclear energy. The high-tech medicalization of childbirth and dying are criticized for penetrating "too far" into zones where nature should be allowed to take its course. Reproductive technologies are under constant attack on religious grounds. Genetic engineering is the ultimate biohazard. In all these cases critics urge us to reject certain technologies, and then ask us to accept the price of preserving traditional or natural ways. This agenda has given rise to both moral and political solutions to the problem of modern technology.

Moral Boundaries

While political conservatives seek to reinvigorate institutions such as the family on a traditional basis, cultural conservatives focus on spiritual values. Ellul and Heidegger, for example, condemn the reduction of our ethical, political, and human existence to a mere instrument for the achievement of wealth and power, and call for a restoration of the holy. Progressives worry about the subversion of democratic institutions by technology. Jürgen Habermas argues that the public life of democratic societies presupposes a commitment by the citizens to engage in rational argument. To the extent that we technicize the public sphere by transferring its functions to experts, we destroy the very meaning of democracy: "The redeeming power of reflection cannot be supplanted by the extension of technically exploitable knowledge" (Habermas, 1970: 61).

Albert Borgmann offers a sophisticated version of the idea of a return to simplicity. He calls for a "two-sector" economy in which an expanding craft sector will take up the slack in employment from an increasingly automated economic core. There is merit in the idea of privileging the growth of craft under industrialism. The need is obvious in domains such as music, where the power of the media to focus all attention on a few stars has devastating consequences for creativity and diminishes the worth of the many talents that fail to make it to the top. Recent developments on the Internet have begun to challenge the system and may in fact open music up to far wider participation.

In principle, Borgmann could accommodate such a symbiosis of craft and progressive technological advance; he does actually endorse a similar position on such consumer goods as hiking boots. But when it comes to production, he falls into an uncritical acceptance of the dominant technological paradigm, which, he asserts, "is perfect in its way" (Borgmann, 1984: 220).[4] But is modern industrial technology really "perfect" in conception and design? Is it not rather a human and environmental disaster? And how can one confine this disaster to its proper sphere, as all these theorists demand, when the problems it creates overflow every boundary and shape the whole framework of social life?

Let me put some order in this barrage of objections. There are at least four reasons to doubt that moral solutions will work.

1. I am in full agreement with a view of technical progress that refuses its imperialism and regards it as only one among the many dimensions of human existence. But it is just as important to conceptualize the progressive transformation of technology as to define its limits. All too often, having defined technology's proper place, criticism fails to see its potential and, in condemning its current form, forecloses its possible future.

2. Suppose, however, that one succeeds in combining limits on technology's reach with an effort to reform it within its own domain. The problem of defining that domain still remains. It is extraordinarily difficult to reach agreement on which activities should be protected from technical mediation: childbirth? the family? politics? ethnic or religious traditions? The only consensus value left in modern societies is efficiency, precisely the value we are attempting to bound so that other values may flourish.

3. Furthermore, by placing spiritual values in rigid opposition to technology, we concede what needs to be defended, that is, the possibility of a technically rational civilization that enhances rather than undermines those values. The moral critique of technology always seems to reopen the tedious debate over "principles" versus "practicality." In a modern society this is no contest but a confession of impotence, since the victory of the practical is so very predictable. What is needed is an alternative practicality more in accord with principle. That is what traditional Marxism promised, but failed to deliver. The question posed for us today is whether we can do any better.

4. Finally, the very project of bounding technology appears suspect. If we *choose* to leave something untouched by technology, is that not a subtler kind of technical control? Have I not domesticated a wild tree or bush or, indeed, a distant mountain peak visible from my garden, if I plant around it in such a way as to bring out its beauty? (This is a standard technique of Japanese gardening called "borrowed scenery.") If I suddenly need meaning in my overly technologized life, and obtain it by returning to my family's religious traditions, am I not *using* religion as a kind of supertechnology? If so, how can I believe in it? How can I ever leave the technical sphere if the very act of bounding a reservation instrumentalizes it?

Political Boundaries

The political solution to the problem of bounding technology turns out to be no more promising. This solution has been tested by those countries that attempt to preserve indigenous values while modernizing. Typically, the rulers argue that the flaws of modern society are the result of a specific instrumentalization of technology. They view Western capitalism and its peculiar technoculture as a system of "values" of the same order as, for instance, Confucianism or Islam. Their goal is to build regional economic and cultural spheres, sheltered from the world market and Western cultural hegemony where modern technology will be in the service of these alternatives (Rybczynski, 1991).

Apart from the many rhetorical gestures in this direction, there have been two serious challenges to Western hegemony. Prewar Japan tested the power of tradition to resist modernization, while the Soviet Union tried to bend modernization to communist goals. The strategy in these cases was remarkably similar despite immense national and ideological differences.

In the late nineteenth century, Japan committed itself to importing and manufacturing Western technology on a vast scale as a means of preserving national independence. Drowning in foreign technology, cultural conservatives could not help wondering what sort of industrial society would have been created by Japanese inventors had they been left alone for another century. Thus the novelist Tanizaki wrote in 1933, "The Orient quite conceivably could have opened up a world of technology entirely its own" (Tanizaki, 1977: 7).

In any case, so successful was the technology transfer that the Japanese came to believe they were destined to lead all Asia, not merely economically and militarily but culturally as well. In the 1940s the struggle to "overcome (European) modernity" (*kindai no chokoku*) attracted the support of many of Japan's most sophisticated writers and philosophers. "The problem was to find a way to conceptualize a modernity that was made in Japan, not in the West" (Harootunian, 1989: 75).

But despite serious reflection, these intellectuals came up with no concrete alternatives, nothing to indicate that a Japanese victory would have opened the way to an original form of modern society. The Japanese defeat in World War II marked the end of the struggle for a specifically Asian form of modern culture, although the idea is periodically brought up in Japan for reconsideration. The failure of Japan's early attempt to preserve its cultural originality foreshadowed all the later struggles to preserve vestiges of tradition and ethnicity in the face of technology's universalizing pressures.[5]

The Soviet experience resembles that of Japan except that the Russian Revolution was oriented toward the future rather than the past. Once again, the protection of original values required the energetic acquisition of existing technology to achieve rapid economic development. Thus, despite certain substantivist implications of the Marxist theory of economic stages, the Soviet regime adopted a typical instrumentalist position on technology, importing and using it as though it were a neutral tool. This is the significance of Lenin's famous remark that communism is "electrification plus soviets." Tight control of economic and cultural interaction with the capitalist world was supposed to open a protected space within which a new culture would be born.

This experiment ended, drained of its heroic ambitions by the banality of bureaucratic corruption, incompetence, and irresponsibility. Under Gorbachev, Russia no longer believed itself capable of organizing an autonomous subregion in the world economy, and called on the West to involve itself directly in the development of the communist economy. The Western media gained access to Russian audiences in this context. The loss of cultural control was soon so complete that no turning back was possible. Meanwhile, economic problems accumulated. Eventually the regime collapsed altogether and with it the communist vision, even in its reformed Gorbachevian version. Capitalist restoration appeared as a nearly irresistible temptation to populations expecting from it the prosperity of the West. Many socialist intellectuals hoped that the difficult transition to capitalism would unleash pressures for a new society that would innovate with respect to both capitalist and communist models. Nothing of the sort occurred. Instead, the former communist regimes introduced capital markets and engaged in a kind of ritualistic imitation of outward features of Western societies. This cargo-cult capitalism led to catastrophe in Russia and the less prepared nations of the former Warsaw Pact. The resulting mess has still not finished teaching us that capitalism is more than markets and depends equally on complex social, cultural, and political preconditions.

Although democratization in China has undoubtedly been slowed by the terrifying example of Soviet disintegration, it is difficult to believe in the rearguard defense of cultural isolationism there. Some sort of transition to capitalism seems probable in the context of intensified economic exchanges with the West, more probable perhaps than the revival of socialism in new forms.

Instrumental theory of technology is not entirely refuted by these experiences, although in each case governments were unable to use technology to further original cultural goals. Defenders of the instrumental view sometimes draw comfort from the conjunction of democratic reform with the decision to Westernize. Ordinary citizens appear to have refused the trade-offs required to sustain traditional or future-oriented values in competition with well-being in the present. The conquest of society by technology is not due to the occult power of the "technical phenomenon"; rather, technology, as a domain of perfected instruments for achieving well-being, is simply a more powerful and persuasive alternative than any ideological commitment.

At this point the specificity of the instrumental theory collapses. If technology is truly neutral, it should be able to serve a plurality of ends. But the close association of democracy with cultural Westernization seems to deny that pluralism, and in fact confirms the arguments of substantive theory. There is little reason to distinguish the two theories if they disagree only in their attitude toward an outcome foreseen by both.

A more interesting argument divides the substantive approach from critical theory. Both can agree that the Japanese and Soviet examples differed only superficially from the Western civilization they professed to transcend. Substantive theorists see this as evidence that no alternative technological civilization is possible. But critical theory, as I develop it here, argues, on the contrary, that an alternative may yet be created on the basis of public participation in technical decisions, workers' control, and requalification of the labor force. If the Japanese and Soviet experiments failed, this is because they rejected this radical democratic path for one convergent with the West.

According to this view, states cannot impose radical alternatives. Their attempts to instrumentalize technology on behalf of original values founder on an internal contradiction. In the face of the technological challenge, only a particularly strong state can create a culturally and economically closed region for the furtherance of original cultural goals. Yet a strong state can sustain itself only by employing the authoritarian technical heritage of capitalism. In so doing, it reproduces all the main features of the civilization it professes to reject: predictably, the means subvert the ends (Fleron, 1977: 471ff.). This argument points toward a democratic reconceptualization of socialism outside the framework of what might be described paradoxically as geographical utopianism.

Critical Theory of Technology

Between Resignation and Utopia

Whatever the merits of placing moral and political limits on technology in particular cases, history seems to show that it is impossible to create a fundamentally different form of modern civilization using the same technology as the West. If this is so, then either Heidegger is right, and "only a god can save us now," or we must invent a politics of technological transformation (Heidegger, 1977b).

The second option characterizes the critical theory of technology. This theory charts a difficult course between resignation and utopia. It analyzes the new forms of oppression associated with modern society and argues that they are subject to new challenges. But, having renounced the illusion of state-sponsored civilizational change, critical theory must engage far more directly with the question of technology than is customary in the humanities. It must cross the cultural barrier that separates the heritage of the radical intelligentsia from the contemporary world of technical expertise and explain how modern technology can be redesigned to adapt it to the needs of a freer society.

The first halting steps in this direction were taken by the early Marxist Lukács and the Frankfurt School. Their theories of "reification," "totalitarian enlightenment," and "one-dimensionality" show that the conquest of nature is not a metaphysical event, but begins in social domination. The remedy is therefore not to be found in spiritual renewal but in a democratic advance. That advance implies a radical reconstruction of the technological base of modern societies. In arguing that the liberation of humanity and the liberation of nature are connected, the Frankfurt School also addressed the fear that socialism might simply universalize the Promethean technicism of modern capitalism. But with the notable exception of Marcuse, these Marxist critics of technology stop short of actually explaining the new relation to nature implied in their program, and even he does not meet the demand his work elicits for a concrete conception of a "new technology."[6] Not surprisingly, given its vagueness, the Frankfurt School's critical focus on technology did not survive Habermas's attack, and for the most part the inheritors of the Frankfurt School regressed to a conformist affirmation of the neutrality of technology (Feenberg, 1999: chap. 8).

I believe this was a wrong turn in the development of critical theory. It is unfortunate that a tradition which began with a philosophically informed critique of contemporary social trends is now frequently left out of the growing public debate over technology. But one cannot simply return to the formulations of Adorno or Marcuse as though the tremendous ferment around environmentalism, medical technology, and computerization had changed nothing of significance. This book therefore constructs a new formulation of the critical theory of technology to address these issues.

This formulation resembles substantive theories in arguing that the technical order is more than a sum of tools and in fact structures the world regardless of users' intentions. In choosing our technology we become what we are, which in turn shapes our future choices. The act of choice is by now so technologically embedded it cannot be understood as a free "use" in the sense intended by instrumental theory. Even so, critical theory denies that modernity is exemplified once and for all by our atomistic, authoritarian, consumerist culture. The choice of civilization is not decided by autonomous technology, but can be affected by human action. There is no one single "technical phenomenon" that can be rejected as a whole in the manner of Ellul.

Thus critical theory agrees with instrumentalism in refusing fatalism. It does not despair in the face of the triumph of technology, nor does it call for a renewal of the human spirit from a realm beyond society such as religion or nature. Political struggle, as a spur to cultural and technical innovation, continues to play a role.

Despite these points of agreement with instrumentalism, critical theory rejects the neutrality of technology and argues instead that "technological rationality has become political rationality" (Marcuse, 1964: xv–xvi). The values of a specific social system and the interests of its ruling classes are installed in the very design of rational procedures and machines even before these are assigned specific goals. The dominant form of technological rationality is neither an ideology (a discursive expression of class interest) nor is it a neutral reflection of natural laws. Rather, it stands at the intersection between ideology and technique where the two come together to control human beings and resources in conformity with what I will call "technical codes." Critical theory shows how these codes invisibly sediment values and interests in rules and procedures, devices and artifacts that routinize the pursuit of power and advantage by a dominant hegemony.

Critical theory argues that technology is not a thing in the ordinary sense of the term, but an "ambivalent" process of development suspended between different possibilities. This ambivalence of technology is distinguished from neutrality by the role it attributes to social values in the design, and not merely the use, of technical systems. On this view, technology is not a destiny but a scene of struggle. It is a social battlefield, or perhaps a better metaphor would be a "parliament of things" in which civilizational alternatives contend (Latour, 1991: 194).

A Multistable System

Civilizations define a human type. Characteristic cultural, social, geographical, and economic conditions shape civilizations and distinguish them from each other. In the past, civilizational alternatives have emerged within every mode of production around differences in the roles of age, sex, or status; the functions of religion, art, or warfare; the available technologies; and so on. There is not just *one* form of tribal life, *one* feudal civilization or absolute monarchy, but a multiplicity in every case. But today, for the first time, there appears to be only one possible modern civilization. It gradually homogenizes every other difference as it obliterates geography and subverts all traditional values.

Critical theory holds that there can be at least two different modern civilizations based on different paths of technical development. The starting points of a new path are not to be sought in speculative fantasies but among marginal elements of the existing system. Technologies corresponding to different civilizations thus coexist uneasily within our society. We can already sense the larger stakes implicit in the technical choice between production by assembly lines or work teams, computers designed to intensify control or to expand communication, cities built around automobiles or public transportation. The instrumentalist notion of "use" does not apply at this level because the consistent pursuit of one or another technical path defines the user as one or another human type, member of one or another civilization.

This point explains the failure of attempts to instrumentalize technology on behalf of tradition and ideology. If a different technological civilization cannot emerge from ethics, ideology, or ethnicity, it must be based on a distinction immanent to the technical sphere itself. As Don Ihde puts it, "Any larger gestalt switch in sensibilities will have to occur from *within* technological cultures" (Ihde, 1990: 200). The most significant such distinction is the power differential between those who command and those who obey in the operation of technical systems. That power differential, organized through a variety of institutions, is one of the foundations of the existing civilization in both its capitalist and communist forms.

Technology is a two-sided phenomenon: on the one hand, there is the operator; on the other, the object. Where both operator and object are human beings, technical action is an exercise of power. Where, further, society is organized around technology, technological power is the principal form of power in the society. One-dimensionality results from the difficulty of criticizing this form of power in terms of traditional concepts of justice, freedom, equality, and so on. But the exercise of technical power evokes resistances of a new type immanent to the one-dimensional technical system. These resistances implicitly challenge the technically based hierarchy. Since the locus of technical control influences technological development, new forms of control from below could set development on an original path.

The conflicts specifically relevant to the transformation of technologically advanced societies thus oppose lay actors to the institutionalized power of those who control the technical mediation of modern life. For my account of these conflicts, I rely heavily on the work of Michel de Certeau (de Certeau, 1980). De Certeau offers an interpretation of Foucault's theory of power that helps to highlight the two-sided nature of technology. He distinguishes between the strategies of groups such as managers and state administrators with an institutional base from which to exercise power and the tactics of those subject to that power and who, lacking a base for acting continuously and legitimately, maneuver and improvise micropolitical resistances.

The strategic standpoint occupied by management privileges considerations of control and efficiency and looks at the world in terms of affordances, precisely what substantive theory criticizes in technology. Modern societies are characterized by the ever expanding effectiveness of strategic control. I analyze this trend in terms of the concept of "operational autonomy," the freedom of management to make independent decisions about how to carry on the activities of the organization it supervises regardless of the views or interests of subordinate actors and the surrounding community.

The tactical standpoint of the managed is far richer than this strategic orientation. It is the everyday life-world of a modern society in which devices form a nearly total environment. The individuals identify and pursue meanings in this environment. Power is only tangentially at stake in most interactions, and when it imposes itself, resistance is temporary and limited in scope. Yet insofar as masses of individuals are enrolled into technical systems, resistances can weigh on the future design and configuration of the systems and their products.

This two-sided interpretation of technology opens up a theory of technical politics better able to give insight into the contemporary world than substantivism, which adopts unthinkingly the strategic standpoint on technology and overlooks its role as a life-world. This is what leads it to such negative judgments and what ultimately explains Heidegger's hope that Nazism could, by mysteriously transforming our relation to technology from above, fulfill his program. Instead, we need a democratic transformation from below.

Is a shift in the locus of technical control possible? There are both cultural and technical objections to this proposal. Radical democratization presupposes the desire for increased responsibility and power, but the citizens of industrial societies today appear to be more anxious to "escape from freedom" than to enlarge its range. I will not argue with this view, but it is simply dogmatic to dismiss the possibility of a reversal of current trends. Things were different as recently as the 1960s and may change in the future as the full scope of worldwide environmental crisis finally sinks in.[7]

The emergence of a *culture of responsibility* would alter non-economic institutions and gender roles as well as the workplace. I do *not* argue that the latter is the determining instance of a general civilizational change. But in an industrial society, where so many social and political choices are made by economic managers, democratization of work is indispensable to a more participatory way of life. And it is precisely in the domain of work that democratization poses the most difficult problems, or at least so it is widely believed.

Modern civilization is supposed to be inherently incompatible with mass participation. Certainly, this is the implication of progress in the sphere of production through the relentless replacement of muscular power, manual skills, and, finally, intelligence by advancing technology. Reduced to passive robots at work, the members of industrial society are unlikely to acquire the educational and characterological qualifications for active citizenship.

This objection points to a deep problem in the usual theories of social democracy, which are primarily concerned with the defense or, in the best case, the extension of the welfare state. These theories often appeal to a negative concept of freedom in opposition to utopian projections, which they dismiss as impractical or even totalitarian. But insofar as social theory merely throws the question of the good life open to debate without proposing its own substantive conception, it avoids utopianism at the expense of trivializing or evading the civilizational issues a leftist politics must confront to carry conviction. Typically, the latest version of the "third way" promises progressive change without challenging the structures of daily life that determine a political culture of passivity and dependency.[8]

But can one go beyond proceduralism without courting the dangers of a positive concept of freedom? The argument depends on the notion that the rather conservative expressed preferences of the population can be distinguished from deeper interests masked by ideological manipulation. This seems an undemocratic position. Perhaps, as Robert Pippin argues, there is nothing below the surface; perhaps citizens respond rationally to the larger cultural context of modernity in preferring a society based on the domination of human beings and nature even as they pay the price of their choice (Pippin, 1995: 54–55).

This argument has particular relevance today in the light of the commonplace belief that a society that achieved morally sanctioned goals, such as increased participation, social justice, or environmental compatibility, would necessarily be the poorer for it economically. Given the widespread passion for consumer goods, there is no hope for socialism if it is merely a utopian ideology against which wealth might be traded off. Brief experiments in heroic virtue of that sort occasionally occur, but sooner or later they collapse in popular exhaustion and thus do not represent a realistic alternative. To escape what I call the "dilemma of development," the hard choice between virtue and prosperity, one must show that there are coherent configurations of human and technical resources that would support a different type of modern civilization.

Once a deep change of this sort has occurred in the pattern of a culture, the ideological motivations for it are no longer a matter of opinion subject to debate and controversy but are simply taken for granted as the "way things are" (Bourdieu, 1977: 164–171). That new culture renders "factually" self-evident what were once speculative claims of ideology and morality. Civilizational change can transcend apparent dilemmas through transforming economic and technical codes. Instead of seeking costly trade-offs between such goals as participation and efficiency, environmentalism and productivity, innovative redesign of technology must bring these goals into harmony. History is full of examples of change in the horizon of economic and technical action no less significant than these and equally difficult to imagine in advance; failing to make allowance for such changes reifies the present state of society as an illusory end of history.

Humanism and History

Technology provides the material framework of modernity. That framework is no neutral background against which individuals pursue their conception of the good life, but instead informs that conception from beginning to end (Borgmann, 1984). Technical arrangements institute a "world" in something like Heidegger's sense, a framework within which practices are generated and perceptions ordered. Different worlds, flowing from different technical arrangements, privilege some aspects of the human being and marginalize others. What it means to be human is thus decided in large part in the shape of our tools. To the extent that we are able to plan and control technical development through various public processes and private choices, we have some control over our own humanity.

The goal of a good society should be to enable human beings to realize their potentialities to the fullest. The most important question to ask about modern societies is therefore what understanding of human life is embodied in the prevailing technical arrangements. I argue here that current technical arrangements place limitations on human development.

Faced with this type of argument, the skeptic will no doubt want to know the grounds for preferring some forms of human development over others. What qualifies an activity as an advance toward human fulfillment? On what basis do we identify some aspects of human being as "capacities" while dismissing others as the result of various failures and limitations, in sum, as "incapacities"?

These are certainly legitimate questions but they admit of no absolute answers. In the absence of absolutes, the best we can hope for is to participate in a still unfinished history and to derive criteria of progress from reflection on its course and direction. In the humanistic tradition certain achievements have the status of paradigmatic guides to the future. Democratic revolutions revealed the capacity of the lower classes to take political responsibility for themselves, and the Civil War and various other political struggles instituted the universality of the human against all distinctions of caste, race, and gender. Universal education demonstrated the potential of the vast majority of human beings to achieve literacy and a significant degree of mental independence. Equally important changes in social and cultural life have also shaped our conception of human fulfillment. Individuality has become an important value through the emergence of the modern family, based on the free choice of partners and the care of children, and creativity is cherished under the influence of the various cultural movements associated with romanticism.

We are the products of this history. Our destiny is inextricably involved with the progressive unfolding of capacities for free self-expression, the invention of the human. Because we belong to the tradition shaped by these achievements, wherever we see similar struggles for a fuller realization of freedom, equality, moral responsibility, individuality, and creativity, we interpret them as contributing to the fuller and wider realization of human capacities.

How do new demands for the realization of hitherto unnoticed or suppressed human potentials manifest themselves? I formulate this problem dynamically in terms of the concept of "participant interests" (Feenberg, 1999: 140ff.). Insofar as one is enrolled in a technical network, one has specific interests corresponding to the potential for good or harm such participation entails. These interests are often served by the existing technical arrangements, but not always, not inevitably. Under these conditions, individuals become aware of dimensions of their being that are ignored, suppressed, or threatened by their technical involvements. When they are able to articulate these interests, an opportunity opens to reconfigure the technical system to take into account a broader range of human needs and capacities. This means: to recognize the intrinsic worth of the human as such in a hitherto suppressed or unnoticed domain.

Note the dialectical character of this conception of participant interests. The kinds of things it seems plausible to propose as advances or alternatives are to a great extent conditioned by the failures of the existing technologies and the possibilities they suggest. The context of struggle is thus the existing level of technical development that successfully represents some aspects of our humanity while suppressing others. Potentialities are identified in terms of the nature and limits of worlds and not on the basis of arbitrary opinions. We become conscious of our potentialities in running up against the specific limits of our time, not in pure utopian speculation. Or rather, our utopias have become "concrete" in the sense that they are rooted in the opportunities of the historical present.

The concept of participant interests informs the notion of 'technical code" that I have introduced to explain general regularities in the design of technologies. A technical code is the realization of an interest in a technically coherent solution to a general type of problem. That solution then serves as a paradigm or exemplar for a whole domain of technical activity. The notion of technical code presupposes that there are many different solutions to technical problems. Some sort of metaranking is therefore necessary to choose between them. In determinist and instrumentalist accounts, efficiency serves as the unique principle of metaranking. But contemporary technology studies contests that view and proposes that many factors besides efficiency play a role in design choice. Technology is "underdetermined" by the criterion of efficiency and responsive to many interests. In my formulation of this thesis, I argue that the intervention of interests does not necessarily reduce efficiency, but biases its achievement according to a broader social program (Feenberg, 1999: chap. 4).

Thus, two different configurations of production technology might each achieve high levels of efficiency, one applying workers' skills and the other eliminating them. Under different social conditions and with different values in view, each could be successful. The technical code would in the one case impose skilled work and in the other deskilling, reflecting the different interests of workers and managers. The humanistic tradition grounds the right of workers to technical advances that protect and develop their skills.

With this in mind, consider society as a scaffolding with three levels. At the center there are social groups acting in defense of interests of one sort or another. Interests are the starting point of the analysis because they are such visible, powerful, and constant moving forces in history. However, interests are not really independent factors, nor do they, by themselves, constitute a society. Without a material framework, there are no interests, and unless some interests are systematically privileged, there is no social order. Thus, interests are institutionalized at two other levels and it is that which gives coherence to social life. These levels are rights as expressed in ethical demands and codified in laws and technical codes.

This perspective suggests a recasting of the traditional fact/value, ought/ is dilemma in terms of the relation of ethical values to technical facts. Ethics is realized not only discursively and in action but also in artifacts.[9] Ethical discourse and ethical demands are often provoked by the limitations of existing technical codes. For example, where safety is not adequately protected by existing product standards, the value of life is brought forward as an ethical claim that advocates attempt to impose on manufacturers. The successful imposition of this claim by law or regulation transforms it from an ethical demand into a technical code and results in the ethical issue sinking beneath the surface in a kind of technological unconscious. Often current technical methods or standards were once discursively formulated as values and at some time in the past translated into the technical codes we take for granted today.

The political implication of this approach has to do with the ethical limits of modern technical codes. To the extent that the system is based on the operational autonomy of management, it is specifically armored against the recognition of many participant interests. That armoring shows up in technical designs that deskill, injure, pollute, and otherwise harm those excluded from a share in technical power. The very same process in which capitalists and technocrats were freed to make technical decisions without regard for the needs of workers and communities generated a wealth of new "values," ethical demands forced to seek voice discursively and realization in the new technical arrangements. Most fundamentally, democratization of technology is about privileging these excluded values and the publics that articulate them.

Technical Politics

Marxism and Post-Marxism

Marx first proposed the idea that an economy controlled by workers would be able to redesign technology to apply high levels of skill to production. He believed that deep changes in education, politics, and social life would flow from the requalification of the labor force. Although communist regimes deferred this prospect into an ever receding future, self-management theorists have long advocated giving worker-controlled firms command of their own technical development.

This approach was given a new lease on life by Marxist theory of the labor process. Harry Braverman (1974), and the generation of theorists who followed his lead, showed that economic interests determine major features of technological design. They argued that capitalism introduced control from above to impose labor discipline on a workforce with no stake in the firm. Technology was gradually redesigned in response to this new form of control to replace skilled workers with more malleable unskilled ones.[10]

Samuel Bowles and Herbert Gintis traced the impact of these economic and technical changes on the educational system, which was reorganized to provide capitalist industrialism with the type of workers it required. "Different levels of education feed workers into different levels within the occupational structure and, correspondingly, tend toward an internal organization comparable to levels in the hierarchical division of labor" (Bowles and Gintis, 1976: 132). Thus the problems identified by Braverman are not confined to the workplace but shape cultural and social life as a whole.

This account reverses the usual order of explanation for the prevalence of the unskilled and uneducated, attributing it not to the general advance of technology or to the natural distribution of intelligence, but instead to social causes. That conclusion suggests the social *contingency* of modern technology, which has unexplored democratic potentialities that might be realized by a better qualified labor force.[11]

Despite this Marxist background, the project of a critical theory of technology will be greeted with skepticism by Marxists who turn to political economy for the serious business of social critique. But an exclusive emphasis on political economy tends to overestimate the rationality and coherence of capitalist strategies and underestimate the significance of resistances, innovations, and reforms in every domain except class struggle, where, unfortunately, there is little to report.

Furthermore, by now we know that a great many fundamental questions of civilization cut across the distinction between economic regimes. Feminists and race theorists have made the point that equality is always an issue. Abolishing discrimination under capitalism will not abolish economic inequality, and it is just as true that a socialist reform of the economy can leave discrimination intact. Environmentalism, too, appears as a challenge to all industrial societies, whatever their economic system.

In recent years, activists involved in environmental politics, and the politics of race and gender, have challenged traditional Marxism and called into question the significance of economic planning and workers' control (Boggs, 1986). The turn away from Marxism is reflected in theory, most notably in the work of Michel Foucault. His historical studies of the rationalization process uncover the roots of modern power structures in a variety of social techniques. He emphasizes the dispersion of power throughout a wide range of institutions such as prisons, hospitals, schools, and so on.

But whatever the merits of these challenges, the new terrains of struggle privileged by "post-Marxism" are also traversed by technical mediations that support power differentials broadly similar to that which characterizes the industrial setting. Change is still promised through substituting control from below for control from above. Foucault's work, in particular, advocates new forms of resistance to the exercise of power through technical strategies. Thus, despite the polemic that opposed Foucault and "the Marxist conception, or at any rate a certain conception currently held to be Marxist," his approach offers an important source for a critical theory of technology (Foucault, 1980: 88).

Foucault's qualified rejection of Marxism suggests the existence of a more interesting version than the usual one we associate with the critique of capitalist political economy. In fact, there is another aspect to Marx, who may be considered the first serious student of resistance to modern technology. He observed that the technical mediation of work accelerated economic growth but also created new social hierarchies. At the same time, Marx argued, technology brought into being a new kind of lower class capable of democratizing the economy. Over a century later, we see technical mediation reaching far beyond the domain of production into every aspect of social life, whether it be medicine, education, child rearing, law, sports, music, the media, and so on. And, while the economic instability of market capitalism has been significantly reduced, everywhere technology goes, centralized, hierarchical social structures follow.

Transforming Technology is situated in this context. It is an attempt to make sense of the political consequences of generalized technical mediation. Under these conditions, technology emerges as a public issue out of a variety of struggles in something like the way in which environmentalism crystallized at an earlier date around hitherto separate issues such as population control, pollution control, nuclear protests, and so on. The enlargement of the public sphere to encompass technology marks a radical change from an earlier consensus that brooked no interference with the decisions of technical experts.

Technical politics today involves a variety of struggles and innovations with significant consequences for the structure of major technical institutions and the self-understanding of ordinary people. We need to develop theory to account for the increasing weight of public actors in technological development. That theory will owe something to Marxism, even if it cannot be qualified as Marxist in the usual sense.

Reconceptualizing Socialism

Is it still reasonable to hope for more than scattered resistances to the existing system? Could these resistances come together and form the basis for a socialist alternative? According to the standard account, the failure of communism has finally awakened us from the socialist dream. Supposedly, public ownership and economic planning are so inherently inefficient that communism was doomed from the outset. The debate over this widespread view is both technical and inconclusive, an unfortunate state of affairs that will not be changed by anything in this book, as I lack the qualifications to intervene in it.[12] It is interesting to note, however, that economists are by no means unanimous in mouthing the free market mantra so often heard from political commentators.

Joseph Stiglitz, for example, has shown how unrealistic are the assumptions supporting the neoclassical faith in markets. While he agrees with mainstream opinion that the communist economies failed for lack of such things as competition, effective incentives, and a realistic price system, he also argues that capitalist economies are not paragons but are fraught with similar, if less severe, problems. An example of his style of argument shows how far he has opened the door to socialism even in a book the intent of which is to bury it as a failed historical experiment.

Stiglitz shows that the supposedly perfect allocational efficiency of competitive markets in neoclassical theory bears little resemblance to actual markets. Yet the imperfect competition that does exist provides vital information to companies about achievable levels of efficiency. The argument for competition is thus persuasive on information-theoretic grounds even as it fails on classical grounds. But the shift in grounds has an interesting consequence: the information-theoretic approach leaves far more room for state regulation and public ownership. If capitalist markets are generally and in principle imperfect rather than approximating perfection as in neoclassical models, then extensive state intervention to preserve their competitiveness is plausible. Still more interesting is Stiglitz's observation that publicly owned firms can be placed in competition to generate the kinds of informational advantages capitalism derives from private ownership (Stiglitz, 1994: chap. 7). He concludes, "The difference between competition and monopoly is the distinction of first order importance, rather than the distinction between private and state ownership" (Stiglitz, 1994: 255).

Despite unresolved disagreements among the experts on such questions, it is impossible to avoid considering the issues and forming an opinion. Mine is in fact formed less on the basis of technical considerations in economic theory than common sense, which tells us that under the right conditions, reasonably clever, honest, and motivated people can achieve economic growth in both systems. If this were not so, the Soviet Union could not have industrialized so quickly and successfully. No doubt planning as implemented there was not efficient enough to make the Soviet Union competitive on the world market, and toward the end the economy was incompetently administered even by Soviet standards, but these considerations are not necessarily decisive so long as we can point to significant examples of growth under public ownership. In this context, it is relevant that large portions of Western economies are or have been administered by the state since World War II without the catastrophic economic consequences of public ownership in the Soviet Union. The French case is particularly noteworthy (Stiglitz, 1994: 233).

It seems obvious that Stalin's tyranny did more damage to the Soviet economy than planning as such. It helps to have an honest civil service and free flows of information, cultural and political factors that cut across the distinction between capitalism and socialism. Without them, managers face the alternative of chaos or excessively centralized controls. It is also critical that what are essentially business firms not become social welfare agencies, providing employees with security and services incompatible with their primary function. And if management is inhibited from harsh disciplinary policies by a degree of worker control, then there must be some connection between compensation and commercial success even in a state-owned enterprise. Finally, it may be necessary to have a fairly large private sector or significant international competition for the public sector to operate well.

Whether mixed economies of the sort that have emerged throughout the advanced capitalist world are optimally efficient in strict market terms, they do work and they can achieve desirable social and political goals. Not free markets but regulation and public ownership make possible educational excellence and medical care for all, communicative freedom and equality in public life, gender and racial equality, attractive and safe cities, and environmental protection. All these goals have long-term implications for welfare that are difficult to measure but not less significant for that matter. Unfortunately, security of employment is among the nonmarket goals most vigorously pursued where power has shifted downward to workers. It is easy to understand why, but beyond a certain point, immobility becomes a tremendous burden on the economy and in any case is largely irrelevant to the long-term civilizational transformation defining for socialism. I will argue in later chapters that that transformation might be furthered by an emphasis on other goals.[13]

The current wave of budget cuts and privatizations has narrow economic benefits insofar as it rationalizes employment, but it sacrifices other important social goals and decisively forecloses the prospects for economic democracy. Were democratization a priority, it would be necessary to extend the reach of state control considerably further as a framework for radical changes in management and technology. Perhaps this new configuration can be called "socialism," it being understood that the word now refers to a society that privileges specific nonmarket goods and employs substantially more extensive regulation and public ownership than the existing capitalist societies to obtain them.

Note that socialism under this new definition does not stand in unmediated opposition to capitalism as we know it. Rather, it represents a possible trajectory of development starting out from the existing welfare states. Some capitalist societies are clearly further along on this trajectory than others and might more easily move toward socialism as a result. The tensions today between different models of capitalism testify to the continuing relevance of the socialist alternative. While many Americans sneer at the supposedly archaic European welfare state, a majority of European voters heartily detest what they hear about American "free market" capitalism and reject attempts to impose it. Nevertheless, vast social and political changes would have to take place before even the most advanced welfare state moved beyond the horizon of capitalism. Those changes are not impossible, but neither are they likely in the near future. Thus, the argument is not about probabilities but rather possibilities. And possibilities are important insofar as they continue to be entertained by large numbers of discontented citizens in the existing capitalist societies.

In sum, while the command economy may be dead, I am not convinced that we have seen the last of the idea of extensive public ownership in the context of a mixed economy. And if it is economically feasible, there are strong political reasons to favor it. The huge concentrations of wealth associated with modern large-scale enterprise weigh heavily in the democratic balance—too heavily. Private control of media conglomerates, the machinery of opinion, is incompatible with serious public debate. The levels of regulation required by the environmental problems of modern societies appear increasingly incompatible with capitalist ownership of certain types of industry, such as the oil industry. And, as I argue throughout this book, capitalist control is incompatible with a long-term evolution of technology favoring skill and democratic participation in the technically mediated institutions of the society. The full implications of this argument are developed in chapter 6.

The Radical Alternatives

The Posthumanist Alternative

That civilizational change requires technological change is a line of argument familiar at least since Mumford and Marcuse; however, its economic and technical implications have not been worked out far enough to carry conviction. This is what I attempt to achieve here. I argue that the existing society contains the suppressed potentiality for a *coherent civilizational alternative* based on mutually supporting transformations of institutions, ideology, economic attitudes, and technology.

The concept of potentiality that is central to this argument can be developed in a variety of ways. There is an influential strand of "green" and "eco-feminist" theory, represented for example by Carolyn Merchant, that formulates the project of technological reform in terms of a recovery of the body and bodily involvement in nature (Merchant, 1980). This view implies a kind of vitalist reenchantment of nature that contradicts the world picture of the modern physical and biological sciences. The potentialities to which these theorists refer are supposed to be ontologically real dimensions of human beings and nature. Although ignored by current science, these dimensions would be identified by a reformed science of the future.

Someday, there may well be a scientific world picture more in accord with the spirit of contemporary ecological thought. But we need not await the reform of science to reform technological design. On the contrary, current scientific and technical knowledge has resources for a very radical reconstruction of the technological heritage. A concept of potentiality rooted in the heritage of actual struggles can guide the process without a foundation in a new concept of nature.

However, most participants in contemporary debates on society and technology regard the very notion of potentiality as outdated and metaphysical. I believe this would be a fair statement of Habermas's objection, and certainly that of many more conservative theorists who, like Habermas, are in full flight from what they perceive as the utopian heritage of Marxism. Unfortunately, most of these theorists lapse back into a conformist view of the neutrality of technology that leaves them little critical margin. Without the concept of potentiality, can one sustain a radical stance? This question divides postmodern critique from critical theory. Postmodernism attacks all forms of totalizing discourse, including talk of potentiality, in the belief that totalization is the logic of technocracy (Lyotard, 1984; Jay, 1984). Freedom and justice are identified with what escapes any sort of fixed definition or control, even the self-definition and self-control of the modern individual.

The most important version of this alternative to a critical theory of technology is the "cyborg" or "nonmodern" critique of humanism. Something similar has been discussed at least since Nietzsche's attack on Christian ethics, democracy, and socialism. Heidegger's critique of metaphysics should also be mentioned in this connection. More recently, Foucault placed posthumanism back on the agenda of the Left. A number of influential thinkers, including Donna Haraway and Bruno Latour, would like to add the moral weight of that tradition to the epistemological innovations of postempiricist philosophy of science in a new constellation of radical theory. Significantly, the idea of potentiality plays no role in these formulations, which seek a different basis for critique.

The posthumanists argue that technology should not be seen as something distinct from humans and nature because technology is "coemergent" with the social and natural worlds. Humans, nature, and technologies can only be distinguished theoretically because they have been first distinguished through various practices in which all, not merely the humans among them, engage. "Collectives" or "hybrids" encompassing humans and nonhumans are both the subject and object of postmodern knowledge: subject, because we know through our technologies and not immediately as in the old paradigm of cognition based on a predefined human-to-nature relation; object, because what we know is a complex of mutually defining human, natural, and technological dimensions (Haraway, 1995).

The posthumanist critique argues convincingly that social groups in a society like ours must be defined in terms of the technical mediations that make it possible for them to form in the first place. This insight can be critically deployed to block essentialist and pseudonaturalistic marginalization of "deviant" ways of being and living. Hence the connection between Haraway's position and an antiessentialist feminism that rejects normalizing assumptions about gender. Latour's posthumanist anthropology of science applies similar premises to the critique of scientism and technocracy, which attempt to place reason beyond the range of social involvements. Latour's work has enraged the defenders of rationalism, a sure sign of its effectiveness.

But posthumanism claims far more than is necessary to make these radical arguments. It wants to get to a deeper level at which not just social groups and technologies "coemerge," but also the human or social and the natural as such. Now, it is true that the boundary between the natural and the social is often a subject of controversy, particularly in medicine and other domains of "body politics." But the work of controversy, which finally draws the boundary, presupposes the general distinction between nature and society. It is in fact this very presupposition that makes it possible to have a controversy in the first place. Why? Because controversy is possible only where the contingency of the social can be distinguished from the necessity of the natural.

Consider, for example, the remarkable Amazonian tribe which believes that after death men are transformed into jaguars, while women and children simply disappear. Clearly, in this context it would be difficult to raise feminist objections to postmortem discrimination as a cultural construct. We can only do so because we know how to distribute effects between the social and the natural.

This ontological presupposition is of course subject to an epistemological critique which points out that it is after all "we" who do the distributing. Some social constructivists have argued that this makes society an ultimate subject and nature merely one of its positings (Vogel, 1996). But the posthumanist line is different. "Subject" is now redefined not as the knower who posits objects but as the "actor," the agent, which effects changes in the world. On those terms, nature is as much a subject as society. The process in which the lines between society and nature are drawn by subjects in this sense involves activity on both sides of the line prior to the drawing of the line. Indeed, since human and natural subjects can only be distinguished once the line between them is drawn, "human" and "natural" cannot be ultimate categories but must be relative to something more fundamental. Latour, for example, calls this foundation the network of "actants." In Haraway, the "cyborg" metaphor plays a similar role. "Hybridity" is another general term often identified with the new ontology.

These notions are notoriously abstract and difficult to pin down. This, I believe, is a sign of a deep problem. How, after all, can the actors act before their existence has been defined by their action? How, one wonders, can we talk about actants without using the language of modernity in which the human and the natural are distinguished a priori? Thus, the ultimate foundation to which the theory implicitly refers seems to be a sublime nothingness about which nothing can be said, that night in which all cows are black, as Hegel complained of Schelling's subject-object identity.

But that is not at all the posthumanists' conclusion. Rather, they have a lot to say about their foundational point of departure. What they say is contained in painstaking local analyses that are supposed to be able to trace the coemergence of society and nature in the processes of scientific and technological development. This *transcendental localism* has opened a new approach to science studies called "actor network theory." In applying this approach, Latour distributes the terms usually attributed to human subjectivity across the boundaries between the human and the nonhuman actors whose coming into existence is itself the object of the story. The most famous example of this rhetorical strategy is Michel Callon's discussion of scientific research on scallops in which the little devils are described as more or less "cooperative" with the researchers (Callon, 1986).

Questionable as are such descriptions, there are still more difficult problems with actor network theory. Despite its contribution to the critique of normalizing assumptions that support modern forms of domination, posthumanism ends up undermining its own critical basis. If the networks are to be a founding reality, it is necessary to refuse the ontological pretensions of everyday language, in which things like human beings and natural objects have an independent existence apart from their mutual involvements. That commonsense approach would lead back to "essentialism." Before you know it, we would be talking about human nature and its potentialities. The new network ontology therefore applies a strict operationalism that forbids the introduction of data that is not effective in the strong sense of decisive for the organization of the network.

This has disturbing normative implications. It means, for example, that the losers' perspective in any struggle disappears from view as it cannot be operationalized in terms of the nature/society distinction realized in the structure of the network (Radder, 1996: 111–112). If our Amazonian feminist protests her status in the afterlife, we cannot find support for her in a rigorous posthumanism for the simple reason that she has no methodological right to refer to a transcendent distinction of nature and society to make her case. True, she can protest the repressive implications of the essentializing assumptions underlying her society, but apparently not in the name of natural equality or human rights. How this protest can lead to a positive program of reform is unclear.

Latour has apparently been troubled by such criticisms and in a recent book attempts to address them. In *Politiques de la nature*, he is anxious to show that his radical replacement for social theory can do the work done by the traditional categories (Latour, 1999). Indeed, he concedes that unless he can do this work as well or better than the old social theory, his argument will fall on deaf ears (Latour, 1999: 148). The effort is a brilliant tour de force, but in the end I fear he remains caught in a bind that characterizes posthumanism generally, the inability to develop criteria of progress out of the analysis of local situations and struggles.

Latour agrees that it must be possible to resist the definition of reality imposed by the victors in the struggle for control of the network. The traditional ground for this is the appeal from the social consensus to a transcendent truth. Latour objects to this appeal on the ground that it is used by scientific elites to block democratic discourse. In fact that is only half the story. The egalitarian sweep of modern history also rests on such appeals, by the lower classes, by women, slaves, the colonized, each of whom has argued successfully that natural differences do not sanction their subordination.

Although this fact of democratic history does not enter Latour's argument with the prominence of his critique of scientific authority, he is well aware of it. But, he argues, considered from a purely operational viewpoint, the democratic appeal to nature has nothing to do with nature as such and everything to do with the procedures of debate and struggle. What we really need is not a clear distinction between "nature" and "society," "fact" and "value," "truth" and "power," but a clear understanding of the legitimate organization of public debate. True democracy must protect public access for entities and persons hitherto excluded from consideration, while also ensuring that new elements and voices be integrated harmoniously with the established structure of the network. In sum, allowance must be made for the intervention of the new and unpredictable while preserving the network from incoherence and collapse (Latour, 1999: 172–173). The significant division of function contrasts not ontological realities (e.g., nature and society) but the procedures Latour calls "the inclusion power," which allows challenges to the boundaries of the network, and "the ordering power," which puts each included entity in its place ("le pouvoir de prise en compte" and "le pouvoir d'ordonnancement") (Latour, 1999: 156). Democracy is thus a matter of maintaining the permanent possibility of contestation.

So far so good. Latour recognizes the problem of participation by subordinate actors and offers a solution. But one would like to know how these actors are to argue for the reforms they desire without reference to any transcendent sanction. Morality in this new theory is now confined to holding the collective open to new claimants and ordering its members in a hierarchy (Latour, 1999: 213). These operations take the place of the old distinction of the right and the good. But they are not exactly equivalent. On Latour's account, morality is no longer based on principles but on these operational rules. The grandiose appeals of the past to equality and human rights are ruled out as impotent modernist inventions. Subordinated actors must now appropriate Latour's theory to articulate their demands on the terms of that very theory. This is a significant problem, but Latour promises that the complicated arguments necessary to support his radical departure from received notions will soon seem obvious as common sense itself is revised to conform with his views (Latour, 1999: 32–33). This is quite unlikely as it depends on the spread of a radical ontological operationalism that eliminates or redefines all the categories of common sense, philosophy, and social science.

There is surely a moment of truth in the antiessentialist demand for permanent contestation, for dispersion and difference, but these negative qualifications cannot provide the basis for a positive approach to technological reform. Normalization is not the only source of modern structures of domination, nor is it sufficient today to denounce the dystopian potential of technocracy. Nuclear weapons, the systematic deskilling of the labor force, the export of pollution to the Third World, these are not the products of rigid bureaucracies the authority of which is sapped by a new postmodern individualism, but of flexible centers of command that are well adapted to the new technologies they have designed and implemented. The opposition to these centers must also oppose the present trend of technological design and suggest an alternative. For that purpose it is important to retain a strong notion of potentiality with which to challenge existing designs.

The Contribution of Critical Theory

Critical Theory's most fundamental insight is the excess of the particular over the universal.[14] Reality, life, the individual are richer in content than the forms that attempt to grasp them and that do effectively grasp them in a social order. Domination consists in the suppression of the individual by the "universal," the "concept." But the critique is not aimed at conceptualization in general. Rather, this is a social critique of the institutionalized concept, historically established by a specific hegemony and therefore contestable. In this framework, "nature" refers not to the object of natural science nor to a higher moral order but to that which escapes conceptualization and inspires resistance. This excess diminishes constantly as technology extends the reach of the universal into the material facts of everyday existence, but it cannot be eliminated. The individual remains as a threatened fiber of potentialities out of which to weave a fabric of transcending demands.

What Adorno called "mindfulness of nature" refers to the act of reflection in which a technologized rationality recalls its limits and recognizes the existence and claims of the nature that lies beyond its grasp (Adorno and Horkheimer, 1972: 40). Marcuse's concept of the "substantive universal" recognizes the individual as a complex being with dynamic developmental potentialities, to a significant extent independent of the given social order and its technological power (Marcuse, 1964: chap. 5). The persistent reference to nature, reflection and individuality as the basis of a critique of the totalitarian power of technology distinguishes critical theory from various forms of postmodernism and posthumanism.

In the absence of power, that is, effective support in the established social networks, potentialities have always been defined in terms of universalistic transcending concepts, such as nature, justice, and humanity. Critical theory continues this tradition along lines first formulated by Marx. Marx objected to universalism for reasons similar to those of contemporary postmodernists, but he historicized values rather than abolishing them. For example, critical theory avoids naturalistic essentialism even as it refers us to nature by emphasizing the negative traces of what society has distorted and damaged. Suppressed nature manifests itself in various forms: resistances, conflict, even humor, but also disease, suffering, and destructive aggression. The diagnosis of social conflicts and ills enables us to identify potentialities that could be released in a different social world. The task of radical social theory is still the one Marx identified, to articulate and explain the historical context of transcending demands, not in order to eliminate them, but to understand how they advance a larger human cause on the basis of premises already in existence.

These themes can help to right the emphasis of contemporary critique. Critical theory recognizes that part of the human actor which overflows any particular network involvement and provides a basis for criticizing the construction of networks. It retains the commonsense notion that human actors have unique reflexive capacities. These capacities make it possible for humans to represent the networks in which they "emerge" and to measure them against unrealized potentialities identified in thought. Reflexivity of this sort is essentially different from the contributions of nonhuman actors, and forms the basis for social struggles that may challenge or disrupt the networks and even reconfigure them in new forms. These reconfigurations have an ethical dimension that cannot be explained on posthumanist terms.

In the remainder of this book I argue that the technical enterprise itself is immanently disposed to address the demands we formulate as potentialities, but that it is artificially truncated in modern societies. Opening technical development to the influence of a wider range of values is a technical project requiring broad democratic participation. Radical democratization can thus be rooted in the very nature of technology, with profound consequences for the organization of modern society. This approach does not involve an ontological challenge to modern science and leaves no opening for the charge of totalitarian utopianism. In strategic terms, it identifies the common ground between critical theory and the scientific and technical professions.

There is some precedent for such an approach in the Frankfurt School tradition. While Adorno and Horkheimer remained resolutely hostile to technology, Benjamin and Marcuse saw democratic potentialities in technological development. Benjamin's famous discussion of the "mechanical reproduction" of art championed the new technologies of film and photography for their ability to move art out of the museum and into the daily lives of the masses (Benjamin, 1969). Marcuse's early essay on technology anticipates his later one-dimensionality thesis, but also points out the democratic potential of modern technology, which does away with the radical differences in aptitude and culture associated with premodern forms of authority (Marcuse, 1941). Later, in One-Dimensional Man and An Essay on Liberation, Marcuse develops a rather sketchy but suggestive account of the new technology of a liberated society (Marcuse, 1964, 1969).

None of these positive evaluations of technology are sufficiently developed to intersect fruitfully with contemporary technology studies. I pursue the argument at a much more concrete level through an analysis of the nature of technology and the technical relation. I show that the control-oriented attributes of technology emphasized in capitalist and communist societies do not exhaust its potentialities. A fundamentally different form of civilization will emphasize other attributes of technology compatible with a wider distribution of cultural qualifications and powers. Such attributes are present in both preindustrial crafts and modern professions. They include the vocational investment of technical subjects in their work, collegial forms of self-organization, and the technical integration of a wide range of life-enhancing values, beyond the mere pursuit of profit or power. Today these dimensions of technology can be brought into play only in the context of the democratic reorganization of industrial society, which they make possible.

I

From Marxism to
Radical Critique

*Marx was the first to unmask the interests behind supposedly technical impera-
tives, showing that capitalist technology is uniquely suited to an alienated society
controlled from above. The first chapter of this section acknowledges this insight
of Marx, but argues that his critique was not completed by a socialist politics of
technology. This is a deep contradiction: as a critique of capitalism, Marxism
shows that politics and technology are inextricably linked, but its concept of
socialism fails to take that connection into account.*

*The politicization of technology can find theoretical support in Marx, but
it did not develop a significant following until the late 1960s and early 1970s.
At this turning point in the public understanding of technology, two major
social thinkers challenged traditional approaches, Herbert Marcuse and
Michel Foucault. In their work, modern society resembles a vast machinery
dominating its members through rational means and procedures. The second
chapter of this section examines Marcuse's analysis of "one-dimensionality"
and Foucault's history of disciplinary power. These theories go significantly
beyond traditional Marxism and its instrumentalist account of the revolution
to analyze modern forms of "technological rationality." But, having refuted
the standard version of revolutionary Marxism, they fail to offer an adequate
alternative account of social transformation.*

*In contrast to these versions of critical theory, I argue that technical systems,
and the modern forms of social domination based on them, are fraught with
internal tensions. Any weakening of organizational control would therefore
open a range of possible futures. Socialist politics must be reconceptualized on
these terms as the creation of a space of social transformation within which the
ambivalence of inherited technology can be freely explored.*

2

Technology and Transition

Marxist Perspectives on Labor and Technology

Exploitation or Domination

Marx created Marxism by conjoining a philosophical critique of alienation with the aspirations of the labor movement. The critique was directed at the enslavement of human beings to machines in modern industrial civilization. Workers' aspirations for democracy and economic justice appeared quite modest in comparison with this speculative attack on industrialism itself. Yet so long as conservative regimes opposed even their most elementary demands, it could be argued that workers' pursuit of a better life depended on general civilizational change.

Toward the end of the nineteenth century, just as they became a significant historical force, expanding socialist parties reinterpreted this link as an order of temporal succession. The canonical conception of the "two phases" of socialism rationalized moderate strategies in the present while holding out utopian prospects for the distant future. The parties focused on short-term reforms embellished with purely rhetorical promises of far larger changes in the "higher phase" of socialism. To be sure, they still believed themselves to be playing a role in the civilizational transformation foreseen by Marx, but they argued that the best way to achieve it was to pursue the more limited goals of the labor movement.

Socialists used the means at hand to gain or remain in power, on the assumption that increasing the political influence of labor was the key that would unlock the door to the future. For the most part this required imitation of capitalist methods rather than the search for innovative ways of organizing social life. The chief exception to this rule was economic planning, a remarkable social invention, but not one capable of shattering such characteristic dilemmas of capitalist civilization as the opposition of individual and society, market and bureaucracy.

As the interests of the socialist movement narrowed, so did those of the interpreters of Marxism. Stalinists and social democrats alike inherited a theory that emphasized the evils of maldistribution, aggravated by capitalist administration of the economy. Marx's critique of alienation fell into eclipse, and was eventually confounded with his moral denunciation of child labor, the hazards of industrial work, and the poverty of the proletariat. After World War II, most social critics accepted this image of Marx and dismissed his critique of industrialism as irrelevant to contemporary debates over the future of technologically advanced societies. The Dickensian problems with which Marx was purportedly concerned had been solved and more interesting ones had arisen, such as the politics of knowledge.

This is, for example, the position of Daniel Bell, whose forty-year-old article "Two Roads from Marx" still defines the horizon of most discussions of Marxism both in the mainstream and to some extent on the left of the academy as well. Under this horizon, Marxists are asked to show their relevance to a "postindustrial" or "postmodern" society no longer wracked by the mortal conflict of labor and capital. This new society, we are told, is tantalized more than tormented by subtle cultural contradictions that emerge against the backdrop of a smoothly running economic machine. So influential is this position that it is worth reconsidering the thesis of Bell's article to establish the relevance of a new look at Marx's critique of industrialism and his cure for its ills.

Bell argues that Marx passed from an early humanistic concern with the alienation of labor to sterile analyses of economic exploitation in his mature writings. "*Alienation*, initially conceived by Marx to be a process whereby an individual lost his capacity to express himself in work, now became seen as *exploitation*, or the appropriation of a laborer's surplus product by the capitalist" (Bell, 1962: 362). This narrowed focus misled the socialist movement into believing that the overthrow of the property relations associated with capitalism would automatically solve all the other problems of workers, including oppression on the job and in society at large. "Marxist thought . . . [developed] along one road, the narrow road of primitivist economic conceptions of men, property and exploitation, while another road, which might have led to new, humanistic conceptions of work and labour, was left unexplored" (Bell, 1962: 386–387).

It is essential to Bell's thesis that *Capital*, the chief work of Marx's maturity, *not* contain a serious discussion of alienation in the Marxian sense, as the laborer's loss of control over the conditions and products of his or her labor.

So Bell argues that "other than as literary references in *Capital*, to the dehumanization of labor and the fragmentation of work, this first aspect of the problem was glossed over by Marx" (Bell, 1962: 367). On this point it is ironic to find Bell anticipating structuralist Marxism. In both cases, the juxtaposition of young and old Marx is employed to show that Marxism properly speaking, as distinguished from a few youthful texts of purely biographical interest, is concerned with economics rather than with human freedom. But this view has been convincingly refuted by Marxist scholars, for example, in Ernest Mandel's thorough study of the evolution of Marx's thought (Mandel, 1967).

Although a subordinate element of Marx's thought, his analysis of the capitalist labor process is surprisingly relevant to contemporary discussions of the social impact of technology. Marx even discusses the characteristic phenomena critics of postindustrial society identify as the nemesis of freedom: the scientization of production and administration, the disqualification of the labor force, and its consequent subordination to the mechanical and bureaucratic systems that organize its common efforts. In fact, *Capital* was the first systematic attempt to carry out Bell's own program for a modern social theory freed from the ideological furies of Marxism: "If one is to deal meaningfully with the loss of self, of the meaning of responsibility in modern life, one must begin again with concrete problems, and among the first of these is the nature of the *work process* itself, the initial source of alienation" (Bell, 1962: 387).

Labor Process Theory 1

Bell's attack on Marxism announced in advance the very agenda for the renewal of Marxism in the 1970s. It was Harry Braverman who argued most persuasively that Marx's mature work contains not one but two related critiques of capitalism. I will call these two critiques a *property theory* and a *labor process theory*, the one based on an economic analysis of capitalism and the other on a sociology of its organizational forms. Braverman focused on the latter and showed that *Capital* and the *Grundrisse* contain an elaborate critique of the labor process that had lain almost completely ignored for generations.[1] Whatever its flaws, Braverman's famous book *Labor and Monopoly Capital* (1974) permanently changed our image of Marx.

Braverman and those who contributed with him to the development of labor process theory wrote in the shadow of the emerging social movements of the late sixties and early seventies. These movements were suffused with an antitechnocratic ideology exemplified by Herbert Marcuse's critique of "one-dimensional man." Industrial civilization was challenged as a whole once again, and not just criticized for failing to live up to its own ideals of affluence and equality. New patterns of dystopian thinking replaced old class theories, reminding Marxist theoreticians such as Braverman of the importance of domination and alienation, long neglected in favor of an exclusive focus on exploitation and economic crisis. The renewed demand for civilizational change made possible the discovery of the "hidden" dimension of Marxism.

Although they rejected many aspects of the New Left, these Marxists hoped to persuade it of the continuing relevance of class by focusing attention on the division of labor. They shifted the debate from the unequal distribution of wealth to the corresponding problem of the unfair distribution of power on the workplace. This shift, which appeared quite daring at first, turned out to have plenty of textual basis in Marx. In Marx's analysis, the continuum of incomes masks a sharp discontinuity of power: the personal wealth of the individual capitalist is inextricably bound up with the "divorce" of workers from the means of production, hence also their subordination in the labor process to the owners of wealth (Marx, 1973: 823).

On this interpretation, Marx was a critic of technocracy *avant la lettre*. By renewing his radical critique of alienation, Marxism was able to participate in the discussion of new types of workers' struggles occurring in the United States and Europe in the late 1960s and early 1970s. These struggles, over the organization of work and management, the distribution of power in the firm, and the innovation process, are still points of reference whenever it is a question of resistance to the prevailing model of industrialism.

Labor process theorists describe the essence of the capitalist organization of labor as "deskilling," the destruction of autonomous craft labor. The goal, as explained by such early management theorists as Andrew Ure, is to simplify tasks into mechanical routines that can be quickly learned. Although deskilling is introduced to reduce labor costs, its impact is not merely economic, but political as well. It is one of several processes that provide a basis for capitalist hegemony in the workplace and in society at large.

Just insofar as the capitalist division of labor restricts the mental horizon associated with each job, capital itself emerges as the "subject" of production. The capitalist occupies a new position in the division of labor, the *post of capital*, which appears as the veritable source and unity of this production process. The cultural incapacity of workers, their inability to understand and master production on the basis of their ever diminishing qualifications, thus becomes the secure foundation on which the hegemony of capital is built.

The craftsman possessed the knowledge required for his work as subjective capacity, but mechanization transforms this knowledge into an objective power owned by another. Thus, in machine industry the subordination of the worker to the conditions of labor is not primarily coercive but is a consequence of the employment of technology. Here the specifically capitalist organization of the labor process "for the first time acquires technical and palpable reality" as "the labourer becomes a mere appendage to an already existing material condition of production" (Marx, 1906: I, 462, 421).

> The development of the means of labour into machinery is not an accidental moment of capital, but is rather the historical reshaping of the traditional, inherited means of labour into a form adequate to capital. The accumulation of knowledge and of skill, of the general productive forces of the social brain, is thus absorbed into capital, as opposed to labour, and hence appears as an attribute of capital. . . . In machinery, knowledge appears as alien, external to him [the worker]; and living labour as subsumed under self-activating objectified labour. (Marx, 1973: 694–695)

The capitalist division of labor is the crucible in which both capitalists and workers are formed as classes. Capitalists obtain a discretionary power over production that I will call *operational autonomy*. As the representative of the collective laborer, the capitalist is empowered to implement a work plan he or she can turn to personal account. This discretionary power grows as the gradual redesign of work increases the dependence of the working population.

The post of capital appears as the source of the excess production made possible by the cooperative labor of the fragmented individuals. The capitalist's hierarchical status is further enhanced by the authority he or she exercises in the name of the group in coordinating its activities, and by his or her role in supplying members of the group with tools and equipment. The capitalist acquires the operational autonomy to reproduce his or her own leadership through these activities, in which this leadership essentially consists. The collective laborer is thus a form of social organization in which *the whole dominates its parts through the activity of one of those parts*.

These considerations suggest an immanent limit on capitalist growth. Might not the pursuit of technical progress at some point come into conflict with the pursuit of power over the worker? What would happen if the division of mental and manual labor on which capital relies became dysfunctional and from a motor of progress became an obstacle? Marx believed that this point had already been reached: once machine technology appears, the maintenance of the old division of labor could only multiply waste and inefficiency (Marx, 1906: I, 461).

The skills and knowledge of the working population, the cultural infrastructure of society, stand in contradiction with the mechanical infrastructure of production. Modern industry "by its very nature . . . necessitates variation of labour, fluency of function, universal mobility of the labourer." A new "law" of economic life has arisen with the new technology, a law that commands "fitness of the labourer for varied work, consequently the greatest possible development of his varied aptitudes." However, by *its* very nature capitalism requires just the opposite, an ignorant and docile labor force tied to highly specialized tasks. This is the "absolute contradiction between the technical necessities of Modern Industry, and the social character inherent in its capitalistic form" (Marx, 1906: I, 533–534).

After a century of industrial progress under conditions excluded by his theory, Marx's argument is undoubtedly less convincing than it was in his own time. Nevertheless, it still contains an important advance in the understanding of the politics of technology, an advance that has been forgotten in the debates over his extravagant claim to have identified a fatal crisis tendency of capitalism.

If the capitalist division of labor is socially relative, rooted in the control problems of capitalism, then it can be replaced by another division of labor in a socialist society freed from these control problems. Indeed, Marx argues that industrial technology is systematically suboptimized in a system where workers have no interest in the firm. In such a system, workers can only be controlled where they have been made dependent through deskilling. These social tensions would be greatly reduced under socialism. Labor discipline "would become superfluous under a social system in which the labourers work for their own account" (Marx, 1959: III, 83). The development of human capacities and productive efficiency would stand in a dynamic, positive relation made possible by an end to the competition of labor and capital for control of the economic resources of the firm.

These hypotheses about the unrealized potential of the existing industrial society are the interesting point for the argument developed here. Thus, where Marx claims that "Modern Industry, indeed, *compels* society, under penalty of death" to adopt a new division of labor, let us merely say that modern industry *permits* society "to replace the detail-worker of today, crippled by lifelong repetition of one and the same trivial operation, and thus reduced to a mere fragment of a man, by the fully developed individual, fit for a variety of labours, ready to face any change of production, and to whom the different social functions he performs, are but so many modes of giving free scope to his own natural and acquired powers" (Marx, 1906: I, 534).

Three Critiques of Technology

The traditional Marxism predominant in the communist world appeals to Marx's property theory of capitalism and completely ignores his critical remarks on the labor process and technology. It holds that the "forces of production" need only be released from capitalist "relations of production" to develop along socialist lines. The all-important distinction between technological forces and social relations thus indicates the boundary between merely capitalist institutions socialism must change and universal achievements of the human race that must be preserved. Advocates of this position are generally determinists of one sort or another, holding that technological progress is apolitical, governed by immanent laws.

A minority view, first clearly formulated within Marxism by Georg Lukács and represented today by labor process theory, socialist environmentalism, and critical theory, argues that Marx was not a technological determinist, but considered both work relations and technologies as forces of production and treated them both as contingent on social interests (Miller, 1984: 188–195). On this account, socialism must change the very machinery of production and not just its administration. The radical theorists emphasize qualitative considerations, such as the nature and direction of progress, rather than quantitative measures of development such as the number and productivity of machinery.

There are so many ambiguities in Marx's writings on technology that both positions can find support there. These ambiguities are due to his occasional attempts to fend off charges of romanticism with a naive instrumentalist account of technology. Thus, he carefully limited his criticism to the "bad use" of machinery and wrote that anyone who objects to such a reasonable critique "implicitly declares his opponent to be stupid enough to contend against, not the capitalistic employment of machinery, but machinery itself" (Marx, 1906: I, 482).

It is easy to understand why Marx did not wish to be tarred with the same brush as the infamous Nedd Ludd, but the distinction between "employment" and technology "in itself" will not save him. In fact *there is no such thing as technology "in itself"* since technologies exist only in the context of one or another sort of employment. This is why every significant dimension of technology can be considered a "use" of some sort. For example, such very different things as hammering a nail, modern war, electric lighting, and the assembly line are all "uses" of technology in different senses. Even the term "machinery" is ambiguous and may refer either to particular technologies used for this or that purpose, or to modern technology as a general field containing various possibilities each of which is a "use."

To say that technology is "badly employed" may therefore refer to problems as different as (1) *what* purpose particular technologies are employed to accomplish, (2) *how* they are employed, whatever the purpose, and

(3) the *way* in which technical principles are employed in designing them in the first place. It is not easy to know which view Marx actually held because he seems to have believed elements of all three without ever clearly distinguishing between them (MacKenzie, 1984: 499–500). By selecting references, which are sometimes obscure in any case, one can easily construct one's own personal Marx. I will briefly review these various positions as they appear in Marx's work or are attributed to him; however, my purpose is less to produce an account of Marx's views than to arrive at a persuasive formulation of a critical theory of technology capable of addressing contemporary concerns. Some aspects of Marx's critique of technology can serve that end.

If Marx intended the first and only the first of these meanings of "badly employed," his critique would be a banal objection to the wastefulness of employing technology for merely private purposes. Marx would have attacked the ends technology serves under capitalism, while approving the means. I will call this the *product critique* of technology because it focuses exclusively on the worth of the products for which technology is used and regards technology "in itself" as unsullied by its role in producing them.

Some Marxists claim that only such a critique of technology is compatible with historical materialism, according to which technology is supposed to be a force of production, an element of the base and not relative to class interests. Yet this is certainly not a full account of Marx's position and rests on a highly selective reading of the texts. Marx frequently denounced the widespread abuses resulting from "the capitalistic employment of machinery," such as harming the soil to extract maximum agricultural yields, and failing to safeguard workers' health.

These problems are due not just to the purposes technology serves but also to factors such as the length of the workday, the pace of work, the provision of inadequate safety equipment and training, and so on. The production process is not merely a means to an end but constitutes an environment for the working population throughout the workday. Subserved to the requirements of class power, this environment becomes a menace to those who must live within it.

This theory represents a second dimension of Marx's critique of technology. While compatible with the product critique, this *process critique* does not describe technology as innocent but asserts, on the contrary, that industrial tools are a constant source of dangers that can be avoided only through scientific study and humane and rational planning unbiased by the drive for power and profit. I will call the combination of these first two theories the "product and process critique." While it cannot explain all Marx's remarks on technology, it represents a plausible interpretation of his views that is routinely attributed to him by Marxists and non-Marxists alike.

Traditional Marxism can live with the product and process critique. If it is correct, the abolition of the capitalist form of property, accompanied by relatively simple health and safety measures, would suffice to resolve the main problems technology causes. Marxist theory has generally confined itself to such proposals while preaching resignation to the alienating effects of machine industry until the distant "higher phase" of communism.

This approach appears to follow from Marx's distinction between the technical and the social "moments" of capitalist production, the one concerned with *efficiency*, the other with the *reproduction* of capitalist power and wealth. Marx employs this conceptual distinction to show that the worst aspects of capitalism, such as widespread occupational disease, depend not on the efficiency criterion but on system reproduction. Hence, a different system might solve those problems without abandoning the use of modern technology (Marx, 1906: I, 363). The customary instrumentalist interpretation of Marx's distinction therefore holds that technical functions are neutral and that meeting the social requirements of capitalism reduces overall efficiency. Capitalism would violate technical norms in pursuit of power and wealth. This formulation maintains a sharp dividing line between technology "in itself"— the actual machines—and its flawed application under capitalism.

For example, Kautsky's *The Class Struggle* discusses the capitalist division of labor and authoritarian management under the general heading of the consequences of technological advance, and promises workers a reduction in labor time under socialism, but no reform in their condition as workers (Kautsky, 1971: 155–160). Similarly, Bebel's classic *Woman under Socialism* treats the reform of wasteful, unpleasant, and hazardous production in considerable detail, but when it comes to discussing technological innovation, we are promised advances such as the automation of stone breaking and the artificial production of food (Bebel, 1904: 283–298). Neither Kautsky nor Bebel foresees fundamental changes in the design of technology and the labor process. Critics of traditional Marxism, such as Albrecht Wellmer, therefore sometimes conclude that Marx was a "latent positivist," who believed in the saving power of pure technology (Wellmer, 1974: chap. 2).[2]

However, this is not quite the whole story. There is evidence from Marx's discussion of the capitalist division of labor that he attributes class bias to technology itself. Capitalist interests control the very design of the technology on Marx's account of innovation, not just the choice of goals or the method of application. While he never states it explicitly, there is thus a third critique in Marx, which is in fact the first "critical theory" of technology.

According to this *design critique*, capitalist technology is shaped by the same bias that governs other aspects of capitalist production, such as management (Gorz, 1978).

Thus, Marx claims that science "is the most powerful weapon for repressing strikes, those periodical revolts of the working class against the autocracy of capital" (Marx, 1906: I, 475). And further, that "it would be possible to write quite a history of inventions, made since 1830, for the sole purpose of supplying capital with weapons against the revolts of the working class" (Marx, 1906: I, 476). These passages seem to say that technology is shaped in its design and development by the social purposes of capital, in particular by the need to maintain a division of labor that keeps the labor force safely under control.

The existence of passages like these should send commentators back to Marx's discussion of the distinction between the technical and the social for a second look. Perhaps he did not mean that these two dimensions of production are materially independent of each other, the one embodied in neutral tools, the other in the class-biased institutions. There is another possible explanation in which they are analytically distinguishable functions *condensed* in capitalist technological design, which simultaneously fulfills social and technical purposes. This interpretation can explain Marx's surprising claim that capitalist technical innovation *both* serves the class interest in increased power over the labor force *and* the generic interest in increased power over nature.

To summarize, this design critique argues that technological progress achieves advances of general utility, but the *concrete form* in which these advances are realized is through and through determined by the social power under which they are made and insures that they also serve the interests of that power. According to this view technology is a dependent variable in the social system, shaped to a purpose by the dominant class, and subject to reshaping to new purposes under a new hegemony.

Labor Process Theory 2

This view now finds wide support in labor process theory. David Noble's research on the history of numerically controlled machine tools offers a particularly clear example of a design critique. The earliest form of numerical control employed a "record/playback" system that facilitated the work of skilled operators by registering their movements on a tape used to guide the equipment through an exact repetition of the desired sequence of motions. General Electric was unable to market this system and eventually dropped it as the digital programming of machine tools came into favor.

That technology took many years to develop and required immense investments, primarily by the military, but it had one significant marketing advantage over the early record/playback system: it promised the elimination of skilled labor on the shop floor. Managers found the prospect of gaining total control so attractive that a consensus quickly formed in favor of the digital systems, long before these were proven and even after it had become apparent that they could not offer all the promised cost savings and productivity increases.

Noble's argument refutes the instrumentalist notion of the neutrality of technology by displaying the actual workings of a major choice that defies conventional economic and technical logic. Instead, Noble demonstrates the powerful role of what he calls "management ideology," which orients development toward the technical alternative that promises to enhance managerial power regardless of its social consequences and even despite significant economic liabilities. Noble explains the outcome as the fruit of a compulsion to total control deeply rooted in the capitalist organization of production (Noble, 1984: part II).

I will have to clarify in later chapters how such a compulsion is translated into technical terms. I introduce the concept of a "condensation" of technical and social functions in a "technical code" governing design for this purpose. Noble's use of the term "ideology" gestures toward such an account in an unsatisfactory way. His conclusion, for example, seems to suggest that managers with a socialist ideology would have stuck with the record/playback approach. But of course the point is not that managers had the wrong politics. It was their understanding of technical issues that was biased, and socialist managers make the same kinds of decisions if they share this understanding, as they often do.

But despite this problem, Noble's example confirms Marx's view that different social contexts can determine different paths of industrial development. Noble has here identified a case in point: the automation of machine tools was underdetermined from a purely technical standpoint and its future decided by social criteria of progress.

Reading Marx in the light of Noble's research and that of other students of the labor process suggests a very different picture from the usual determinist accounts. The evolution of technology can no longer be regarded as an autonomous process but must be rooted in interests and social forces. According to this view capitalist interests generate a division of labor and a conception of technical progress incompatible with the full development of workers' individuality. The working class, on the contrary, has a long-range interest in the abolition of the division of mental and manual labor and the related wage system. A workers' power would further that interest by creating an industrial society favorable to individual development. Capitalists *must* impose a division of labor that *only* workers can overcome.[3]

Is there any truth to these claims? While capitalism has proven to be far more flexible than Marxists usually allow, it does reach some sort of limit in terms of the quality of work. There is considerable social scientific evidence that workers under capitalism experience discontent with a work process designed in view of maintaining control rather than in function of their needs (*Work in America*, 1973). Workers could be motivated by this situation to demand a transformation of the production system. And no group other than workers can consistently support an end to control from above, since such a change is subversive of every way of organizing the economy from outside the labor process itself. Thus socialism can only be created by workers' control and not, for example, by an enlightened dictatorship of Marxists.

Marx's deterministic predictions concerning the direction of development of industrial society is not persuasive in their original formulation, but they can be reconceptualized more modestly as a theory about the possible impact of different economic cultures on technological development. On this account, we can reformulate Marx's theory of the transition in ideal-typical terms. It is unnecessary to prove that working-class rule guarantees a socialist evolution of society. The interesting point is the *possibility* that workers in some socialist society might choose an original technological future corresponding in its main outlines with the Marxian transition. Workers' actual understanding of their own welfare *may* become the basis for the adaptation of technology to socialist purposes where it approximates to the hypothetical "interests" Marx imputes to them. I will return to this suggestion in chapter 6.

Critique and Transition

The argument so far enables us to sketch two rather different Marxisms (Gouldner, 1980). The version Bell criticizes is a form of technological determinism. Marx's maximum thesis of inevitable capitalist crisis is combined with the product and process critique of technology to yield an optimistic vision of the future in which the proletariat rides a wave of technological progress to certain victory. Inconvenient bits and pieces that don't fit, such as Marx's critique of the capitalist division of labor and technological design, fall by the wayside.

The critical alternative to this version of Marxism argues that industrial society cannot be democratized through a merely formal change in the ownership of capital because the technical inheritance is peculiarly adapted to hierarchical control. Undemocratic aspects of capitalist technology and division of labor would also have to be transformed. Transitional policy therefore cannot be guided by the classical distinction between base and superstructure because after a socialist revolution technology would have to be reconstructed much like the state, law, and other institutions inherited from capitalism. That reconstruction would not be determined by immanent laws of technological development, but on the contrary by social and political choices. Advocates of this version of the theory must ignore Marx's endorsement of a two-phase transition to socialism based on the prolonged employment of the capitalist division of labor and technology.

Surprisingly, then, radical theory did not have to wait for Daniel Bell to articulate a critique of Marxism's exclusive focus on ownership and exploitation. Bell's attack on Marxism was anticipated long ago by none other than Marx himself. Yet, when all is said and done, Bell's misperception of Marxism as a deterministic theory of economic redistribution is not arbitrary. It has roots in the theory of the transition to socialism and the implementation of that theory in communist societies.

As noted earlier, traditional Marxism reserved radical technological change for the distinctly remote "higher phase" of socialism, and most of the little that Marx has to say about the politics of the transition abstracts completely from the implications of his own critique of industrialism. Once workers have seized the state, they will introduce public ownership of industry, plan production, and promote the rapid growth of productive forces. This view of the transition implies a position on technology not so different from the one Bell attributes to Marx, a position that can be held partly responsible for the deradicalization of the socialist movements.

How could Marx have failed to take into account his own critique of technology in conceiving the transition to socialism? How could Marxists in power persist in this error when faced with workers' resistance to the imposition of a system of control from above? Recall that Marx proposed both a property and a labor process theory of capitalism. The one criticizes private ownership as an obstacle to economic rationalization, and the other offers a parallel critique of capitalism as a social technology of domination. The coexistence of these two "moments" of capitalist power is due to the condensation of ownership and "appropriation," or control, in the same persons.

Etienne Balibar argues that Marx had difficulty distinguishing these two aspects of his theory because under capitalism both ownership and control involve the "separation" of the worker from the means of production. The relationship between these two types of "separation" is unclear from this vocabulary (Balibar, 1965: II, 210; Poulantzas, 1968: I, 20–24). Logically, the transition to socialism requires reuniting the workers with the means of production in *both* senses. But theoretical texts such as *Capital* do not say which is fundamental, while programmatic and historical writings usually stress the property system and the role of the state in supporting it. It is these latter writings that have shaped Marxism until quite recently, with the result that it ceased to be concerned with one of the most basic forms of power in industrial societies, including communist ones.

Although Marx was aware of the trends leading to modern bureaucratic forms of social organization, such as the separation of management from ownership, he believed he could attack control from above by attacking private property as the legal condition for the exercise of that control. But the further development of industrial societies split apart the legal form of property and the effective system of authority far more completely than he anticipated. History has shown that no transition to socialism is possible on the basis of a capitalist organization of labor and that planning is no substitute for workers' control.

Today the economic aspect of Marx's argument is overshadowed by his sociology of organization, which applies more generally than he ever dreamed, not only to capitalist social relations but to bureaucratic administration in general. The remainder of this chapter will consider the consequences of this strange turn of events for the theory of the transition to socialism.

Contradictions of the Transition

The Concept of Ambivalence

According to the Marxist theory of the transition to socialism, the revolution, like Archimedes, can move the world if only it can find a place to stand. This "place" is the institutional and technological base that socialism inherits from capitalism. Here are the most important examples of such inheritances:

1. Political institutions such as voting, taken over from the bourgeois republic, serve as the basis for a democratic socialist state. This socialist state is not an end in itself but merely a means to the end of abolishing the state altogether.
2. Similarly, even such a basic capitalist institution as the wage system is reformed and retained during the transition as a step toward the socialist goal of distribution according to need.

3. Capitalist management, subordinated to the will of the "assembled producers," is employed to run industry during the transition to a new type of industrial society that transcends the division of mental and manual labor.

4. The technology of alienation taken over from capitalism is used to produce a different technological apparatus, a technology of liberation in which work becomes "life's prime want."

These claims are not based on the idea that technological means are neutral. A means can only be "neutral" as between goals that fall under the goal-horizon it is designed to serve. But the transition to socialism refers to the possibility of transforming the goal-horizon itself, that is to say, generating a framework for the achievement of goals not supported by the existing means. Thus, the issue is not what different *ends* may be directly served by a given institution or technology, but what new institutional or technological *means* it may produce, in a culturally and technically feasible sequence leading from one type of industrial society to quite a different type. I will call this relation the *ambivalence* of means with respect to *civilizational projects*.

The concept of ambivalence depends on the distinction between production and reproduction. The socialist regime controls not only day-to-day production, which must be based at first on inherited means, but also long-term social reproduction in the course of which that inheritance may be bent to new purposes. For example, technology can be reshaped as machines developed under capitalism are employed to produce a new generation of machines adapted to socialist purposes. Class power determines which of the ambivalent potentialities of the heritage will be realized. An undemocratic power such as that of the capitalist class eliminates institutional and technical innovations that threaten its control. Since, under socialism, workers are in charge, they can change the very nature of technology, which, for the first time in history, concerns a ruling class with an interest in democracy on the workplace.

The theory of ambivalence resolves the dilemma opposing political realism and utopia by identifying the raw materials of socialism among the inheritances of capitalism. It asserts the possibility of *bootstrapping* from capitalism to socialism. As far as technology is concerned, it is difficult to imagine an alternative to an ambivalent process of change. A whole new technology cannot spring pure from the sweaty brow of the proletariat as Athena did from Zeus's forehead.

But Marx's critics argue from the actual evolution of the Soviet Union that the continuity of domination is not interrupted but perpetuated by reliance on inherited means. This criticism is unfair. In what follows, I will argue that Marx's theory of ambivalence was never actually tested in the USSR. The course of Soviet development is not due to theoretical ambiguities in Marx but rather to the uncritical employment of Western methods and technology to shore up a modernizing dictatorship. In the process the idea of a transition to socialism was travestied and transformed into an apologetic state doctrine.

Like much else about Marxism, the theory of ambivalence can still interest us today only if it is disassociated from these distortions. The aim of the theory is not apologetic but strategic and consists in guiding the evolution of institutions, equipment and techniques developed under capitalism toward new forms. As such, the theory is of general interest for any radical project of civilizational change. One can gather a rough idea of Marx's approach from his design critique of technology and his theory of the labor process. But, as I will show in the remainder of this chapter, he failed to apply these conceptual advances to the transition to socialism.

From Social to Political Revolution

Socialist revolution is a conscious project by its very nature. To be transformed, ambivalent inheritances must be grasped by an agent with a will. But what kind of agent is capable of creating a socialist society? Marx and Engels assure us that the working class is that agent, but this answer raises still more questions. How is the class will shaped and applied? Can its agency express itself in the forms defined by capitalist institutions, based on operational autonomy and control from above? If so, how can the self-organization of the class be distinguished from its alienated cooperation in capitalist society? If not, what other forms of agency and organization does socialism involve?

There are no clear answers to these questions in the work of Marx and Engels, and the main teaching of the history of the socialist movement is the negative lesson of Stalinism. Yet there are hints of a positive alternative in certain writings and historical experiences. Reflection on these hints suggests a way of making sense of an ambivalent process of change.

Marx's first attempt to distinguish the subjects of socialism and capitalism appears in his early critique of the French Revolution. In the 1844 essay "Critical Notes on 'The King of Prussia and Social Reform'" Marx distinguishes between "political" and "social" action, the one representing control from above, the other control from below. The essence of socialism, Marx argues, is the dissolution of all power relations in free cooperation, the very opposite of "Jacobin" voluntarism. "The principle of politics is *will*. The more one-sided and thus the more perfected *political* thought is, the more it believes in the *omnipotence* of will, the blinder it is to *natural* and spiritual *restrictions* on the will, and the more incapable it is of discovering the source of social ills" (Marx, 1967: 350). This source is the alienated sociability of capitalism that draws individuals together under an oppressive power they themselves unwittingly create.

In this early essay all alienated organization from above is identified with "politics," which cannot therefore liberate the proletariat from alienation. In fact, Marx argues, politics plays only a negative role in proletarian revolution. Force opposes force and compulsion is ended by compulsion, but "where its organizing activity begins, where its own aim and spirit emerge, there socialism throws the political hull away" (Marx, 1967: 357). Workers need a "social" revolution to consciously transform their alienated interactions and recapture their "common forces."

The contrast between a political and a social revolution refers us to two different types of subjects, an alienated subject of will and a "human" subject of need. But at this point in his career, Marx has no very definite idea what this latter form of subjectivity entails. Although he is scandalized by the sheer physical deprivation of the proletariat, he does not want to rest his case on the merely natural needs of an animal subject. In the *Paris Manuscripts*, Marx hints at a notion of need based on the development and expression of specifically social potentialities, but the "aim and spirit" of socialism is still an abstract quasi-ethical demand.[4]

The idea of social revolution as the dissolution of alienated political organization from above influences Marx's later economic writings, inspiring his theory of the labor process (Mandel, 1967: 172). That theory implies a new subject of production based not on control from above but on the voluntary self-organization of the "assembled producers." Alienation is to be overcome through the suppression of private ownership and, eventually, through overcoming the division of mental and manual labor.

Surprisingly, Marx's most important mature writing on revolution, "The Civil War in France," does not build on these implications of the economic works, but instead reveals a curious displacement. We have seen that in his early discussion of revolution, politics is to be replaced by "social" activity, but Marx does not yet know in what that activity consists. By 1871, Marx has laid the basis for a theory of "social" activity as disalienation of the production system. But his discussion of the Commune of Paris was influenced only formally by his critique of economic alienation. When he comes to reconsider the question of social revolution, he concludes that it is disalienation of . . . the state.

"The Civil War in France" largely ignores production, and instead generalizes the attack on the split between conception and execution in the economy to embrace the corresponding division of executive and legislative, policy and operations in the state: "The Commune was to be a working, not a parliamentary body, executive and legislative at the same time" (Marx, 1969: 291). The representatives' operational autonomy was to be limited by the clear assignment of responsibility, the publicity of decision making, and the complete subordination of government to the voters. In the model Marx derived from the experience of the Commune, the state continues to exist during the transition, but as the *political* leadership of a *social* movement.

This discussion shows that Marx's views are incompatible with the single-party state as implemented in the Soviet Union. But what are the implications of Marx's theory of the transition for economic practice? Paris was not yet a major industrial city, and its revolution lasted only a few months. In the economic domain, the Commune did little more than abolish abuses such as night work. Marx seems to have concluded that socialism's "organizing activity" is radical democratic politics, and so leaves us in suspense as to what form of economic and labor organization should replace capitalist practice in the first phase of socialism.

Later libertarian socialism applied Marx's democratic image of the Commune to the factory in order to recover his early antistatist insight into the difference between social and political revolution. But despite the internal consistency of the resulting concept of industrial democracy, Marx himself had only vague sympathy for workers' control. Although he advocated industrial cooperatives and bitterly criticized the despotic character of capitalist management, he never insisted on early changes in the exercise of economic authority. There is, however, a passage in which he notes ironically that capitalist management is "unaccompanied by that division of responsibility, in other matters so much approved by the bourgeoisie, and unaccompanied by the still more approved representative system" (Marx, 1906: I, 463–464).

These hesitations are reflected in Engels's ominously entitled essay "On Authority," which argues for the necessity of maintaining a separate management under socialism. This text, perhaps because of its title, has often been interpreted as authoritarian, but in fact Engels gestures here toward some sort of workplace democracy. At one point he says that production problems may be "settled by decision of a delegate placed at the head of each branch of labor or, if possible, by a majority vote" (Engels, 1959: 483). At another point he mentions the need for "a dominant will that settles all subordinate questions, whether this will is represented by a single delegate or a committee charged with the execution of the resolutions of the majority of persons interested" (Engels, 1959: 484). It is clear from the conditional form of these remarks that workplace democracy is desirable within practical limits, but not as a matter of principle.

Having discovered the central importance of the division of labor, why didn't Marx and Engels propose an antiauthoritarian strategy of resistance to work arising spontaneously around class struggle in the factory? This would have given a concrete content to the idea of a specifically socialist "organizing activity" animated by an original "aim and spirit." It would have clarified the distinction between the willful subject of capitalist control and the needy subject of socialist cooperation.

Had they proposed such a strategy, they would have anticipated a recurrent pattern of struggle in industrial societies that began with the formation of workers' councils ("soviets") in the Russian Revolution of 1905. In the brief period after World War I when workers mobilized to seize power throughout Russia, Central Europe, and Northern Italy, these councils led general strikes accompanied by factory occupations and in some cases partial resumption of production under workers' control. Despite attempts by several theoreticians to show that such activities are specific to a transcended craft stage of industrialism, comparable struggles have occurred as recently as the French May Events of 1968 (Feenberg and Freedman, 2001).

One can only conjecture that Marx's failure to formulate such a strategy was due to the difficulty of imagining a constructive transformation of technical practices. During Marx's lifetime, there were no large-scale radical struggles to overcome workplace alienation comparable to the Commune of Paris. Because Marx refused to engage in utopian speculation, his critique of the factory system remained primarily negative and his projection of technical disalienation in the "higher phase" of socialism appeared to have no implications for the present.

Since he published no powerful and persuasive document on the subject of workplace disalienation, Marx's critique of the labor process was quickly forgotten, overshadowed by his attack on the other aspect of capitalist power, ownership, and the proposed remedy, the nationalization of capitalist property by a democratized state. There were, after all, precedents in the French and American revolutions for the conscious transformation of political practices and institutions. Thus, while hinting at the possibility of democratizing the economy, Marx and Engels rely primarily on a strategy of radical political disalienation to initiate the transition.

As a result, when workers' councils finally emerged as the industrial equivalent of the Commune, practically no one saw how neatly they joined together Marx's theories of social revolution and his critique of the labor process. The victorious Russian revolutionaries had no higher ambition than to operate and expand the industrial apparatus inherited from capitalism. When they found that early experiments in workers' control reduced efficiency, they did not consider adapting the conditions of production to new social requirements but rather quickly reintroduced "one-man" management.[5]

These measures were motivated less by theory than by an emergency situation. But soon the leading German theoretician of social ownership, Eduard Heimann, could write that "the introduction of factory councils has conceptually nothing to do with socialization" (quoted in Kellner, 1971: 132). Communist leaders came to believe in the imperative requirements of the existing technology and division of labor. They defined capitalism as a form of ownership, and they identified its mode of appropriation with the general technical requirements of industrial production. Authoritarian economic control appeared as necessary to most socialists as it did to capitalists.

The hesitations and ambiguities of the Marxist theory of the transition were finally resolved in an uncompromising emphasis on control from above. The subject of the revolution turns out to be merely political after all, and its will is law. The demands of economic planning resonate with this emphasis: the planning of capital investment seems obviously to require a command system based on scientific evaluation of social needs. Indeed, for a whole generation the creation of a planned economy appears as the sine qua non of socialism no matter who exercises power and how.

At the extreme limit of this authoritarian emphasis lie such outlandish ideas as Trotsky's early proposal for the "militarization" of the Soviet labor force. If capital is scientifically allocated from above, why not labor as well? (Anderson, 1963: 140–147) Something not so very different from Trotsky's proposal was eventually implemented in Russia. With the passage of time the disappearance of that freedom of movement which was for Engels the foundation of the mental independence of the working class came to be seen as an intrinsic part of the socialist heritage.[6]

Rethinking the Transition

Although the Russian case cannot be regarded as a true test of the Marxian theory of the transition to socialism, it does bring out the hidden tension in that theory. For Marx, the autonomy of operational decision making is the foundation of alienated power in both the economy and state. It is institutionalized in the systems of political and managerial representation socialism inherits from capitalism. These systems can be employed transitionally by reducing the autonomy of the representatives through new and more democratic procedures. This disalienating strategy appears most applicable to the state, while a comparable transformation of the economy would run up against the inherited division of mental and manual labor. Marx and Engels therefore defer the latter transformation to a future "higher phase."

Neither the work of Marx and Engels, nor that of Lenin contains a satisfactory theory of the ambivalent employment of the capitalist economic and technical heritage. As a result, Marxism lacks an account of the *historical* connection between the theory of the socialist state in the first phase of socialism and the theory of the transcendence of the division of mental and manual labor in the "higher phase" of socialism. The confusion becomes clear as soon as one compares Marx's two principal writings on the transition, "The Civil War in France" and "The Critique of the Gotha Program." These texts offer two entirely independent scenarios of revolution that coexist in unresolved tension in Marxist projections of the future. In his reflections on the Paris Commune, the transition appears as a purely political process, while his comments on the Gotha Program emphasize overcoming the division of mental and manual labor. We are never told how the two sides are related, and in fact the division of socialism into "phases," the one characterized by political struggle, the other by technological change, isolates these two aspects of the process from each other.

In *The State and Revolution*, Lenin copies Marx's incoherence faithfully and presents the passage to communism twice. On the one hand, the transition is described as a near-term result of proletarian victory in the struggle to master the still-bourgeois administrative apparatus inherited from capitalism. With the achievement of proletarian self-administration, the state becomes obsolete and dissolves into the mass (Lenin, 1967a: II, 345). On the other hand, Lenin follows "The Critique of the Gotha Program" to the letter in asserting that the passage to communism requires a technological transformation, for so long as work is odious and goods are scarce, a state will be required to impose distribution according to merit (Lenin, 1967a: II, 342). What is the connection between these two forms of passage? What guarantees that they will be coordinated in time? In Lenin's conception, in fact, political struggle for the higher phase of socialism appears to be drastically foreshortened, while the technical progress he expects is unforeseeable.

After the October Revolution, Lenin applies these Marxian premises and argues for the early abolition of professional state administration. At the same time, with typical Marxian caution on technical issues, he sees the factory soviets less as instruments of economic democracy than as the legitimating basis of the state. The outcome of this attempt to apply the theory of the transition is disastrous: no sooner abolished, the professional state administration is reconstituted, and the soviets, reduced to a largely symbolic role, never supply the framework for democratizing either politics or economics. The transition is blocked. This outcome appears to confirm Weber's gloomiest predictions of universal bureaucratization.

Socialist emancipation in Marx's sense cannot consist in the implementation of policies, however "socialist," by the new subjects of capital's accumulated operational autonomy. Every such agent finds itself in precisely the position of the capitalist, obliged to use similar means of repression to extract labor power from an unwilling working class. *The solution to the problem of exercising power from above is contained in the very division of labor Marx criticized, and so any system based on top-down control will inevitably reproduce that division of labor, whatever its ostensible policy or purpose.*

This conclusion is illustrated by the fate of the USSR, trapped between socialist ideology and the capitalist heritage.[7] In theory, the ideology was supposed to instrumentalize the heritage, subordinating it to socialist purposes, but in practice the new Soviet elite was unable consistently to carry out either a socialist or a capitalist mission. Its socialist ideology prevented it from implementing a capitalistic civilizational project even though it occupied the post of capital it had expropriated from the previous ruling groups. But it was also unable to create a socialist society. In consolidating its power, the "socialist" regime suppressed the creative process of civilizational change. Now it could only implement socialist policies where these were compatible with the maintenance of a power rooted in capitalist social relations.

Since alienated administration offers the general solution to the problem of operating an industrial society from above, the Soviet system was bound to converge increasingly with the capitalist societies it struggled to overtake. This relative convergence was not so much an effect of modernization per se as of the impossibility of creating a truly new form of civilization on the basis of old methods of organization. Not surprisingly, having adopted those methods, Soviet society could solve its social and economic problems only by following in the footsteps of the advanced capitalist nations. The actual evolution of the Soviet Union confirms that socialism cannot be imposed by law and administrative fiat. Socialism is not a policy, but a movement of social change that can be created only from below.

The sharp distinction between politics and technology that guided the Russian revolutionaries is most un-Marxist. The two "phases," corresponding to political and technological disalienation, reflect not so much real historical periods as an unresolved theoretical tension. Marx is unclear on the transitional roles of the complementary bases of capitalist power, ownership and control. This unresolved tension is covered up by historicizing the relation between the expropriation of capital by the state and the end of the capitalist division of labor.

Yet we can see another possibility, toward which the whole shaky theoretical edifice tends and which, in the light of historical experience, makes a great deal more sense. In this alternative conception, the transition is conceived as an extended period of *democratic struggle over technology and administration* with the aim of bringing the strata located in the post of capital under social control. Socialism would gradually reduce the operational autonomy of managerial and expert personnel and reconstruct the divided and deskilled labor process they command. This reconstruction would be the essential content of the transition, not a distant utopia.

The Limits of Marxism

Marx made the great discovery that technology is a universal mediation of social life in modern society. He also understood that workers are strategically placed to modify that mediation and to create a fundamentally different type of society in which work favors rather than suppresses individual development. A clear and persuasive line of argument leads from these premises to Marx's conclusion that capitalism must go. If the operational autonomy of industrial leadership is reduced and technical design altered to favor further democratic advances, the firm will not be controllable by private owners and so will cease to yield a profit. Social ownership is the logical response to this situation.

However, it is no longer possible to agree with Marx that opposition to the existing society is primarily the mission of the working class and that its goals are best pursued through seizing state power. Even though most people are now employees, their common interests as such do not override their other concerns. Hence, struggles emerge around many issues, all of them traversed by technical mediations, but only a few of them primarily labor issues. Labor struggle is simply not the only "organizing activity" that corresponds to Marx's critique of modern industrialism.

Marx mistook the emergence of universal technical mediation for the creation of a compact social subject that would be able to rule the state in the universal interest. His focus shifted away from technique toward the political stage on which classes act and play their role. But it is now clear that technical politics is not a contingent struggle of a particular class, but, rather, is a basic form of resistance that lies at the core of many types of social struggle in advanced societies.

From this standpoint labor appears to be involved in one among many sectoral struggles. The theory of the "new social movements" hails the demotion of labor from the vanguard to a mere item on the list of discontents. But it is important not to confuse the current weakness of the classical labor movement with an argument for the unimportance of the issues with which it has been concerned. It is clear that no one movement, including the labor movement, totalizes all social struggles, but that does not mean that class issues are outmoded or reactionary.

In an industrial society, the problems of the work world are of such immense scope and moment that it is difficult to conceive a fundamental civilizational advance that would not address them. Furthermore, given the strategic weight of industry in the organization of modern states, the control of production is a source of power that cannot be ignored. This is why it is still necessary to pose the problem of *capitalist* hegemony and why no fundamental change is likely to occur without the reemergence of new forms of class politics alongside the innovative social movements of recent years.

The story told in this chapter implies a fundamental shift in perspective. I have exposed the link between Marx's daring call for a total transformation of the state and his relative timidity in the face of the technical challenges of the revolution. The rejection here of Marxism's most radical attack on the state appears to be a retreat. But our story suggests a different conclusion: the disalienation of the state is not the scene of effective struggle to change capitalist civilization. When Marx abandoned his original notion of social revolution for a more conventional emphasis on politics, *that* was the original retreat from which the socialist movement has still not recovered. That shift burdened the state with impossibly ambitious tasks it either abandoned in social-democratic managerialism or implemented through voluntaristic excesses and state terror. A different path opens once the socialist state is seen again as Marx originally conceived it, not as the salvation of the whole, but as a protective umbrella under which social creativity can operate at the microlevel of particular institutions and workplaces. A new society can be born only of an immense multiplicity of such activities, not from a politically enforced plan.

3

The Bias of Technology

Means and Ends

Instrumentalist theory of technology in both its Marxist and non-Marxist forms shares the commonsense assumption that the subjects of action—for example, the worker or the state—can be defined independently of their means. But in reality subjects and means are dialectically intertwined: the carpenter and the hammer appear accidentally related only so long as one does not consider carpentry as a vocation shaping the carpenter through a relation to the tools of the trade. The army is not merely accidentally related to its weapons, but is structured around the activities they support. Similarly, the school does not "use" its teachers or their knowledge as means to its educational goals, but is constituted qua actor by these "means." In these cases of collective action, the agent *is* its means of action viewed from another angle.

If this is true, sociotechnical transformation cannot be conceived in terms of instrumental categories because the very act of using technology reproduces what is supposed to be transformed. Hence the well-known limitations of liberal management techniques such as job enrichment and quality circles. This is the *paradox of reform from above*: since technology is not neutral but fundamentally biased toward a particular hegemony, all action undertaken within its framework tends to reproduce that hegemony.

Traditional Marxism founders on this paradox. It claims that a workers' state can instrumentalize the inherited technological base in the creation of a new republic of skill. But this program involves a conceptually incoherent interaction between a social actor and the very division of labor that forms it as such in the first place. A similar contradiction refutes the claim that "postindustrial" capitalism will evolve spontaneously into a participatory, skill-based society. Both authoritarian socialism and reformist capitalism can evolve only within the rather narrow limits of top-down control. But what alternative is there to these discredited formulations? How can social actors alter the system that defines their very being?

The previous chapter suggested an answer to these questions in terms of new theories of design, ambivalence, and technical politics. These theories are based on the notion that technologies "condense" social and technical functions. The design critique explains this condensation as it affects technologies shaped in the past by the power of the ruling groups, while the theory of ambivalence asserts that technical features determined by a social function are subject to social change. In this conception, a socialist state might create a more favorable political environment for technological change, but would not by itself resolve the tensions in the industrial system. These can only be grasped from "within," by individuals immediately engaged in technically mediated activities and able to actualize ambivalent potentialities previously suppressed by an authoritarian technological rationality.

Ideas such as these could have provided the basis for understanding the transitional role of workers' councils in the period after World War I. Today, adapted to a situation in which technology is no longer just a labor issue, these ideas can still revive the critical theory of society. The purpose of this chapter is to reach a coherent formulation of this radical alternative to instrumentalist versions of Marxism.

As we have seen, Marx's design critique agrees with substantive theory of technology that machines and artifacts embody values. But there is an important difference. Substantive theory identifies the values embodied in current designs with the essence of technology as such. From that standpoint, no transition to a fundamentally different form of modern society is possible since all imaginable modernities will employ technology and hence express the selfsame essence. By contrast, the design critique relates the values embodied in technology to a social hegemony. But what depends on a social force can be changed by another social force: technology is not destiny. The major attempts to work out a philosophy of technology on this basis are to be found in Marcuse and Foucault. They treated technology as an expression of the historical development of the dominant paradigm of rationality, and reconceptualized social conflict as the result of internal tensions in that paradigm. The idea of internal tensions promises to fulfill Marx's original hopes for a theory of social revolution, but it needs a great deal of further refinement before it can replace instrumentalist notions of political change.

For both Marcuse and Foucault society is a gigantic machinery regimenting its members. Presumably, liberation depends on reversing the balance of power between the system and individual resistance. But whether and how this is possible remains unclear. Marcuse wavers between instrumental and substantive interpretations of his "one-dimensionality" thesis, and Foucault's theory of resistance is vaguer still. Despite these problems, Marcuse and Foucault present the most powerful accounts of modern forms of domination. I will examine their critical theories in the next two sections and attempt to complete their rather sketchy accounts of radical change in the remainder of this chapter.

Marcuse and Foucault

Marcuse formulated his theory of technological rationality under the influence of and in reaction against the Weberian theory of rationalization. Weber distinguished two different types of rationality corresponding to two types of social thought and action.[1] Rationality is "substantive" to the extent that it realizes a specific value such as feeding a population or maintaining the social hierarchy. The "formal" rationality of capitalism refers to those economic arrangements which optimize calculability and control. Formally rational systems lie under technical norms that have to do with the efficiency of means rather than the choice of ends.

Weber's concept of the "rationalization" of modern societies refers to the generalization of formal rationality at the expense of traditional substantively rational modes of action. This is a cultural change with important social consequences. Weber recognizes that rationalization is favorable to the ambitions of capitalists and bureaucrats, who rise to the top in any rationalized society. Yet he wants us to believe that only substantive rationality contains valuative biases, that formal rationality is in itself value-free.

Weber's sociology of rationality appears to open a whole new field, but no sooner does he offer us a glimpse of this exciting realm than he shuts the door. Substantive rationality remains a vague, practically contentless concept, while Weber's attention is focused on formal rationality, which, because it is value-free, is not really subject to sociological explanation.

Yet it is puzzling that the generalization of a neutral form of rationality should produce a socially biased outcome. Today, in a completely rationalized society, this puzzle is no longer just a scientific curiosity. As technical mediations spread into every nook and cranny of social life, mastery of the machine becomes the principal source of power. Is it simply an accident of "progress" that rationalization concentrates that power in a few hands?

Technological Rationality

The critical theory of technology is suspicious of the advantages the benefi-
ciaries of technological advance derive from the claim that, like justice, technology is socially blind. This suspicion motivates Marcuse's attack on Weber.
Marcuse argues that the prevailing forms of technology are subject to the same
sort of demystifying critique that Marx applied to the market. Like market
rationality, "technological rationality" constitutes the basis for elite control
of society. That control is not simply an extrinsic purpose served by neutral
systems and machines but is internal to their very structure. The concept of
technological rationality "presupposes the separation of the workers from
the means of production . . . (as) a *technical* necessity requiring the individual
and private direction and control of the means of production. . . . The highly
material, historical fact of the private-capitalist enterprise thus becomes . . .
a *formal* structural element of capitalism and of *rational* economic activity
itself" (Marcuse, 1968: 212).

Technological rationality is indelibly marked by the presupposition that
production goes hand in hand with social domination. The trace of this presupposition can be found in economic thought, managerial methods, and
the very design of technology. The concept of "efficiency," for example, is
usually applied against an unexamined assumption about worker resistance
to work. The point is not that this assumption is false; it is often true. But
that is the result of unquestioned structures of ownership and control that
exclude workers from any interest in the firm, resulting in difficult problems
of labor discipline. Insofar as this background is ignored or suppressed, the
concept of efficiency becomes ideological in the application.

The concept of technological rationality expresses the condensation of
social and technical functions implicit in Marx's design critique of technology. It explains how rules and procedures that achieve a certain kind of universality may also represent private interests through the assumptions that
form their horizon. These interests are overlooked because they are not expressed through orders or commands, but are technically embodied, for
example, in apparently neutral management rules or technical designs.

One-Dimensional Man discusses the ideological function of this capitalist-
distorted rationality. Marcuse argues that it is not just biased in its operational employment but also legitimates social domination. This argument
carries us well beyond the original Marxian critique of the inefficiency of
capitalism. Marx believed that alienation was not only inhumane but was also
an obstacle to the growth of the productive forces; therefore, the normative
demand for a more humane society was congruent with the technical pur-

suit of productivity. Marcuse argues that the economic success of contemporary capitalism has invalidated Marx's position. Technological rationality no longer serves, as it still did for Marx, as the basis of a critique of the relations of production, but becomes the legitimating discourse of the society. Habermas summarizes this aspect of Marcuse's theory: "At the stage of their scientific-technical development, then, the forces of production appear to enter a new constellation with the relations of production. Now they no longer function as the basis of a critique of prevailing legitimations in the interest of political enlightenment, but become instead the basis of legitimation. *This* is what Marcuse conceives of as world-historically new" (Habermas, 1970: 84).

Under these conditions, the condensation of social and technical determinations tends more and more to appear as the very definition of rationality. Not only is technical progress distorted by the requirements of capitalist control but the "universe of discourse," public and eventually even private speech and thought, is limited to posing and resolving technical problems. "When technics becomes the universal form of material production, it circumscribes an entire culture; it projects a historical totality—a 'world'" (Marcuse, 1964: 154). There is no place for critical consciousness in this world: it is "one-dimensional." The normative critique is thus forced to appear explicitly and independently; it can no longer hide behind the Marxian demand for a liberation of the productive forces. This explains why Marcuse not only attacks the dominant social interests but also criticizes technology, breaking with the traditional radical faith in progress.

Power/Knowledge

Marcuse's theory of rationality provides a general framework for discussing the condensation of technical and social functions. Once rationality is treated as a social phenomenon, its concrete sociological forms are open to study. But, like much Frankfurt School social theory, Marcuse has plenty of brilliant insights, but they remain very general. In this respect, Foucault provides a useful corrective. Although he does not appear to have been directly influenced by either Weber or Critical Theory, his approach is similar. He, too, argues that power is organized, exercised, and legitimated through forms of rationality that are open to historical investigation.

Foucault applied this approach to studying the origins of the modern social, administrative, and medical sciences in various practices of social control that emerged from the seventeenth century on. He calls these practices "microtechniques," punctual controls that spread without any overall decision or plan. They include examining, drilling, measuring individual growth patterns, isolating individuals for inspection, dossiers and files, and so on. These practices first develop in settings as diverse as armies, convents, hospitals, schools, prisons, and factories. A "disciplinary power" arises from their proliferation.

Foucault rejects the neutrality thesis: knowledge and technology are not value-free tools that may be put to a good or bad use. Truth and power are not two independent things that meet contingently in the moment of application. Social sciences such as psychology and criminology are outgrowths of specific institutions such as hospitals or prisons. New forms of knowledge and new forms of social control are connected at the origin. Foucault's clearest example of this connection is Bentham's Panopticon, an architectural solution to the problem of placing large numbers of subjected individuals under the gaze of a few supervisors. Here the glance that examines and judges reveals the "truth" in constraining its object. The "regime of truth" is the logic of this inextricable relation between knowledge and power.

This theory has a Kuhnian twist. For Kuhn, scientific paradigms include not only concepts and theories but also standard procedures that define objects in measuring and controlling them. Similarly, for Foucault the social sciences are rooted in paradigmatic ways of observing and collecting data (Dreyfus and Rabinow, 1983: 197ff.). But where the object of investigation is another human being, such procedures are not and cannot be socially neutral. For example, in the prison setting, what the psychologist calls "observing the subject," the subject experiences as just another form of forced confinement. Knowledge, at least of human affairs, is obtained through cognitive procedures that are also exercises of power. The dual nature of such procedures, at once cognitive and social, resembles the social/technical duality that Marcuse identifies in the repressive rationality of ostensibly neutral tools such as the assembly line.

According to Foucault, power/knowledge is a web of social forces and tensions in which everyone is caught as both subject and object. This web is constructed around techniques, some of them materialized in machines, architecture or other devices, others embodied in standardized forms of behavior that do not so much coerce and suppress the individuals as guide them toward the most productive use of their bodies. Although Foucault does not focus often on technology, his approach to the Panopticon can be plausibly generalized to other types of devices.[2] On this account, technology is just one among many similar mechanisms of social control, all based on pretensions to neutral knowledge, all having asymmetrical effects on social power.

This explains why the social imperatives of capitalism are experienced as technical constraints rather than as political coercion. Surveillance, disciplinary power, normalization, all make possible the factory system and the capitalist society founded upon it. They "condense" technical and social functions at the level of everyday behavior, even before that functional duality is transferred to the design of machinery. Eventually these sociotechnical constraints are embodied in mechanical structures that determine workers' action more effectively than rules and commands by determining their reflexes, skills and attitudes.

> The exercise of power is not added on from the outside, like a rigid, heavy constraint, to the functions it invests, but is so subtly present in them as to increase their efficiency by itself increasing its own points of contact. The panoptic mechanism is not simply a hinge, a point of exchange between a mechanism of power and a function; it is a way of making power relations function in a function, and of making a function function through those power relations. (Foucault, 1977: 206–207)

Dystopian Paradoxes

Although frequently accused of irrationalism, Foucault and the Frankfurt School claim to make "a rational critique of rationality" (Foucault, 1988: 27). This position implies that rationality is not singular but plural. Accordingly, they favor "isolating the form of rationality presented as dominant, and endowed with the status of the one-and-only reason, in order to show that it is only *one* possible form among others" (Foucault, 1988: 27). The critical theory of technology applies this approach to the analysis of technical design and so recapitulates many of the familiar problems in wider ranging social critiques of rationality. Two of these problems are discussed in this section:

1. Both Foucault and Marcuse have a difficult time sustaining our belief in the possibility of resistance even as they appeal to us to oppose the closed world they describe.
2. Neither Foucault nor Marcuse is an irrationalist, yet they find it difficult to grant any sort of validity to knowledge, having demystified its social neutrality.

One-Dimensionality

Like Marx, Marcuse and Foucault share a system theory of capitalist alienation. Capitalists and workers are not the primary units of explanation in this theory, but are, rather, the *bearers* of the procedures underlying the system. Workers produce capital and, in turn, "personified capital, the capitalist, takes care that the labourer does his work regularly and with the proper degree of intensity" (Marx, 1906: I, 338). Capitalism is a kind of collective automaton, the parts of which are human beings organized into a self-reproducing, self-expanding system of dependencies.

We are far indeed from the traditional Marxist account that explains how one group of historical actors, capitalists, gains control over another group, workers, *using* the division of labor and machinery as its instrument. On the contrary, here capitalists and workers are defined by their place in the division of labor, which is a more fundamental *structure* establishing the conditions of their existence. The ruling class is not the origin of the system of social domination but must be located in a preexisting field of instrumentalities it exploits. The emphasis here is not on the deeds and misdeeds of classes but on what Foucault calls a "machinery of power," an order of ideas and practices that creates a network of constraints and opportunities within which individual and collective subjects emerge as actors.[3]

Both Foucault and Marcuse support this system theory with a new conception of the relation of individual to society. Their accounts aim to show, as Foucault explains it, that power is not merely repressive but constructs a productive subjectivity in the dominated. Foucault emphasizes the role of "normalization" in achieving this result, while Marcuse has a fundamentally similar theory, the "integration" of the individual through "repressive desublimation."[4]

But there is a difficulty with this position that Marcuse and Foucault do not squarely face: having abandoned naive notions of individuality and natural instinct, neither can identify the locus of resistance to the system, the flaws of which they analyze so persuasively. Their theories open no space within which opposition could emerge; they provide no structural basis for understanding the operations in which the dominated might resist domination. Hence, they have no way to block the closure toward which the system tends, which Marcuse calls its "one-dimensionality."

Foucault's overly ambitious theory of power ends in this impasse. He argues that subjects emerge as individuals through subjection to modern forms of social power. In Foucault's terminology, subjection is "subjectification": "The individual . . . is not the *vis-a-vis* of power; it is, I believe, one of its prime effects" (Foucault, 1980: 98). But if subjects do not preexist subjugation, but are created by it, then the very word "power" loses any meaning because it has nothing to which to oppose itself.

Deleuze attempts to save Foucault from this difficulty by asking: "Is not the force that comes from outside a certain idea of Life, a certain vitalism, in which Foucault's thought culminates?" (Deleuze, 1986: 92–93)[5] One can only hope the answer to this question is negative. The reference to an amorphous subject of resistance constituted prior to the cultural encoding of individuality offers only a prerational basis for opposition: chaos or madness as a metaphor for political opposition.[6]

Foucault believed for a time that a lingering dialectical prejudice explained our tendency to dismiss such spontaneous resistances (Foucault, 1980: 143–144). Presumably, if society does not form a "totality," the opposition need not be totalizing either and so need not possess a rational grasp of the whole. Foucault hoped to valorize the particularism of local struggles by abandoning the dialectical requirement that action transcend the system.

This new orientation was undoubtedly liberating for the French Left, obsessively focused on the state. But so involved was Foucault in a polemic against the French Communist Party's conception of the intellectual that his spontaneist strategy ignored important aspects of his own theory. That theory not only analyzes microtechniques against which spontaneous local resistance is inevitable but also recognizes a level of strategic coordination by hegemonies that instrumentalize and integrate the elementary forms of resistance. These hegemonies construct "metapowers," such as corporations and states, which mobilize the available microtechniques through a rationalized system of domination. Thus, Foucault writes, "one must rather conduct an *ascending* analysis of power, starting, that is, from its infinitesimal mechanisms, which each have their own history, their own trajectory, their own techniques and tactics, and then see how these mechanisms of power have been—and continue to be—invested, colonised, utilised, involuted, transformed, displaced, extended etc., by ever more general mechanisms and by forms of global domination" (Foucault, 1980: 99).

It seems obvious that resistance must operate not merely on the level of microtechniques, but at the level of the metapowers if it is to counter this constructive movement of capitalist hegemony. This is clearly not a task for the unaided life-force and so we are back to the necessity of unions, parties, and so on.

Marcuse confronts the problem directly. He admits that most forms of resistance, vital or not, can be absorbed by the system, and that, far from threatening it, they contribute to its dynamism. Capitalism no longer merely promises ideal compensations for real miseries, but "delivers the goods" to a working class that is effectively incorporated into the system. The constellation formed by authoritarian management, a technology adapted to its needs, and a ready supply of consumer goods cannot be broken. The essential sources of opposition have dried up, and so Marcuse seeks validation for his critique among marginal groups, the weakness of which he acknowledges in principle. The theory subverts itself by canceling the idea of transcending action and appears to reinstate the fatalism of a Heidegger or an Ellul.[7]

Despite his sympathy for the new social movements, Marcuse was never a spontaneist. Revolution requires not an end to culture and individuality but their reappropriation. It is not outside power but is a transformation operated in the field of power. Foucault himself recognizes this when he writes that "there are many different kinds of revolution, roughly speaking as many kinds as there are possible subversive recodifications of power relations" (Foucault, 1980: 122–123). On these terms, "life," if indeed that is the correct word for the force against which hegemonies impose themselves, is not preindividual but represents an alternative form of individuality elaborated in a variety of social activities, not the least of which is resistance to social domination. Foucault's later work, with its emphasis on "self-mastery," appears to support this reading and draws it close in spirit to Critical Theory (Foucault, 1988).

Irrationalism

Marcuse's critique of rationality is formulated in a dangerous flirtation with a substantive theory of technology. Marcuse approaches substantivism from Marxism by extending the critique of ideology. Traditionally that critique refutes the claim to rational universality of superstructures such as art or law, but Marcuse applies it to technology as well. When he writes, for example, that science is "political" or that technology is "ideological," he makes the strong point that "technology as such cannot be isolated from the use to which it is put" (Marcuse, 1964: xvi). Yet in making his point in this way, he might be taken to mean that, as ideology, science and technology are merely expressions of the interests of the ruling class. Then radical opposition would include the utopian demand that capitalist technoscience be quite simply junked as just another instance of ideology. This is not at all Marcuse's intent. Despite his sharp criticism of "technological rationality," he still maintains the old Marxist faith in the liberating potential of the technological inheritance:

> If the completion of the technological project involves a break with the prevailing technological rationality, the break in turn depends on the continued existence of the technical base itself. For it is this base which has rendered possible the satisfaction of needs and the reduction of toil—it remains the very base of all forms of human freedom. The qualitative change rather lies in the reconstruction of this base—that is, in its development with a view of different ends. . . . The new ends, as technical ends, would then operate in

the project and in the construction of the machinery, and not only in its utilization. (Marcuse, 1964: 231–232)

As can be seen from this passage, Marcuse avoids irrationalism only by offering correctives to his strongest critical claims. Here the correctives hint at a theory of ambivalence, but elsewhere he ends up asserting the neutrality, validity, and instrumental effectiveness of science and technology despite their "ideological" character. At one point he writes that "basic needs" will continue to be served under socialism by the very "technological rationality" he condemns elsewhere for its connection to domination (Marcuse, 1964: 251). But this assertion contradicts his claim that a reconstructed technology can be made to contribute to freedom precisely through serving basic needs in a new way. That requires a new direction for progress, not the addition of a thin veneer of "humanized" technology on the surface of a world engineered in all its essential features to the destruction of man and nature.

Marcuse's contradictions are summed up in two brief remarks that assert with equal assurance that "technology has become the great vehicle of *reification*" and that "science and technology are the great vehicles of liberation" (Marcuse, 1964: 168; Marcuse, 1969: 12). The mutually canceling formulae do actually add up to a theory, but it is buried in the interplay of the inadequate concepts used to present it. In any case, Marcuse's rhetorical strategy is clear enough: from a variant of the Marxist position, he extracts results that one would expect from the substantivist position. He has his conceptual cake and eats it, making the strongest possible critique of technology without paying the "Luddist" price. The ambiguous results reveal the limitations of Marcuse's approach.

Like Marcuse, Foucault strays into puzzling epistemological difficulties. He argues that "Truth is a thing of this world," and he identifies power and knowledge without worrying much about the reflexive paradox into which this position precipitates his own theory: if all truth merely reflects a position of power, then Foucault's argument appears to subvert itself (Foucault, 1980: 131).[8]

There is a way out of this paradox, and Foucault takes it by distinguishing *power* from *domination*. Power is a kind of life-force that opens perspectives on the real in Nietzschean fashion, while domination is institutional closure, premature totalization. On this account, there is a knowledge rooted in the suppressed potentialities and self-understanding of the dominated distinct from the forms of knowledge linked to domination. Thus, in certain passages Foucault refers to an "insurrection of subjugated knowledges" to which his own critical work contributes (Foucault, 1980: 81). His "genealogical method" attempts to recover the "local, discontinuous, disqualified, illegitimate knowledges" of the dominated in opposition to the "unitary body of theory which would filter, hierarchise and order them in the name of some true knowledge and some arbitrary idea of what constitutes a science and its objects" (Foucault, 1980: 83).

Although Foucault's method is very different, his critique is similar to Marcuse's, not absolutist to be sure, but at least internally consistent in offering reasons for its claims. But because Foucault continually plays on the ambiguity of power and domination, we are never sure how far he intends to go toward a relativistic reduction of knowledge claims to social positions. Like Marcuse's, Foucault's rhetorical strategy lends force to his condemnation of the established technocracy while blurring essential issues.

Marcuse and Foucault offer a persuasive account of the condensation of the social and the technical, and they propose a system theory of social action that appears more applicable to contemporary societies than the traditional Marxist class theory. But their very advances plunge them into insuperable difficulties. Their theories of the bias of knowledge threaten rationality as a whole; their accounts of social order seem to exclude resistance. Is there any way to preserve the essential insights of these thinkers while avoiding their shortcomings?

In the remainder of this chapter I will argue that Marcuse and Foucault encounter these difficulties because they lack a theory of *technological hegemony* capable of explaining the relationship of social organizations to ideology/science and power/knowledge. As a result, they invoke a substantivist rhetoric that immediately identifies science and ideology, knowledge and power. These identifications give a particular dystopian pathos to their theories. Indeed, if the problem is knowledge as such, or the very existence of discipline, then criticism and resistance are equally hopeless. For all the rhetorical power of these images of a closed world, they cannot explain the possibility of critical knowledge of society and systematic resistance. That will require a theory of those hegemonic mediations responsible for the problems Marcuse and Foucault appear to blame on knowledge and technology per se.

The Technical Code

Double Aspect Theory

Despite many ambiguities, one thing is clear about the position of Marcuse and Foucault: they reject the accustomed terms of the rationalism/relativism debate and affirm *both* that rationality is integral to a system of domination *and* that it nevertheless achieves cognitive success. Although this position appears contradictory, they finesse the difficulties with the notion that knowledge and power share a common foundation but have different destinies. For Marcuse that foundation is a method of abstraction rooted in the will to domination. His critique of that method will be discussed in the last chapter of this book. For Foucault, it is the common fund of microtechniques that establish both a disciplinary society and a social science and technology adapted to it.

As we have seen, neither Marcuse nor Foucault pursues this line of argument consistently. In this section, I will therefore leave behind the details of their positions to sketch an approach to the study of technology suggested by their work. I will call this approach a "double aspect" theory of power/knowledge or ideology/science because it treats hegemonic and cognitive functions as complementary aspects of a single underlying source rather than as separate things.

The place to begin this discussion is with the function of rationality in modern hegemonies. An effective hegemony is one that need not be imposed in a continuing struggle between self-conscious agents but that is reproduced unreflectively by the standard beliefs and practices of the society it dominates. Tradition and religion played that role for millennia; today, forms of rationality supply the hegemonic beliefs and practices. This is the sense in which knowledge has become a kind of power, not merely a tool of those in power, *without losing its character as knowledge.* This change in the status of knowledge is rooted in distinctive structures of capitalism.

In precapitalist societies workers had traditional tasks and established codes of self-expression; they owned their own tools and formed a natural community. The labor process was so completely enveloped in regulations and responsibilities that precapitalist elites could rule only by escaping the economic domain to exercise what Foucault calls "sovereign" power, the negative power of the state.

Capitalism frees itself from these limitations to an unprecedented degree by building workforces and markets out of atomized individuals, much like the prisons and asylums studied by Foucault but on a far wider scale. Released from all traditional rules and familial restraints, the capitalist has a great deal more freedom of action than had the leaders of traditional work groups. In chapter 2, I called this special kind of freedom the capitalist's "operational autonomy." It is not primarily a property of individuals but of organizations that mobilize an array of microtechniques.

Operational autonomy is the power to make strategic choices among alternative rationalizations without regard for externalities, customary practice,

workers' preferences, or the impact of decisions on their households. Whatever other goals the capitalist pursues, all viable strategies implemented from
his peculiar position in the social system must reproduce his operational
autonomy. The "metagoal" of preserving and enlarging autonomy is gradually incorporated into the standard ways of doing things, biasing the solution to every practical problem toward certain typical responses. In industrial societies, strategies of domination consist primarily in embedding these
constancies in technical procedures, standards, and artifacts in order to establish a framework in which day-to-day technical activity serves the interests of capital.

Capitalism is unique in that its hegemony is largely based on reproducing its own operational autonomy through technical decisions. This is usually sufficient because power in modern societies can be wielded through
technical control without titles of nobility or religious sanctions. The "will"
that Marx identified with Jacobin "politics" is to be found here, in the expansive dynamic of modern organizations, driven ever further toward the
accumulation of autonomous possibilities of action.

Capitalist social and technical requirements are condensed in a "technological rationality" or a "regime of truth" that brings the construction and
interpretation of technical systems into conformity with the requirements
of a system of domination. I will call this phenomenon the social code of
technology or, more briefly, the *technical code* of capitalism. Capitalist hegemony, on this account, is an effect of its code.[9]

In this sociological context, the term "code" has at least two different
meanings. First, it may signify a rule that simultaneously (1) classifies activities as permitted or forbidden and (2) associates them with a certain meaning or purpose that explains (1). The traffic code defines permitted driving
behavior by distinguishing the safe from the unsafe. Technical manuals are
full of similar codes that determine the rule under which operations are to
be performed in service to a variety of ends such as reliability, strength,
human factors, efficiency, and so on. It is characteristic of a bureaucratized
society such as ours that we have written records of many codes regulating
behavior.

Economic codes are nowhere recorded in a manual but are implicit in
behavior and attitudes, and signify a broader range of values than the permitted and the forbidden. An act of interpretation is required to extract the
meaning of this second type of code from its various manifestations. Consider, for example, the prestige hierarchy of goods such as automobiles: we
"know" that Cadillacs are "better" than Fords, Mercedes "better" than
Volkswagens. In displaying one or the other car we send a message about

ourselves to others. As is clear from this example, such codes have a communicative function.

The technical code combines elements of both types. It is most essentially the rule under which technical choices are made in view of preserving operational autonomy (i.e., the freedom to make similar choices in the future). This invariant requirement of the code is not generally explicit, although like the prestige hierarchy it can be brought to the surface without much difficulty. The goal of enhancing operational autonomy is implicit in the basic technical procedures of fields that serve the needs of business enterprises and other similarly structured organizations. Noble's account of numerical control, discussed in chapter 2, is a clear example. As in that case, the preferred designs are usually signified as "efficient" with the class bias Marcuse identified in his critique of Weber. And since efficiency is such a widely shared value, that signification has a legitimating function that constitutes the communicative aspect of the code.

The technical code has (social) ontological significance in a society where domination is based on control of technology. It is not merely the rule under which means are chosen. Much more than that, it is the principle of organizational identity and survival. Marc Guillaume thus defines social codes "as the ensemble of associations between signifiers (objects, services, acts . . .) and that which they signify in society, associations created or controlled by organizations as a basis of their existence and if possible their development" (Guillaume, 1975: 64). However, in the case of the technical code, it is necessary to go beyond this formulation. To exist, organizations must encode their technical base, not merely associating technology with certain signifiers but installing these signifiers in their very structure.[10] How is this achieved? This question can be answered only by carrying the theory of the condensation of the social and the technical one step further. In the process, we will see how the dual aspects of power/knowledge are reconciled in technical objects.

Everyone who develops modern technologies or studies their history knows that they are built up from concatenations of more or less loosely connected parts. The parts themselves arise out of discoveries so basic that, although they may first have served one or another specific purpose, they can be used for very different purposes in a wide variety of contexts. Thus, we distinguish between the principles embodied in technologies and the form of their concrete realization in this or that actual device.

I will reserve the term "technical element" for the specific principles, such as the spring, the lever or the electric circuit. These are in themselves "relatively" neutral, if not with respect to all social purposes, at least with respect to the ends of ruling and subordinate social groups. The work of discovering such elements is to some extent autonomized in the research process. Once discovered, they are like the vocabulary of a language; they can be strung together—encoded—to form a variety of "sentences" with different meanings and intentions.

Individual technologies are constructed from just such decontextualized technical elements combined in unique configurations to make specific devices. The process of invention is not purely technical: the abstract technical elements must enter a context of social constraints. Technologies, as developed ensembles of technical elements, are thus greater than the sum of their parts. They meet social criteria of purpose in the very selection and arrangement of the elements from which they are built up.[11]

These social purposes are embodied in the technology and are not therefore mere extrinsic ends to which a neutral tool might be put. The embodiment of specific purposes is achieved through the "fit" of the technology and its social environment. The technical ideas combined in the technology are relatively neutral, but one can trace in it the impress of a mesh of social determinations that preconstruct a domain of social activity in accordance with certain interests or values.

Bruno Latour makes a similar point. He argues that each technology draws together a "sociogram" of alliances of social interests around a specific configuration of technical elements, which he calls the "technogram." Latour argues that "every piece of information you obtain on one system is also information on other" (Latour, 1987: 138).[12] Sociogram and technogram are essentially just two sides of the same coin; a particular technical configuration reflects the influence of a particular network of actors. A precise definition of a specific technology can therefore only be found at the intersection of the two systems.

The technical code of capitalism can now be defined as a general rule for correlating sociogram and technogram. The assumption that, as nonowners, workers are indifferent to the welfare of the firm is the most important social factor that infiltrates itself into the definition of technical reason through this code. The assembly line is an excellent example of a technology influenced by this assumption: a strategy of technologically enforced labor discipline forms the glue that holds together the elements from which it is composed. This asymmetrical effect on power is characteristic of a strategically encoded technology.

This example also illustrates the historical relativity of the process of rationalization. The assembly line only appears as technical progress because it extends the kind of administrative rationality on which capitalism already depends. It might not be perceived as an advance in the context of an economy based on workers' cooperatives in which labor discipline was self-imposed rather than imposed from above.

Of course, the parts of an invention like the assembly line have a technical coherence of their own that in no way depends on politics or class relations. Technology is not reduced in this example to production relations nor technical knowledge to ideology. The first term in each of these pairs has its own logic; technology must really *work*. But it is not merely because a device works that it is chosen for development over many other equally coherent configurations of technical elements. Were that the case, then by analogy one could also explain the choice of individual sentences in speech by their grammatical coherence. The social character of technology lies not in the logic of its inner workings, but in the relation of that logic to a social context.

This is even true of the social technologies Foucault studies. Techniques of discipline and normalization do not determine a single organization of society, but open possibilities that are disputed between dominated and dominating social groups. Foucault did not despair because, whatever the outcome of the struggle, modern societies will inevitably employ some variant of these techniques. On the contrary, his goal was to find a way "which would allow these games of power to be played with a minimum of domination" (Foucault, 1988: 18).

Despite radically different purposes and institutional structures, modern sciences, technologies, and social organizations share a similar method of abstraction and similar microtechnical foundations. Because of this, scientific and technical disciplines are able to supply the hegemony they serve with the applications it requires. But the lower we descend toward the foundations, the more ambiguous are the elements from which these applications are constructed. This is the source of the ambivalence of technology. Thus, a technical code is needed to bind applications to hegemonic purposes since science and technique can be integrated to several different hegemonic orders. That is also why new technology can threaten the hegemony of the ruling groups until it has been strategically encoded. And that is why hegemonic claims to monopolize rationality are subject to rational critique. The double aspect theory can thus demystify the neutrality of knowledge and technology without also asserting that, like ideology, they are invalidated by their service to particular interests.

In Marcuse and Foucault, the relation between technical knowledge and society is unclear. Because their double aspect theory of technology is implicit, they lack an appropriate terminology in which to express it. At times they appear to be saying that knowledge is merely a projection of social power;

and yet they also want to distinguish knowledge from mere prejudices and ideologies. These hesitations are an attempt to suggest the preestablished harmony of knowledge and hegemony without reducing one to the other. I argue here that the connection between knowledge and power, technique and hegemony lies in the code that ensures that they are coordinated in the application.

Formal Bias

The theory of the technical code offers a paradoxical challenge to the conventional idea of the neutrality of technology. It is usually assumed that since technology is founded on a generic interest, it is indifferent with respect to particular social interests. As we saw above, Marcuse and Foucault reject this familiar approach. Their double aspect theory of technology attributes a certain neutrality to basic techniques, if not with respect to ends in general, at least with respect to different encodings. Technical codes responding to a specific social interest select one technically coherent configuration of these basic techniques from among a variety of alternatives. This is what makes possible modern hegemonies based on technical knowledge.

The critical theory of technology thus implies that in certain cases neutrality and bias are not opposites, but merely different aspects of a single concrete object (Marcuse, 1964: 156; Dreyfus and Rabinow, 1983: 203). This approach appears to be very difficult to communicate, and not uncommonly the double aspects are collapsed back into a single one—usually it is bias— on the assumption that the critique is an irrationalist attack on objective knowledge. How can the coexistence of neutrality and bias be more clearly explained to avoid such misinterpretations?

The problem is due to the fact that we usually conceive of bias as a deviation from fairness, which, in common usage, refers to the application of the same standard to all regardless of personal feelings. This background explains why the notion of bias suggests particularity subverting universality, for example, nepotism or prejudice slanting a hiring decision that ought to be made on the universal ground of qualifications for the job. Neutrality, as a property of the universal, therefore appears opposed to bias. On these terms, it is impossible to make sense of the notion of biased technology since the rationality inherent in technical devices is incommensurable with personal partiality by definition. However, there is another more subtle form of bias that consists in applying the same standard to individuals who cannot be compared or under conditions that favor some at the expense of others. This type of bias is often difficult to identify because the application of a single standard gives the appearance of fairness. In this case neutrality is not the opposite of bias but its essential precondition.[13]

I will borrow a distinction from Weber's theory of rationality to designate these types of bias, and call the first "substantive" bias and the second "formal" bias. As one would expect from these terms, the second type is peculiarly characteristic of modern societies. For example, it characterizes conditions in which "formal" equality contradicts social "content," such as where equality before the law is systematically frustrated by the unequal ability to pay for legal representation, or where equal educational opportunity is denied not by discriminatory exclusions but by administering class or ethnically biased tests.

In the case of biased technical arrangements, the valuative bias does not appear as such but governs the "fit" of the formally rational subsystems and society as a whole. The assembly line can again serve as an example. In Marx's terms, it is guilty of "supplying capital with weapons against the revolts of the working class," and so is clearly a biased technology (Marx, 1906: I, 476.) Yet the objective workings of this technology are as blind to social distinctions as the computer that grades a culturally biased test. The bias, in such cases, originates not in the technical elements but in their specific configuration in a real world of times, places, historical inheritances—in sum, a world of concrete contingencies. The essence of formal bias is the prejudicial choice of the *time, place, and manner of the introduction of a system composed of relatively neutral elements.*

These two types of bias are open to criticism on very different grounds. Substantive bias, based on the application of unequal standards, is most often associated with prejudice, with explicit norms that discriminate between people of different classes, races, sexes, or nationalities. However, since unfair treatment cannot be justified on the basis of mere personal preferences, such norms are generally represented as factual judgments attributing abilities or merits, disabilities or demerits to the more- or less-favored groups. The critique of substantive bias proceeds by showing up its pseudofactual judgments as "rationalizations," or, where they are highly elaborated, as "ideologies."

Formal bias implies no necessary feeling of prejudice, nor is it associated with factual errors based on rationalized feelings. On the contrary, the facts generally support claims of fairness aimed at justifying this type of bias so long as embarrassing contextual considerations are ignored. Outside the larger context, fair treatment seems to be rendered through an equal application of the same standards to all. But in that context, it becomes clear that the apparent fairness of the system, taken in isolation, hides systematic unfairness of another sort.

Criticism of formal bias requires redefining the domain of considerations relevant to judging the action or institution in question. It is not the particular factual claims advanced in favor of the discriminatory activity that are challenged, but the *horizon* under which those facts are defined. The enlargement of the cognitive horizon in such cases involves passing from arbitrarily isolated elements to a larger system in which they have a functional significance. Thus to show discrimination in the case of a technological choice or a culturally biased test, it is necessary to demonstrate that the discriminatory outcome is no accident but reproduces a relationship of domination.

The traditional neutrality thesis reifies technology by abstracting from all contextual considerations. This approach is relatively persuasive because, as in other instances of formal bias, the decontextualized elements from which the biased system is built up *are* in fact neutral in their abstract form. The gears and levers of the assembly line, like the bricks and mortar of the Panopticon, possess no intrinsic valuative implications. The illusion that technology is neutral arises when actual machines and systems are understood on the model of the abstract technical elements they unite in value-laden combinations. Critical theory shatters the illusion by recovering the forgotten contexts and developing a historically concrete understanding of technology.

That understanding is critical, but it contrasts sharply with the one-sided condemnations of substantive theory. Ellul and Heidegger attribute substantive bias to technology and treat it quite literally as a kind of materialized metaphysics. Their approach confounds the essence of technology with the hegemonic code that shapes its contemporary forms, denying the existence of subordinated technical potentialities that could support an essentially different type of development.

The same deficiency is often attributed to Marcuse too. This may explain why his critics accuse him of being irrationalist and, like Habermas, beat a hasty retreat into the conformist view of technology. But a one-sided critique is not improved by abandoning critique altogether. What is needed is a theoretical account of the "other" side, that is, those progressive dimensions of technology that would come to the fore in the course of reconstructing the technical base. I address this question in parts II and III of this book.

Technological Figurations

The theory of the technical code and its bias establishes the social relativity of the existing technology. But if technological domination is a contestable hegemony rather than a dispensation of being, one would expect it to be associated with specific forms of opposition and resistance. What would it mean to make a counterhegemonic use of knowledge or technology? How would such a use differ from the mere instrumentalization of neutral tools for new purposes?

Modern ideas of resistance were originally formed in the political sphere rather than in reflection on the dialectic of technological subjects and their means. Political struggle lends itself to the sort of instrumentalist accounts I have criticized as inappropriate to the study of technology. Substantivism recognizes the failure of the instrumental view and responds with the dystopian metaphor of society as a gigantic machine. But mechanical imagery describes a far more stable and harmonious social order than the one in which we live. A satisfactory model must reflect not only society's power to shape its members but also the tensions and resistances it evokes.

In the search for such a model, some theorists have chosen to compare society with a game rather than with a machine. Games define the players' range of action without determining any particular move. This metaphor can be usefully applied to technology, which sets up a framework of permitted and forbidden "moves" in much the same way games do. The technical code might be reconceptualized on these terms as the most general rule of the technical game, a rule that, however, biases the play toward the dominant contestant.[14]

The game metaphor is ambiguous, like the society it describes. Thus, Michael Buroway holds that "playing a game generates consent with respect to its rules," but he also notes that "participation in a game can undermine the conditions of its reproduction" (Buroway, 1979: 81, 94). Buroway's study of the shop-floor "game" of "making out" illustrates this ambiguity. He wonders whether what appears to be a struggle for free time *against* the system may actually be functional *within* it. These two positions are personified by Cornelius Castoriadis and Marcuse.

> But is making out as radical as Castoriadis claims? Or is it, as Herbert Marcuse would argue, a mode of adaptation that reproduces "the voluntary servitude" of workers to capital? Are these freedoms and needs, generated and partially satisfied in the context of work, and harnessed to the production of surplus value, a challenge to "capitalist principles"? Does making out present an anticipation of something new, the potential for human self-organization, or is it wholly contained with the reproduction of capitalist relations? (Buroway, 1979: 73)

In the remainder of this section I draw on the ideas of Michel de Certeau and Norbert Elias to develop a theory of resistance explaining these ambiguities. I will apply their insights to a noninstrumentalist account of subversive practice.[15]

De Certeau's contribution belongs to a certain phase in the breakdown of French structuralism. As coded objects, cultural artifacts resemble a syntax regulating behavior that, like speech, follows the rules of the code. For example, knives, forks, and spoons are not just strips of metal, but imply a whole system of eating behavior with respect to which each actual meal is a performance. Clothing, cars, technical devices, are all subject to a similar analysis.

This approach has a deterministic cast, but some semiologists—for example, Roland Barthes—offered looser formulations, applicable to culture, in which speech practice can modify syntax (Barthes, 1969: 103–104). De Certeau was influenced by Foucault in attempting to develop a similar theory of cultural change. The game metaphor serves in this context to soften the deterministic rigors of the then dominant linguistic model of society.

"Strategies," according to de Certeau, are the institutionalized controls embodied in social and technological systems such as corporations or government agencies (de Certeau, 1980: I, 85). The techniques of power are not tools wielded by elites; rather, they open a space, an "interiority," from out of which those elites act on society. The social distance implied in the metaphoric pair—interior/exterior—is vertical: it creates a position "above" society from which to see and control it. To that position corresponds what I have called the operational autonomy of a hegemonic subject. With certain modifications, this account could be generalized to any technically mediated activity in modern societies.

Social groups that lack a base from which to act on an exteriority respond "tactically" to the strategies to which they are subjected, that is to say with punctual, temporary, shifting actions that fall more or less under the control of the dominant strategy but subtly alter its significance or direction. Tactics are the inevitable response of the dominated to their domination, unfolding on the terrain of the Other and operating in the "usage" of the hegemonic system (de Certeau, 1980: I, 59–60).

Just as operational autonomy serves as the structural basis of domination, so a different type of autonomy is won by the dominated, an autonomy that works with the "play" in the system to redefine and modify its forms, rhythms, and purposes. I call this reactive autonomy "margin of maneuver." It may be used for a variety of purposes in technically mediated organizations, including controlling work pace, protecting colleagues, unauthorized productive improvisations, informal rationalizations and innovations, and so on. Action on the margin may be reincorporated into strategies, sometimes in ways that restructure domination at a higher level, sometimes in ways that weaken its control. Foucault's "subjugated knowledges" are elaborated in the "space" of tactical involvement, the margin of maneuver opened by strategies. De Certeau offers examples such as practices in which workers exploit materials and tools from their workplace to make objects for their own use (*la perruque*), or the investment of Christianity by local rites in colonial situations (de Certeau, 1980: I, 68ff., 106–107).

De Certeau sheds a new light on the metaphoric identification of societies with machines and games. These two metaphors are in fact angles of vision on social activity. The mechanical metaphor describes a smoothly working system from the point of view of those who manage it. The view of the dominated partner is exemplified in the game, and especially in the peculiar counterhegemonic "move" that changes the rules. The two metaphors together thus embrace the complementary perspectives of actors located in different positions in the system. They exemplify the opposing self-understandings associated with operational autonomy and margin of maneuver.

De Certeau's distinction between strategies and tactics offers an alternative to both instrumental and substantive theories of technology. His theory of strategies exposes the bias of the apparently neutral technical management of modern organizations. His analysis of the role of tactics brings out the inherent limits of dystopian rationalization. At the same time, it suggests a new way of understanding resistance as neither individual moral opposition nor as just another policy, indistinguishable except for the accidents of political fortune from the dominant one. Both morality and policy are functions of strategic will. Resistance, as a tactical modification to which strategies are subject, belongs to another order entirely, that order which Marx attempted to signify with his early notion of the social.

This approach has a larger context in social theory: the attempt to transcend the dilemma of methodological individualism versus structuralism. A third position, sketched variously by Pierre Bourdieu, Norbert Elias, and a number of other social theorists, argues that individual and society, considered as separate entities, are abstractions from a more concrete unity. That unity is a structured process of human relations. Norbert Elias calls this process a "figuration," an ordered "pattern of bonding" among the "semi-autonomous" individuals who make up society (Elias, 1978: 6). No individual exists outside such a framework, nor are the frameworks themselves conceivable other than as systems of human interdependencies. In our society, these relations are asymmetrical and position a few leaders to "manage" the others.

Elias uses imaginary games to illustrate these contests for power. In a game in which one player, A, is much more successful than his opponent, B, A not only has power over B but "*in addition*, a high degree of control over the game as such. Though his control of the game is not absolute, he can determine its course (the game process) and therefore also the result of the game to a very great extent" (Elias, 1978: 81). This second-order control over the game is very similar to what I have called "operational autonomy," the power to select the procedures and devices (rules) that govern the behavior of those within the system.

But Elias also allows for the case in which the dominated are able to use their discretionary margin to strengthen their position. Then the outcome of the play becomes increasingly unpredictable. It no longer looks like the result of a strategy but comes to resemble ordinary social interaction. Elias imagines a multitiered game, very much like a modern society, in which a small number of players has the advantage over a larger number of weak players. He describes power shifts in such a game in the following terms:

> As long as power differentials are great, it will appear to people on the upper level as if the whole game and the lower-level players in particular are there for their benefit. As power balances shift, this state of affairs changes. Increasingly it appears to all participants as though the upper-level players are there for the benefit of the lower-level players. The former gradually become more openly and unambiguously functionaries, spokesmen or representatives of one or other of the lower-level groups. (Elias, 1978: 90)

Elias's model has interesting applications to the politics of technology. Where the rules of his multitiered game are technologically embedded, they establish a biased system within which the dominant players functionalize the subordinate players' moves. Subordinates' initiatives tend to cancel out as they implement the dominant players' strategy, giving the impression that the "system" is effective in its own right rather than as a pattern of human relations. The stronger players experience the play as the implementation of their own strategy, which itself coincides with a specific technical rationale, and the subordination of the weaker players then appears as an impersonal technical necessity.

Technical mediation, however, has unforeseeable consequences. Technological strategies create a framework of activity, a field of play, but they do not determine every move. Like all plans or rules, they are coarse grained compared with the actual detail of concrete activity. Furthermore, the technical system is not just a plan in the heads of a few administrators; it is a real thing with its own properties, its own logic. To the extent that this logic has not been perfectly anticipated and mastered—and it never can be—there will be breakdowns, imperfections in the order of the plan. The "weaker players," those whose lives or work are structured by the technical mediations selected by management, are constantly solicited to operate in this range of unpredictable effects.[16] As a result, tactical responsiveness is not something imported into the technically mediated game from the outside ("life," instincts, etc.), but is a form of *socially necessary freedom* generated immanently within the game itself (Feenberg, 1970).

Struggles over control of technical activities can now be reconceptualized as tactical responses in the margin of maneuver of the dominated. Just because a measure of discretion is associated with the implementation of any plan, the use the dominated make of their position in the system is inherently difficult to foresee and control. It has no predetermined revolutionary or integrative implications as such, but, like all tactical responses to strategies, is essentially ambiguous. These "usages" of the capitalist technical code are both necessary to its implementation and germs of a new society. Their contradictory potentialities are more or less contained by management depending on the extent of its operational autonomy. A strong management can cancel the potentially subversive long-term impacts of tactical maneuvers. If management is forced to compromise with its subordinates over a long period, they can transform the technical process through iterative tactical responses that gradually weaken management's control and bend its strategic line. This explains why in technical politics there are no clear "sides" in struggles for identity that stretch all parties between their own contradictory potentialities.

Workers' control simply carries this process to the limit. It is not a new state power, but is rather a negative condition for a flowering of tactical initiative, the "organizing activity" specific to socialism. The ambivalent employment of the technical heritage depends entirely on maintaining and enlarging the margin of maneuver required to alter the strategies encoded in the division of labor and technology.

In sum, modern technology opens a space within which action can be functionalized in either one of two social systems, capitalism or socialism. It is an ambivalent or "multistable" system that can be organized around at least two hegemonies, two poles of power between which it can "tilt" (Ihde, 1990: 144). From this standpoint the concepts of "capitalism" and "socialism" are no longer mutually exclusive "modes of production," nor is their moral significance captured in the manichean conflict between a prisonlike society and the individual in revolt. They are, rather, ideal-types lying at the extremes of a continuum of changes in the technical codes of advanced societies. As such, they are constantly at issue in struggles over all sorts of technical problems: at work, in education, medicine, ecology, and, as I will argue in the next two chapters, in the development of a new technology such as the computer. This position offers a way of understanding the continuing struggle for radical change in a world that no longer believes a new civilization can be created by ordinary political action, or geographically localized in this or that country or block.

II

The Ambivalence of the Computer

The last ten years has been characterized by the very rapid computerization of society not only in the United States, Europe, and Japan but around the world. With the spread of the technology, discourses and projects originally associated with production reach into every aspect of social life. For example, deskilling and automation can now be extended to such areas as education, medicine, even food service. The computer seems to promise the final triumph of the Heideggerian enframing.

Yet computers can also be employed to develop and apply skills and initiative. Instead of reducing individuals to mere appendages of the machine, computerization can provide a role for communicative skills and collective intelligence. Computer design thus involves a choice between two different conceptions of the relation of rational systems to human action and between two corresponding conceptions of what it is to be human in a technological society.

The first chapter of this part develops this theme in relation to early theoretical debates over automation and artificial intelligence. These debates reflect profoundly different potentials of modernity that contend for the soul of a computerized society. A second chapter then applies the resulting perspective to current debates over online education. Here is an issue that clearly illustrates both the threat and the promise of computerization. On the one hand, the production mentality follows the computer into the ivied halls of academe. On the other hand, online education could contribute to a radical redistribution of cultural and technical competences in a more democratic form of modern society.

4

Postindustrial Discourses

The Ambivalent Computer

Early commentaries on the computerization of society projected either optimistic scenarios of social salvation or nightmares of impending dystopia. The optimists argued that computers would eliminate routine and painful work and democratize industrial society. The pessimists argued, on the contrary, that computers would put millions out of work and bring universal surveillance and control.[1]

There is a third alternative: perhaps the computer is neither good nor evil, but both. By this I mean not merely that computers can be used for either domination or democratization but that they can evolve into very different technologies under the influence of different strategies of development. My purpose here is to review a wide range of discourses representing the ambivalence of the computer in order to test the theory of the bias of technology introduced in the previous chapter. By way of introduction, let's consider the contradictory potentialities of computerization in more detail.

The computer's structure bears an ominous resemblance to mechanistic rationalization. Computers work under the control of programs devised outside the technology by human agents who command it from above. Unlike other machines, the computer is an automaton that realizes a plan installed in its core rather than simply responding to external controls. This explains the authoritarian connotation of the metaphoric "programming" of people and social systems. What is the significance of this curious structural parallel between the computer and a hierarchical organization of society? Is the computer predestined to strengthen the administrative grip of the powers-that-be? Or does it contain democratic potentialities obscured in the dominant understanding of the technology?

As we have learned from the Internet, computers are useful not only for control but also for communication, and any technology that enhances human contact has democratic potentialities. But this function of the computer was largely invisible to the general public until this decade and is still treated with suspicion by those whose power is based on a knowledge deficit it could subvert. The computer's communicative capabilities could attenuate the distinction between mental and manual labor. New forms of sociability could emerge that would become a medium for democratic self-organization.

The ambivalence of computer technology can be summarized in two principles that describe the social implications of technological advance. I call the first of these the "principle of the conservation of hierarchy." According to this principle, the social hierarchy can generally be preserved and reproduced as new technology is introduced. Computerization of record keeping is a case in point, intensifying surveillance and control. A second "principle of democratic rationalization" holds that new technology can often be used to undermine the existing social hierarchy. Most major innovations open possibilities of democratization that may or may not be realized depending on the margin of maneuver of the dominated. Thus, in many workplaces the drive to computerize has excited and sometimes fulfilled participatory expectations.

This kind of argument was first presented by Marx over a century ago, not specifically in relation to automation but as a theory of the ambivalence of industrial development in general.[2] While well aware of capitalist deskilling, Marx argued that the productivity of machine technology can generally be enhanced by inputs of knowledge and skill. More "intelligent" means of production based on a deeper understanding of nature can be used to maximum advantage only by more intelligent producers. Automation is merely an instance of this general proposition. Marx concluded that with mechanization, "Labour no longer appears so much to be included within the production process; rather, the human being comes to relate more as watchman and regulator to the production process itself. . . . [The worker] steps to the side of the production process instead of being its chief actor" (Marx, 1973: 705).[3]

How much validity does Marx's argument retain over a century after its initial formulation? Surprisingly, current reflections on automation reproduce its very structure. Thus, if the information age appears full of unprecedented threats and emancipatory potentials, that may be an effect of historical amnesia. We can learn from Marx that every stage in the development of industrial technology was haunted by missed opportunities for democratic progress. These opportunities are due to the impact of mechanization on the *potential* economic contribution of cultural advance. In the next section, I will explore past and current discourses of automation in the light of this connection between economics and culture.

Automation and Ideology

In a famous book called *Automation*, published in 1952, John Diebold foresaw a new day dawning for workers. Automation, he wrote, "means . . . that to a great extent the jobs in which the worker is tied to and paced by the machine will be taken over by other machines. The worker will be released for work permitting development of his inherent human capacities" (Diebold, 1952: 162). Diebold hinted that management might have trouble adjusting to the change: "The humility that management needs . . . is a quality that, although always essential in administration, will be of even greater importance in the future" (Diebold, 1952: 163).

Over the years several studies cast doubt on Diebold's predictions (Buckingham, 1961: 96ff.). Some thirty-five years later, Harley Shaiken reviewed the results of a generation of automation in American industry. He concludes *Work Transformed* with reflections on the following theme:

> It is ironic that computers and microelectronics should be used to create a more authoritarian workplace. They could just as easily be deployed to make jobs more creative and increase shop floor decision-making. Rather than pace workers, systems could be designed to provide them with more information about the production operation in general and their own jobs in particular. The technology could be used to bring the work under the more complete control of the people who do it rather than the other way around. (Shaiken, 1984: 267)

The reason for the dismal failure to realize the promise of automation? According to Shaiken, it is "the use of technology to extend managerial power" (Shaiken, 1984: 268).

Shaiken's comments belong to a discourse of automation that articulates the conflict between technical potential and management resistance. We are told now that automation requires a new type of labor process based on new machine designs, but we are still trapped in Taylorism by various institutional lags. In this section I will present conjointly two influential texts of this approach, a social scientific work by Larry Hirschhorn and a similarly inspired business best-seller by Shoshanna Zuboff (Hirschhorn, 1984; Zuboff, 1988).

In *Beyond Mechanization*, Hirschhorn offers a historical account of how postindustrial work has been determined by the development of modern production technology. He argues that such undesirable social consequences of early mechanization such as Taylorism were due to technical limitations we can now surpass. The old mechanical technology was extremely rigid because it employed built-in mechanical controls such as gearing and cams. For that reason its efficient application required hierarchical management and sharply divided labor. The new postindustrial technology employs electronic controls that can be operated separately from the machines they govern. The technical system becomes flexible both in operation and goals, with far-reaching consequences, including an increasing role for workers with new types of skills.

Shoshanna Zuboff's book on the computerization of the workplace, *In the Age of the Smart Machine*, develops a similar argument. Zuboff claims that computers make possible two distinct transformations of the workplace. On the one hand, they can be used to automate production, relieving human beings of physical effort and replacing skilled with unskilled labor. On the other hand, they can be used to "informate," Zuboff's term for the integration of workers and machines in a reskilled labor process. Informating is not exactly an alternative to automation in the usual sense, but a better way of automating that realizes the human potentialities of the workforce as well as the technical potentialities of the computer.

Hirschhorn and Zuboff attempt to pinpoint the unique properties of computers that can support the demand for increased skill. Hirschhorn argues that as mechanical control relaxes and the control system separates out, "the machine has developed into a communications apparatus. The transmission of information, not power, has become its primary purpose. . . . Only through reinterpretation and reconstruction as a communications device can the machine play an effective role in feedback-based production" (Hirschhorn, 1984: 37).

According to Zuboff, information technology not only produces products but also represents the world on which it acts. This communicative or "reflexive" dimension of information technology gives rise to a "textualized" work process that increasingly blurs the distinction between mental and manual labor. A process of automation that emphasizes the replacement of man by machine rests on the mechanical capabilities of information technology alone and "could lead to chronic suboptimization of the technology's potential" (Zuboff, 1988: 66).[4]

In Hirschhorn's account, the key to the "reinterpretation and reconstruction" of automated systems lies in their very imperfections. Although they can handle the routine problems their designers anticipate, they can never achieve the ideal of self-regulation engineers and managers have set for them. Unforeseeable "second-order" breakdowns arise from the vagaries of wear and tear, materials quality, operator error, and changes in production systems. Work in a postindustrial society consists in dealing effectively with these second-order breakdowns. Hence, Hirschhorn rejects "the wistful utopianism" of engineers attempting to build the perfect system. "Machine systems inevitably fail, given the realities of materials and human behavior. Once we accept failure as a part of technological reality, we will gain a clearer perspective on postindustrial work" (Hirschhorn, 1984: 86).

Workers in "symbolically mediated environments" have very different needs from those in mechanical ones. Describing an automated pulp factory, Hirschhorn writes, "The operators were engaged in second-order work, the management of novelty, even as the machinery of production became more automated and the process became more continuous" (Hirschhorn, 1984: 100). This sort of activity requires a redefinition of work as a process engaging the worker's capacities as much as the machinery of production. Learning and work merge in this new technical environment.

Zuboff argues that the heritage of Taylorism is the chief obstacle to this redefinition of work. The new approach to work does not sit well with management, the very existence of which is rooted in the expropriation of skills: "Rationalized knowledge was the occasion for the expansion of middle management and became the basis for its legitimation" (Zuboff, 1988: 232). Formal education and intellective skills were monopolized by management and distinguished it from workers. Thus, it has become "second nature for managers to use technology to delimit worker discretion and, in this process, to concentrate knowledge within the managerial domain" (Zuboff, 1988: 69). But the informating process requires the reverse, and it can succeed only where management designs training and organizational structure to spread intellective skill as widely as possible. Zuboff continues, "Without this strategic commitment, the hierarchy will use technology to reproduce itself. Technological developments, in the absence of organizational innovation, will be assimilated into the status quo" (Zuboff, 1988: 309–310). Unfortunately, those with the most to lose, at least in terms of their traditional self-understanding, are the very ones on whom change depends.

Hirschhorn discusses engineering in similar terms, as haunted by the old mechanistic conception of work. "The very character of postindustrial work, of second-order control tasks, of monitoring and evaluating signals and data, increases the significance of group processes. Yet managers and engineers continue to make work-design decisions as if group life did not exist" (Hirschhorn, 1984: 159). It is once again the heritage of Taylorism that blocks adaptation to the new world of postindustrial technology. Taylorism is incompatible with a "learning approach to machine installation and development" (Hirschhorn, 1984: 57). Engineers must get beyond the notion that there is always a "technical fix" and come to terms with the complexity of the social system in which their tools will be employed. Hirschhorn concludes:

> There is more at stake here than competing philosophies of engineering design. Each principle sets the stage for a different conception of work. The principle of integration and utopian design reinforces a Taylorist view: the more perfect the machine, the simpler and more rational the job. Systems theory, control engineering, utopian thinking, and Taylorist prescriptions all converge to limit the worker's skill. In contrast, the principle of flexibility creates a conception of work in which the worker's capacity to learn, to adapt, and to regulate the evolving controls becomes central to the machine system's developmental potential. (Hirschhorn, 1984: 57–58)

Although Hirschhorn and Zuboff do not blame capitalism for the problems they discuss, their critique of the high cost of authoritarian management generally parallels that of Marx. They show that the computer is an ambivalent technology available for alternative developments. Automation increases management's autonomy only at the expense of creating new problems that justify workers' demands for an enlarged margin of maneuver. That margin may be opened to improve the quality of self-directed activity or it may remain closed to optimize control. As Zuboff writes, "Technological design embodies assumptions that can either invite or extinguish a human contribution" (Zuboff, 1988: 182).

Computers, Communication, and Artificial Intelligence

From automation to artificial intelligence (AI) appears a great leap indeed, but both fields are divided by similar ambivalences. Of course, AI has no precise equivalent for the ideologies of automatism and participation, but the various currents in this field reflect a parallel conflict in the vision of human life.

Recent debates over artificial intelligence also raise interesting philosophical questions concerning the nature of rationality. Roughly formulated, the problem concerns the similarities and differences between human thought and information processing. To the extent that similarities can be found, computerized automata can replace people for many sophisticated purposes. To the extent that differences appear, greater philosophical precision is introduced into the notion of human thinking, clearly distinguished from man-made simulacra.

These similarities and differences are not merely theoretical but also concern computer design and programming, AI is a unique field in which connections can be made between the technical preoccupations of practitioners and the social theory of technology. And, since computer programming and design are probably the most completely "textualized" forms of work today, this discussion also lends support to the argument of the previous section.

The Myth of Artificial Intelligence

There are at least three different senses of the term "artificial intelligence." In the first place, AI is a type of computer program that, despite wild overselling, has certain concrete results to its credit. AI has been used in medicine, for example, to analyze laboratory test results. Whatever philosophers may think of artificial intelligence, there is no reason to expect technical progress in simulating certain intellectual functions to slow down soon.

Second, AI has inspired a new field in psychology that takes the computer as a model of the mind. This approach suits the dominant rationalistic outlook of our society. Philosophers and psychologists are pleased to find that, having conceived of thinking as a kind of machinery, machinery in fact turns out to be the perfect image of the process of thought. Despite the implausibility of this premise, researchers have gained useful insight into mental functioning.

Third, AI is the slogan of an ideological movement for reconceptualizing man on the model of his own automata.[5] At the highest level of abstraction, this is a philosophical enterprise remote from social interests. Participants in this movement therefore have the sense of doing "science" much like their other colleagues in the university and tend to attribute the prestige of their research program to its inherent virtues. But the social reception of these speculations is an entirely different matter. Why have the most exaggerated claims of AI become grist for popular psychology and to what practical project can they be linked?

The theoretical advances of cognitive science affect the lives of ordinary people only indirectly, through the plausibility they give to metaphors that identify human beings with computers. The popularity of these metaphors is disturbing: if computers are the very image of man, then the mechanical world forms a closed system in which we are no more nor less than a working part. The technological obsolescence of mankind has never been closer to achievement. Certainly the progressive political and ethical advances of the last few hundred years cannot survive the discovery that human beings are, after all, merely computational devices.

It is true that the French Enlightenment long ago declared that "man is a machine." The Enlightenment made a progressive use of demystifying materialism, but the renewal of that doctrine today is not a response to religious obscurantism. Rather, contemporary materialism appears to be the theoretical expression of the obsession with total control that David Noble identifies in the managerial world.

What is the self-understanding of a machine supposed to be like? Perhaps the answer is supplied by the theory of the "new narcissism," the intensified pursuit of personal pleasure by individuals who have less identity than ever before. The collapse of public life and the decline of the family seem to cut individuality loose from its institutional moorings. No longer concretized through real bonds and obligations, the person becomes a discontented spectator on his or her own life, engaged in strategies of manipulation and control directed toward the self and others alike (Lasch, 1979). The computerization of the human self-image places the subject now in the position of programmed device, now in the position of programmer. The discourse of human relations in this new age of narcissism brings home the desolation of mechanical man. People "push each other's buttons" today where once they might have been sentimentally described as falling in love (Turkle, 1984: chap. 8).

Computer-Mediated Communication

There is one audience that has a unique perspective on the AI debate since it applies theories of intelligence in its work. Among computer programmers and designers, discussions about the nature of intelligence are not merely theoretical but also express tensions in the self-understanding of a profession. Its members rely for the most part on unreflected projections of the engineering culture in which they are socialized. These projections define the "real" function of computers and the best way of using them.

The ordinary computer user is sheltered to some extent from this culture by the higher level interfaces of application programs such as Microsoft Word, but one still gets a hint of the engineers' world from these programs. It is a rationalistic world that bears little or no connection to everyday experience, in which thinking consists in linear operations on unambiguous representations of artificial, decontextualized, and well-defined objects; problems are clear-cut and solutions definitively testable. To be sure, this is a world in which cars, power plants, and bridges are successfully built, but it is a specialized instance of intelligence and not its paradigmatic case.

These rationalistic assumptions are embodied in the technical code of the computer profession, the rules and procedures on the basis of which standard design decisions are made. It is this technical code that defines the computer as a system of control, an automaton. The AI debate brings hidden premises of this underlying code to conscious awareness.

The computer world is an especially favorable setting for the ideology of automatism, but even there the ambiguities of the information age have an impact. The functions of mainframe computers include communication, usually in the form of electronic mail. Programmers and designers "live" in an *environment* defined by the computer programs they use, exchange, and discuss online. Computing is a web of communications, a social as well as a technical network.[6]

In its application to communication, the computer has an astonishing power to form the medium for a parallel world. The participants in regular online discussions find their lives doubled into a "real" and a "virtual" segment. In their everyday world they relate to people who are geographically close, but in the virtual world, social contacts are chosen without reference to geography, exclusively on the basis of shared interests or work. Despite a certain simplification of social interaction that results from its decontextualization, online communication shares the ineradicable complexity and ambiguity of speech in natural language (Feenberg, 1989). It does not conform with the computer culture's standard model of intelligence any more than would the conversation around the Coke machine in the programmers' office. Yet this online world is not extraneous to the computer but is the form of its symbolic mediation in the contemporary labor process.

We are familiar on the Internet with online work and discussion groups. These "computer conferences" or "discussion forums" are typically "asynchronous," meaning that messages are stored on a server and made available to members at their terminals whenever they call in. The earliest version of this new medium, computer conferencing, dates from 1974 when it was introduced as an improvement on simple person-to-person electronic mail. Its first successes were in computer companies, where employees could understand the programs and had easy access to the necessary equipment. These applications are a perfect illustration of Hirschhorn and Zuboff's argument that postindustrial work is essentially a process of communicating and learning organized around the "reflexivity" of computer technology.

Computer conferencing at the Digital Equipment Corporation (DEC) is a case in point. DEC gambled very early on what is called "distributed networking," that is to say, the linking up of computers in integrated systems. Instead of building huge "mainframe" computers, like IBM, each standing in solitary splendor at the center of its own world, DEC's middle-sized "minicomputers" were designed to be interconnected to share files and tasks. But connecting computers means connecting those who use them, including designers working on the company's products. DEC's industrial strategy reacted back on the company itself, amplifying a preexisting culture based on horizontal ties and coalitions.

In the mid-1980s DEC's 125,000 employees were scattered all over the world and linked together by a corporate computer network. In 1986, engineers developed the first version of the VAX Notes computer conferencing system to improve the functioning of networked project groups. Eventually the system grew to 15,000 conferences with tens of thousands of members, and VAX Notes itself was polished up and distributed as a DEC software product.

The company declined to control the content of the network: conferencing at DEC evolved entirely in function of the users' interests. In addition to work-related conferences, many others were formed: clubs and sports groups, employees with multiple sclerosis, executives writing international restaurant reviews, and so on. In short, the real social world of DEC was doubled by a "virtual" community.

Here, then, is an unsuspected aspect of computer work. The contradiction between automatism and communication built into computer practitioners' daily experience offered a certain margin of maneuver that they were able to use to modify their social insertion and activities. One of the many VAX Notes conferences was especially symptomatic of these contradictions: a discussion of Heidegger's philosophy. A leading design engineer and his coworkers started the conference because they had lost faith in their rationalistic assumptions about human beings. Heidegger's phenomenology of human action seemed to promise an escape from their naive engineering culture toward a more realistic approach to designing interfaces and equipment (Whiteside and Wixon, 1988).

I discuss some of the implications of this surprising turn in the next section. This reaction testifies to a tension in technical professions between widely accepted rationalistic technical codes and the everyday realities of human thought and action. This tension was articulated in 1989, when the philosopher Hubert Dreyfus organized an "Applied Heidegger Conference" at the University of California, Berkeley, attended by hundreds of professionals not only from the computer world but from fields as diverse as nursing and management.

These are "specific intellectuals" in Foucault's sense, intellectuals whose resistances and revolts are rooted in their social function and its associated knowledge base rather than in the language of politics and justice employed by the literary intellectuals of earlier times (Foucault, 1980: 127–128). In calling such intellectuals "specific," Foucault does not imply that their action lacks universal significance, but that it grows out of a local situation in the technical division of labor. In the terminology introduced here, specific intellectuals act in the margin of maneuver associated with a technical domain in order to transform the code establishing that domain. I would like to turn now to a consideration of an early attempt in the AI community to articulate the foundations of an alternative code.

Toward a New Paradigm

The AI field is divided into two camps, a majority "cognitivist" camp and a "neoconnectionist" minority. Cognitivists attempt to simulate the essential operations of human thought with very powerful computers of conventional design. These "serial computers" move quickly from one operation to the next, manipulating symbols in sequence according to syntactic rules contained in their programs. So-called expert systems work in this way, sorting, classifying, and calculating with symbolic materials supplied by the users. Such computers finally beat the world chess champion in 1997.

Neoconnectionism's best argument against this approach is the fact that the human mind does not think in linear sequences, but "processes" data in complex parallel operations. "Parallel processing" appears to be essential to such activities as vision, which would explain why it is easier for a serial computer to beat Kasparov than to imitate the eye of a fly.

The neoconnectionists hope that their "neural networks" can overcome these limits although so far there has been far less progress than promised a decade ago. This is a new computing technique that applies parallel processing to tasks for which ordinary programs seem in principle unsuited. The operation of these networks more nearly resembles an apprenticeship through trial and error than a programmed processing of symbols. The neural network interacts with the environment in such a way as to reorganize its own internal state in a coherent manner that can be used for some purpose such as recognizing or imitating patterns. Because it is based on statistical regularities, it can work with approximations and improve its own performance. A few products have been developed using these techniques, but the field is still in its infancy.

The Paradox of Self-Organization

According to Jean-Pierre Dupuy, this division in the AI research community was prefigured in the debates of the cybernetics movement that preceded it. Mainstream cybernetics attempted to show that self-organizing systems such as living things could be explained on the basis of the same principles of feedback, homeostasis, and control that apply to machines. Meanwhile, a smaller group attempted to distinguish between self-organizing systems and mechanical ones, but at first only the study of mechanical systems prospered (Dupuy, 1985).[7]

The theory of self-organization was taken up again by a group of original thinkers with better approaches in recent years. This emerging field, which Heinz Von Foerster calls a "second cybernetics," is represented principally by Von Foerster himself, and Henri Atlan, Humberto Maturana, and Francisco Varela (Dupuy, 1982: 227). Dupuy argues that this "second cybernetics" is in the process of resolving fundamental problems in the heritage of the first.

Early cybernetics bequeathed biology and neurology a set of concepts derived from mechanical models, such as the notions of genetic "codes" and mental "programs." Whatever the fruitfulness of such concepts in particular applications, insofar as biological and mental life are self-organizing systems they are fundamentally different from machinery, even such sophisticated machinery as computers.

As machines, computers are turned on the one side toward action in the world and on the other side toward a human user. Like a hammer, which possesses a head for striking and a handle for holding, the computer's very structure implies an operator who intervenes in the mechanical environment but is not a part of it. This structure—control from above—appears self-evident: the programmer operates the computer and not vice versa. When the order is reversed, when the operator is also the object of action, as, for example, when the hammerer strikes his own thumb, the operation falls outside the domain of technical action proper and is counted as a mistake.

Russell and Whitehead explored the logical structure of such irreversible hierarchies. They wanted to eliminate reflexive paradoxes, such as the famous "liar's paradox," which occur when certain types of propositions refer to themselves. The logical equivalent of hammering on one's own thumb is exemplified by the statement "This sentence is false." Russell and Whitehead introduced the "theory of types" to expunge such paradoxes from language. This theory requires a clean separation between levels of discourse. In the accepted terminology, the higher-level "metalanguage" refers to the lower-level "object language" but it cannot refer to itself. Russell and Whitehead permit Sentence A (the metastatement) to claim that Sentence B (the object statement) is false only if A and B are different, thereby avoiding the liar's paradox.

But, however inconvenient reflexivity is in logic, it is essential to the world as we know it. Living things are "programmed" by genetic materials that are themselves the objects on which the genetic program operates (Atlan, 1979: 21–23). And, although some mental operations are describable in terms of the metaphor of external programming, the brain as a system largely "creates" itself by operating on its own states; human thought more nearly resembles a neoconnectionist neural network than an ordinary computer. We are, in short, self-programming beings, an apparent contradiction in terms (Varela, 1984).

Social applications of the concepts of the "first cybernetics" resonate with the ideology of total control. The separation of the (controlling) metalevel of the programmer or operator and the (controlled) object level reflects the split between conception and execution in modern technical systems. In contrast, the idea of a self-programming or self-organizing system has a paradoxical structure and emancipatory implications: in a democracy all individuals are both objects of administration and administrators of each other.

Ontological Designing

We appear to have wandered far afield from artificial intelligence, but in fact the divisions in AI can be reformulated in terms of the concept of self-organization. Two Chilean neurophysiologists, Humberto Maturana and Francisco Varela, joined the debate with an innovative conception of the brain as a self-organizing system (Maturana and Varela, 1987). Their theories influenced a small group of computer scientists and designers who challenged the dominant rationalistic technical code. This influence was primarily mediated through the account of Maturana's theories in *Understanding Computers and Cognition* by Fernando Flores and Terry Winograd (Winograd and Flores, 1987).

Maturana rejects the prevailing model of mental functioning according to which the mind is essentially an observer of the world. On that account the mind forms mental representations of what it observes, and these representations then serve as mediations between sensory inputs and outputs of action. Mental "programs" are said to organize the construction of such representations and the response to them. Maturana's theory of the nervous system breaks with this representationalist paradigm of cognition and conceives the mind not as an observer but as an actor immediately engaged with reality.

Operationally considered, cognition is not the construction of representations in the brain but the patterning of behavior. Such patterning aims at the preservation of the structure of the organism in and through interaction with the environment. To this end, the organism must achieve what Maturana calls "structural coupling" with the world around it (i.e., effective responses to the perturbations it experiences). To explain the brain as a self-organizing system is to show how it continually reproduces itself under these dynamic conditions (Maturana and Varela, 1987: 75–80).

According to Varela, the mind is not basically a manipulator of symbolic representations like a computer. He observes that "only a predefined world can be represented," but, as he points out, we do not live in such a world (Varela, 1988: 92). The world is not given to us as a collection of well-defined objects and problems but as an infinitely rich context of action. We do not discover the unambiguous truth of that context in knowledge but "enact" a viable "world" on the basis of our experience and culture. This is what human intelligence is all about and it is quite different from representing a world the outlines of which are clear prior to action.

Varela and Maturana show that the representationalist paradigm of knowledge presupposed by expert systems works only against a background of practical involvements it cannot explain. They agree, of course, that we are able to construct representations of aspects of the real world, but a category mistake is involved in treating those representations and the expert systems based on them as general models of the world and intelligence. Accordingly, Winograd and Flores argue that

> the current discourse about computers is based on a misinterpretation of the nature of human cognition and language. Computers designed on the basis of this misconception provide only impoverished possibilities for modeling and enlarging the scope of human understanding. They are restricted to representing knowledge as the acquisition and manipulation of facts, and communication as the transferring of information. As a result, we are now witnessing a major breakdown in the design of computer technology. (Winograd and Flores, 1987: 78)[8]

Winograd and Flores conclude that what is needed is "new ground for rationality—one that is as rigorous as the rationalistic tradition in its aspirations but that does not share the presuppositions behind it" (Winograd and Flores, 1987: 8). For the authors this alternative tradition is represented by Martin Heidegger. It is interesting to note that these technologists have no use for Heidegger's later substantive theory of technology; they are concerned only with the early theory of action developed in *Being and Time*, which they apply to the human relation to computers. There Heidegger argues that being and subjectivity are inextricably intertwined in "being-in-the-world." We are "thrown" into the world, obliged to establish our own meanings and objects, always already in the midst of action. The objective representation of "things," in the specific sense of stable, independent objects, is a secondary process and not our basic relation to reality.

Maturana appears to be making similar claims. The representational model of cognition, in which things and their properties are presumed to precede activity, is a theoretical construct built by observers who are outside the situation of active involvement they describe. In fact, cognition occurs against a background of practical assumptions, called "preunderstandings" by hermeneutics, that construct the domain of experience as an action domain. Knowledge articulates distinctions already made at the practical level; but these distinctions cannot be explained after the fact by reference to the very objectivities that they establish in establishing a world.

So far the theory seems quite abstruse, but Winograd and Flores operationalize it through focusing on Heidegger's concept of "breakdown." Heidegger holds that action is not a simple response to the objective qualities of things. Rather, what we take for things in a contemplative mode actually arises from the "breakdown" of practical behaviors in which we engage with reality at a more fundamental level.[9] In breakdown, the "ready-to-hand" objects of action become "present-at-hand," that is, they are viewed from a distance *as* things and not experienced immediately as a dimension of an action system. This theory has a certain similarity to Maturana's concept of structural coupling, which involves a kind of "readiness-to-hand." "What really *is* is not defined by an objective omniscient observer, nor is it defined by an individual . . . but rather by a space of potential for human concern and action" (Winograd and Flores, 1987: 37).

These concepts suggest a very different paradigm of computer design from the rationalistic tradition, with its emphasis on thought, planning, and decision. Rather than constructing an exhaustive rational map of the program for the user, "the designer of a computer tool must work in the domain generated by the space of potential breakdown in that [structural] coupling" (Winograd and Flores, 1987: 72).[10] This is reminiscent of Hirschhorn's discussion of industrial design. Because of the inevitability of breakdown, "the allocation of responsibility between the controls or computer and the operator must be dynamic, based on the operator's learning needs as well as the performance requirements of the system" (Hirschhorn, 1984: 97).

Heidegger's phenomenology of action can contribute to these technical discussions because it looks at the world from the standpoint of the involved subject rather than from that of the external observer. That subject has appeared in our discussion before as the individual engaged in tactical maneuvers in an environment shaped by an alien rationality. In that context, the theory of breakdown refers not to a purely contingent feature of the human relation to tools, but more specifically to the limits of control from above. These themes now come together in the idea of an alternative rationality, a rationality of implementation rather than of planning and control, based on self-referential processes of communicating and learning in the course of using and modifying tools.

Winograd and Flores argue that computers are not automata, artificial intelligences, but "machines for acting in language" (Winograd and Flores, 1987: 178). AI needs to lower its sights considerably if this is true. From this standpoint, "The relevant questions are not those comparing computers to people, but those opening up a potential for computers that play a meaningful role in human life and work" (Winograd and Flores, 1987: 12). It makes more sense to compare expert systems to word processing than to treat them as mental prostheses. Word processors are not intelligent but enable us to act effectively in a particular domain, the preparation of text. Expert systems that supply aids for accomplishing definite tasks have a similar relation to professional activities.

These aids make possible a new form of human-machine interaction that gives the illusion of partnership. But however "intelligent" it may appear to be, the computer is not a mind but "a *structured dynamic communication medium* that is qualitatively different from earlier media such as print and telephones" (Winograd and Flores, 1987: 176). It is the programmer and those who use it who are engaged in communication, not the computer system.

This view leads to a revalorization of the communicative functions of computers. A new field of "collaborative technologies" has emerged to adapt computer programs to the needs of work groups. Instead of appearing as tools for individuals, programs are designed as "groupware" for use by a whole team (Johansen, 1988). The social and technical dimensions of computerized activity are integrated here in a way that recalls Hirschhorn's communication theory of automated machinery and Zuboff's discussion of the textualization of work.

The stakes in this debate over artificial intelligence are not merely technical. If we understand computers rationalistically, as automata, we prepare a revised self-understanding along the same lines. People become information processors and decision makers, rather than participants in shared communicative activity. "Computer systems can easily reinforce this interpretation, and working with them can reinforce patterns of acting that are consistent with it" (Winograd and Flores, 1987: 178).

Considered as a communication medium, the computer is an environment for an increasing share of daily life. In this conception, computers are not "images of man" but domains in which we act and which shape us in return. As Hirschhorn suggests, postindustrial "technology can potentiate latent cultural trends. Control system failures may help to bring out in the culture a developmental concept of the self, a concept that leads people to seek out learning opportunities throughout their lives" (Hirschhorn, 1984: 4). One of the chief obstacles in this path is the hidden cultural agenda of industrial design. "In their search for fail-safe systems engineers demonstrate the hubris of most design professions. The designers of a machine, a building, or a policy are attempting to imprint their minds on other people's lives" (Hirschhorn, 1984: 86). This attempt is not merely a theoretical error but reflects the practical requirements of the capitalist technical code, with its overriding emphasis on operational autonomy.

The design of computers is thus humanly significant as well as instrumentally important, for "in designing tools we are designing ways of being" (Winograd and Flores, 1987: xi). Winograd and Flores call this "ontological designing." They write, "In ontological designing, we are doing more than asking what can be built. We are engaged in a philosophical discourse about the self—about what we can do and what we can be" (Winograd and Flores, 1987: 179). That discourse, I would add, is also political.

This discussion of artificial intelligence leads to the same conclusion as the earlier discussion of automation. The place computers are intended to hold in social life is intimately connected with their design. Systems designed for hierarchical control are congruent with rationalistic assumptions that treat the computer as an automaton intended to command or replace workers in decision-making roles. Democratically designed systems must instead respond to the communicative dimension of the computer. As a medium it facilitates the self-organization of human communities, including those technical communities the control of which founds modern hegemonies.

The Myth of Automatism

Although technologies are first and foremost tools for solving practical problems, they are not fully understandable in functional terms. This is especially true in cases where their function is itself in dispute. As we have seen with computers, these disputes are not merely technical but go to the cultural significance of the technology. The critical theory of technology is therefore a cultural theory.

Jean Baudrillard suggests a semiological approach to understanding cultural investments in technology. He argues that technical objects have an equivalent of "denotation" through their function, and "connotation" through their relation to the fantasies and sociopsychological needs of those they serve (Baudrillard, 1968: 15–16). Ambiguities in the definition of a technology such as the computer are resolved through interactions between designers and users in which the still fluid boundary between connotations and denotations is fixed.[11]

For his understanding of the functional aspect of technologies Baudrillard relies on the French philosopher of technology Gilbert Simondon. According to Simondon, technical objects generally begin as loose concatenations of separate mechanical structures, each devoted to a single function. As the object becomes more technically elegant, single structures incorporate multiple functions, and powerful synergisms emerge from the interactions between structures. This type of development, which Simondon calls "concretization," defines an immanent criterion of progress (Simondon, 1958: chap. 1).

Technological "connotations," on the other hand, lack a basis in the structure of technical development and may invest machines with inappropriate functions (Baudrillard, 1968: 14). Where this occurs, the technical object does not advance toward a higher stage, but instead becomes complex and cumbersome. The evolution of the automobile in the 1950s offers a case in point. As cars became symbols of prosperity and sexual prowess, they grew in size and weight; their gadget-encrusted bodies were burdened with fishtails and heavy chrome bumpers. Needless to say, these dinosaurs were less efficient as means of transportation precisely to the extent that they were better at serving their symbolic functions.

These theories are interesting, but they are too deterministic: they assume the existence of purely technical criteria of progress, but technical development generally opens onto several different paths of concretization. The alternatives are signified first in connotations that gradually determine shifts in the very definition of the technology. Thus, some of the goals that were clumsily pursued by the automobile industry in the 1950s, such as improved comfort, have been attained today through concretizing innovations in design. The floating living room is gone, but more appropriate solutions to the problem have been found through improving suspensions and seat design.

The case of the computer suggests, however, that not all paths are equal: the managerial ideology of total control, like the rationalistic ideology of artificial intelligence, responds to fantasies that distort technical development for political purposes. These ideologies are expressed in the discourse of "automatism." Here we can see a connotative dimension of a new technology in the very process of conversion into a denotation. Ancient dreams of power, embodied until modern times in emblematic objects designed to exemplify the human capacity for godlike creativity, are confounded with the actual workings of society and the mind as automatism captures the modern imagination. The fantasy of the totally automated factory, cleansed of human effort and the necessity of employing obstreperous workers to supply it, replaces the innocent dreams of earlier times. As Noble puts it, "Thus did the capitalist mentality appropriate the primitive enchantment with automation and turn it to practical and pecuniary ends, where it now fueled fantasies not of automatic birds and musicians but of automatic factories" (Noble, 1984: 58). These same dehumanizing connotations of the computer appear in the notion of a mechanical mind.

What is the peculiar fascination of automatic functioning? Baudrillard addresses this question in an interesting discussion of its symbolic significance. He begins by dismissing the idea that the pursuit of automaticity is technically motivated. Automatism does not respond to the rational drive toward increasing efficiency and technical concreteness. In fact, it complicates objects needlessly, making them more effective as symbols of pure technicity at the price of rendering them ever more elaborate, fragile, and rigid. Machines actually progress not through automatism but through increased flexibility and responsiveness to more subtle external instruction. Automatism is thus not rational but contains "the imaginary truth of the object," our fantasy of mechanical perfection (Baudrillard, 1968: 156).

Carried to the limit of its possibilities, automatism is exemplified in the useless gadget, a marvel of purposeless complexity. Baudrillard calls this the "functional delirium" of technique, a kind of baroque predilection for complexity that encrusts otherwise useful devices. The gadget is a technical object that "no longer obeys any other necessity than that of functioning" (Baudrillard, 1968: 159–160). It may possess some ostensible purpose, for example, to lock or unlock car doors from a distance, but in reality it exists simply to display its own workings.

Automatism is a fantastic way of experiencing "technicity," that is to say, what is *essentially* technical in machines. Through automatism, technicity appears as a symbol of pure operativity, signifying not some specific technical function but an imaginary investment of the world as a whole by technique: "Automatism is the object acquiring the connotation of an absolute in its particular function" (Baudrillard, 1968: 153–154). The clever device that automatically cores apples or magnetically suspends a pen in an upright position serves not so much a practical need as a sort of functional superstition that is comforted by the thought of "nature as a whole reinvented according to the technical reality principle" (Baudrillard, 1968: 164).

Baudrillard rejects the widespread belief that our problems are due to the rapid advance of technology while social science and moral reflection stagnate. With the fantastic demand for automatism, technology and morality are both caught up in the same contradiction. "In our technical civilization . . . techniques and objects suffer the same servitudes as men" (Baudrillard, 1968: 175). Consumer society exemplifies technical failure as well as moral regression through the corruption of design and conception by symbolic demands that block the concretization of technology. Baudrillard concludes: "Between men and the world, technique can be an effective mediation: that is the hardest path. The easiest path is that of a system of objects which interposes itself as an imaginary solution to every sort of contradiction, which short-circuits, so to speak, the technical order and the order of individual needs, exhausting the energies of the two systems" (Baudrillard, 1968: 183).

Baudrillard's analysis converges with that of Norbert Wiener, one of the founders of cybernetics and a skeptical observer of early automation. Wiener warned that any machine capable of making decisions would either have no capacity to learn, in which case we would not be wise to place much reliance on it, or it would have such a capacity—it would be a true automaton—in which case there is no guarantee its decisions would be acceptable to us. "For the man who is not aware of this, to throw the problem of his responsibility on the machine, whether it can learn or not, is to cast his responsibility to the winds, and to find it coming back seated on the whirlwind" (Wiener, 1950: 212).

Technology and Finitude

The rationalization of modern societies has been carried out by subjects— capitalists or government bureaucrats—whose defining characteristic is their operational autonomy. This fact is articulated through images drawn from the sphere of technique because modern power relations resemble the operation of a machine. Thus, Lukács argues that modernity brought with it a specific type of formal rationalism that, in the seventeenth century, identified the workings of the universe with the mechanical creations of the human hand and brain. The scientific logic of classification and calculation is the metaphoric equivalent of the techno-logic of machinery. The input of data, the raw material, is worked over by the axiomatic of the system, yielding an output of truths, goods, or wealth. The identity of syllogistic-mathematical procedures with mechanism inspired science and technology, and gave a distinctive practical aspect to modern Reason that culminates in the computer.

Descartes was the first to articulate the self-understanding of the subjects of this new form of rationality. De Certeau calls the shaping of an "interiority" from which to act on a correlated "exterior" the "Cartesian gesture" (de Certeau, 1980: 85). This gesture lays the foundation of leadership in modern societies. One manages organizations from without, rather than as a full member of the community. There is thus an inner link between the "possessive individualism" of emerging capitalist society and the Cartesian *cogito*, which is also a figure of alienation from immediate involvements.[12] The structural parallel between these subject positions is the basis for the social generalization of modern Reason, its transformation from an intellectual method into the cultural basis of modern society. A technical paradigm of thought and action triumphed in this transformation.

A finite subject is constituted by its own actions on the world. In using technique it is shaped by technique and becomes something quite different from what it intends. Meanwhile, as it incorporates its objects into technical systems, it changes them from immediate "natural" objects into mediated social objects. Thus, prior to the actual unfolding of any particular technical action, the subject and object have already been restructured. Modernity is the general collapse of religious and folk tradition in the face of this process. As a vision of the world, it is characterized by the fundamental misrecognition of finitude associated with the naive self-understanding of technical subjects.

A little god, the modern subject sees itself as autonomous, as independent of the system on which it operates through technical means. The modern subject places itself beyond the web of consequences of its own actions. From this beyond it elaborates projects based on formal, mechanistic thinking and a representation of reality as essentially an object of technical control. But as Adorno and Horkheimer argue, what ultimately conquers humanity in these projects is not a particular elite but a new form of life based on total technologization.

One of the paradoxes of the twentieth century is that, just as the entire world was enrolled into Western technological rationalism, the foundations of science and philosophy changed radically, undermining the assumption that the subject can remain external to the systems it designs and operates. Modern physics, philosophy, and biology, not to mention avant garde art and literature, increasingly challenge what Heidegger calls the "onto-theological" constitution of the subject as "beyond" objectivity (Heidegger, 1977a). These challenges demystify the procedures by which the illusion of technical interiority is produced and suggest the need for a new understanding of rationality. Although not always progressive, these theoretical innovations open potential political challenges; reason appears as inherently ambivalent and can either support a technocratic order or subvert it depending on how it is deployed socially.

Yet the new ideas have had little lasting social impact. Heidegger and Lukács lent their thinking to totalitarian schemes that exaggerated to the breaking point the very things they were attempting to overcome. The relatively justified reaction in favor of liberalism that began after World War II continues with ups and downs to this day. At its best, it saves what can be saved within the existing system, but liberalism appears now as a practical necessity, in the absence of workable alternatives, rather than as a solution to the fundamental problems of modernity.

As a culture, modern technological rationality is not dependent on science and philosophy but on hierarchical forms of social organization and technologies such as the computer. As hierarchy obtains a technical function, social subjects are placed in a technical interiority from which they control the systems on which they act. To attack the belief that hierarchy is destiny is an essential philosophical task requiring new concepts of social and technical action based on a radical acceptance of human finitude. Ethics has always involved the recognition that our actions on the world are ultimately actions on ourselves, on our way of being in the world and on our very nature. This insight must now be extended to technology as well.

At the beginning of the democratic era, Saint-Just expressed this contradictory structure through the figure of speech called "paradoxisme" in the rhetorical theory of his day. The National Assembly "ingeniously enchained the people with their own freedom"; "The people is a submissive monarch and a free subject" (Saint-Just, 1963: 27, 39). These are paradoxes of reflection in which the subject is also the object. They express the emergence of political rationality in the peculiarly modern form of self-consciousness.

This reflexive logic is diametrically opposed to the one-way movement down a Russellian hierarchy from metalanguage to object language. The politics of self-organization has the form of a "strange loop," which Douglas Hofstadter describes as a "phenomenon [that] occurs whenever, by moving upwards (or downwards) through the levels of some hierarchical system, we unexpectedly find ourselves right back where we started" (Hofstadter, 1979: 10). The most elegant illustration of Hofstadter's concept is Escher's "Drawing Hands," an etching of two hands, each of which holds a pencil and draws the other. Strange loops play many roles in our lives, appearing in various reversals of agency with which we are all familiar. For example, the child on whom we impose rules may insist *we* follow them. Or consider the case of President Clinton's rising ratings during the impeachment, which pollsters concluded was due to an attempt by those polled to use polling to stop the process, regardless of their opinion of Clinton. Controlling people exposes the controllers to a counteraction on the part of their human objects and the strange loop is closed.

Political democracy institutionalizes such reversals in the electoral subordination of the rulers to the ruled. Democratic notions of management and political organization can be rethought on these terms as rational systems without assuming an external source of control (Jantsch and Waddington, 1976). A self-referential logic of action is needed to grasp a democratic process that would have as its goal not escape from the community to a commanding position above it but internal self-development in common with others.

5

The Factory or the City
Which Model for Online Education?

Technology and Modernity

Much recent discussion of the Internet emphasizes its promise of epoch-making changes in our lives. In no domain are these anticipated changes more radical than in education. We are told that the substantive content of instruction can now be delivered better by computers than by teachers. Are we on the verge of a fundamental transformation of all our assumptions about education as we enter a postindustrial information age, or are we instead witnessing significant but more modest changes in education as we know it? As a participant in the early development of online education, I hope to be able to bring a touch of realism to the debate.

The debate is not limited to education, which is simply one among several fronts in the struggle to define the society of the future. The meaning of modernity is at stake in this struggle. One possible outcome is a society reflecting in all its institutions the logic of modern production, obsessed by efficiency achieved through mechanization and management. The Internet could serve this technocratic project in hitherto protected domains such as education. But one can also envisage a very different outcome modeled not on the factory but on another modern institution, the city.

The city is the place of cosmopolitan interactions and enhanced communication. Its god is not efficiency but freedom. It is not dedicated to the rigid reproduction of the same, the "one best way," but to the flexible testing of possibilities and the development of the new—not hierarchical control but unplanned horizontal contacts; not simplification and standardization but variety and the growth of the capacities required to live in a more complex world.[1] The Internet extends this urban logic in a radically new way.

The question implied in the debate over educational technology is therefore: Which model, the factory or the city, will shape the future of education? Online education can serve either strategy in different technical configurations. Automated education is certainly possible although at the price of a redefinition of education itself. The generalization on the Internet of a more traditional concept of education centered on human interaction would facilitate participation by underserved groups and might raise the cultural level of the population at large.

This latter prospect recalls a significant precedent. It is clear that the gradual disappearance of child labor and the consequent establishment of universal education has transformed modern societies and shapes the kind of people who inhabit them. To the extent that we are capable of understanding the complex technologized world around us and acting independently within it, this is owing to the extended time for learning modern societies allow.

However, there is a strong link between education and the division of labor, with the latter determining the former over long periods. Where deskilled production governs educational expectations, cultural levels remain relatively low. Marx saw no escape from this situation so long as capitalism survived to impose its division of labor. But capitalism is alive and well long after the demand for skill has risen to encompass a significant fraction of the labor force. The consequence has been tremendous educational dynamism. Adult education, for example, now embraces more than half the students in American college programs, a reflection of the shortage of competencies in the labor pool.

Yet one wonders how far this trend can go under capitalism. In the first place, the growing demand for educated labor in the advanced capitalist world is accompanied by the export of manufacturing to poor countries. While skilled and unionized manufacturing workers suffer steep declines in income and job security in the advanced countries, old-fashioned patterns of industrialization appear everywhere else. The net effect may well be a global increase in deskilled work despite the contrary appearance in places such as Silicon Valley. Second, business leaders appear to be increasingly alarmed by the high cost of education, which is now the largest budget item in practically every advanced capitalist nation. In the United States, the promise of the Internet has inspired an ideological offensive in favor of automating and deskilling education. These problems suggest the continuing relevance of critical theory to educational policy.

The Meanings of the Internet

One of the first educational technologies was writing, and like every subsequent educational technology, it had its critics. Plato denounced the
medium for its inability to re-create the give-and-take of spoken discourse.
Writing is analogous to painting, he has Socrates argue in *The Phaedrus* (a
text that, fittingly, depicts an intimate conversation between teacher and
student): "The painters' products stand before us as though they were alive,
but if you question them, they maintain the most majestic silence. It is the
same with written words; they seem to talk to you as though they were intelligent, but if you ask them anything about what they say, from a desire
to be instructed, they go on telling you just the same thing forever" (Plato,
1961: 521).

In short, Plato holds that the technology of writing has the power to destroy the dialogic relationship that ought to join teacher and student. Technology in the form of writing is the enemy of the human touch, a position
familiar from critics of modern life today. How often have we heard that
technology alienates, "enframes" and dehumanizes, that technical systems
intrude on human relations, depersonalizing social life and neutralizing its
normative implications? Could it be that the humanistic bias against the
computer can be traced back to Plato?

Ironically, Plato used a written text as the vehicle for his critique of writing, setting a precedent that we continue to follow in present-day debates
about educational technology: many of the most vociferous attacks on Web-
based media circulate *on the Internet* (Noble, 1997).

As Plato sees it, the medium in which we communicate determines the
quality of our interactions. But this is a deeply flawed view, as we have seen
in the case of the Internet. Rather, the social impact of technology depends
on how it is designed and used. Writing can lend itself to ongoing dialogues
between teachers and students, and speech can easily become one-sided.

However, while Plato's condemnation of writing was unfair, he alerts us
to a real issue: whenever a new educational technology is introduced, arguments emerge for substituting interaction with the technology for the process of intellectual exchange. But there is something about dialogue, and the
active involvement of the teacher, that is fundamental to the educational
process and that should be woven into the design of every new instructional
tool. Any break with this assumption would amount to an epochal change
in the communication between the generations. Ultimately, then, the question comes down to whether we can still defend an understanding of education like Plato's or whether the Internet, a more powerful technology than

writing, has finally rendered his conception obsolete. Neither television nor stand-alone computers ever managed to accomplish this feat, but many believe that such possibilities await us just a few miles down the information superhighway.

The optimism of these advocates of automated education fuels long-standing humanistic distrust of computers. As discussed in the last chapter, the computer appears as the very emblem of the modern experiment in total rational control. It is this image of the computer that inspires much of the current rhetoric of online education, both for and against.

To the extent that social thinkers fear or anticipate an automated society, they loathe or admire the computer. While technocrats hail the power of the computer to render social life transparent and controllable, humanists foresee the domination of man by the machine. In 1962, Heidegger offered a typical example of this pessimistic view. He explains the difference between language as saying, as revealing the world by showing and pointing, and language as mere sign, transmitting a message, a fragment of already constituted information. The perfection of speech is poetry, which opens language to being. The perfection of the sign is the unambiguous position of a switch, on or off, as in Morse code or the memory of a computer. Heidegger writes,

> The construction and the effectiveness of mainframe computers rests on the basis of the techno-calculative principles of this transformation of language as saying into language as message and as the mere production of signs. The decisive point for our reflection is that the technical possibilities of the machine prescribe how language can and should be language. The type and style of language is determined according to the technical possibilities of the formal production of signs, a production which consists in executing a continuous sequence of yes-no decisions with the greatest possible speed. . . . The mode of language is determined by technique. (Heidegger, 1998: 140, translation modified)

And Heidegger goes on to announce the end of Man under the impact of the computer. Lyotard concurred in his 1979 book on *The Postmodern Condition*. Here is his account:

> Knowledge cannot enter these new [computer] channels . . . unless it is capable of being translated into quantities of information. It is predictable that everything belonging to the constituted body of knowledge that is not so translatable will be abandoned, and that the orientation of new research will be subordinated to the condition that the eventual results be translatable into machine language. . . . Consequently, one can expect that knowledge will be rigorously externalized with respect to the "knower." (Lyotard, 1979: 13, my trans.)

Lyotard foresees the disappearance of humanistic culture and the complete commodification of knowledge in a postmodern society (Feenberg, 1995: chap. 6).

These thinkers bring out the difference between knowledge considered as pure data—mere information—and knowledge as a living process of discovery, growth, and communication between human beings. A critique of automated education could be built on this basis, but it would be far too encompassing. Heidegger and Lyotard blame the problem on the structure of the computer as such and not on particular designs or applications. If they are right, there can be no alternative realizations of the technology with different social consequences. It is digitization itself that is the villain.

All this makes fun reading for philosophers, but it is embarrassingly wide of the mark. What has actually happened to language in a world more and more dominated by computers? Has it in fact been reified into a technical discourse purified of human significance? On the contrary, the Internet now carries a veritable tidal wave of "saying," of language used for expression as always in the past.[2] Of course, we may not be interested in much of this online talk, but that is another story. The simple fact of the case is that these philosophical reflections on the computer were wrong. They not only failed to foresee the transformation of the computer into a communication medium but they precluded that possibility for essential reasons.

It was only in the 1980s that electronic communication by computer exploded, moving beyond the corporate settings to which it had been largely confined and entering the home. The first breakthrough occurred in France, where the Minitel system quickly attracted millions of users. Within a decade the Internet was to forever change the image of the computer. It was mainly nonprofessionals (or professionals not associated with the design and management of the systems) who pioneered these unexpected uses of the new technologies. And they succeeded because ordinary people wanted computers to serve personal goals and not just the official functions emphasized by experts. In the process they refuted widespread deterministic assumptions about the rationalizing implications of the computer and revealed its communicative potential.

The Minitel was the first large-scale domestic computing network. In the early 1980s, the French telephone company distributed six million terminals connected to a packet switching network to which servers could be easily hooked up. This was a national anticipation of what the Internet became on a global scale. The system was designed by telephone company technocrats who conceived it as a means of modernizing French society through improving citizen access to information resources. Human communication over computer networks was not originally part of the design or, where it was mentioned in early documents, it was far down on the list of priority functionalities. As a result, hardware and software were biased against human communication, although it was not technically impossible. Very quickly, hackers opened the network to human communication, which soon became one of its central functionalities (Feenberg, 1995: chap. 7). This case is emblematic of the democratic transformation of technical networks by the human actors they enroll, innovating novel social forms.

But is this transformation really significant from a democratic point of view? Isn't this just a "market rationalization" responding to commercial motivations? After all, most of the online communication supported by the Minitel system, as later with the Internet, is of no public significance. But transpose the case to a university campus and the point is clear. Suppose that the chancellor promulgated a new rule forbidding all unofficial conversation on campus. That would surely be perceived as undemocratic, indeed, as positively totalitarian. And why? For two reasons: first, because it would reduce complex living persons to the simple functions they serve inside a specific institution; and second, because it would make it nearly impossible to articulate complaints that might lead to changes in the institution. Absurd as this example must seem, it may well apply to virtual campuses in which automated learning systems are substituted for human contact.

In any case, this analogy illuminates the Minitel case. The doubling of real social space by the virtual space of computer networks opens new communicative possibilities for everyone. Limiting interaction to an official subset, such as business and government communication, has undemocratic implications online just as it would on campus. Fortunately, such limits have not been imposed.

In the similar case of the Internet, the stakes reach well beyond the Minitel example. Corporate and government organizations globalize on the Internet today without restraint. Obstacles to human communication on computer networks, had they been introduced, would have prevented a comparable globalization of citizen critique. Events such as the World Trade Organization protests would have been that much less likely in an environment where business was ever more cosmopolitan and citizens still provincial in their contacts and attitudes. This is of course not to say that the Internet causes or determines anything in particular on either side of the lines of battle drawn in Seattle. But the exclusion of ordinary human communication from the Internet would certainly have had undemocratic consequences.

This is the context in which to evaluate the opening of the networks by users to innovative communicative applications. Wise after the fact, we look back on the history of computing with the certainty that it was always meant to facilitate human contacts and then complain that it doesn't do as good a job as it should. If we "follow the actors," as Bruno Latour advocates, we discover a very different picture in which the networks are invented and re-invented by users as places of human encounter.

Just twenty years ago, few imagined what the future would hold for ap-parently trivial applications such as email. But it seems obvious today that the computer is a vital medium of communication, and not just a calculat-ing and information storage device. Its *definition* has changed in a direction determined by a social process. And the story is not yet over. The computer is not yet a finished product. It is still in flux, its evolution subject to a wide range of social influences and demands. But this fact also means that to the extent we depend on computers the very definition of modern life is still up for grabs.

As universities move into online education, they are becoming one of the most significant fronts in this struggle over the meaning of modernity. The new computer-based initiatives polarize around two alternative understand-ings of the computer as an educational technology. Is it an engine of control or a medium of communication? The choice that faced Minitel and Internet users decades ago returns today as a live option in the world of education. The automation of education relies on the first option; an informating solu-tion that incorporates human-to-human teaching relies on the second. In the remainder of this chapter, I will argue for that second solution as a pro-gressive technical alternative.

Automating Education

Why would one want to automate highly skilled educational tasks? Some may argue that technology can deliver education more effectively than can fac-ulty, empowering the learner, who is presumed to be oppressed or at the least badly served by the teacher. Others would claim that automated instruction offers "consumer-friendly" options for working adults. Automated educa-tion is said to foster postindustrial virtues such as temporal and spatial flex-ibility, individualized products, and personal control. But in the final analy-sis, the main reason for automating is obvious: to cut costs.

Costs, of course, are the concern of administrators and for too many of them the big issues in online education are not educational but financial. They hope to use new technology to finesse the coming crisis in higher education spending, and to accommodate exploding enrollments of young people and returning students. Automated online education is supposed to improve quality while cutting costs of delivery. Students in virtual classrooms need no new parking structures. What is more, courses can be packaged and marketed, generating a continuous revenue stream without further investment.

All this should have a familiar ring since it describes traditional correspondence schools. These schools fed written documents or television and radio broadcasts to isolated students studying in their homes. Compared to classroom education, the economies of scale in the production of documents and broadcasts yield tremendous cost savings. Labor costs approach zero as the school acquires a body of reusable materials and substitutes low-wage graders for professional teachers.

The Internet can raise the level of correspondence education inexpensively by improving the materials available to the student. To the extent that earlier attempts at replacing teachers failed for purely technical reasons, the Internet does show promise. In its ability to transmit graphically exciting materials and programs, as well as text, it represents a considerable advance over the correspondence schools of the past. It can even offer crude imitations of teacher-intensive tasks, such as answering questions using Frequently Asked Question lists (FAQ's) and "Ask the Expert" help programs. "Intelligent agents" can adapt computer-based programs to students' learning styles (Kearsley, 1993). And, incredibly enough, it may even be possible to automate the grading of some types of essay tests, as Peter Foltz and Thomas Landauer claim in describing their "Intelligent Essay Assessor," based on a technique called "Latent Semantic Analysis" (Foltz, 1996). According to a Coopers & Lybrand white paper, this kind of software will soon have a radical impact upon the daily realities of higher education. A "mere 25 courses" of packaged instructional software could handle 80 percent of enrollment in core undergraduate courses; a twenty-four-hour help desk would add a personal touch (Coopers & Lybrand, 1997).

The key to automation is to separate out informational "content" from "process." A small number of well-paid "content experts" will work as "star" performers, while the delivery process is deskilled so that inexpensive tutors can handle interaction with students. In a really low-cost solution, discussion can be replaced by automated exercises. Eventually it will be possible to dispense with campuses altogether. Students will pick out courses at an educational equivalent of Blockbuster and "do" college at home without ever meeting a faculty member or fellow student (Agre, 1999).

As we saw in the last chapter, strategies of automation go way back. Skilled workers are expensive, and automation is a time-honored strategy for cutting costs. The story begins in the early nineteenth century, when textile manufacturers in northern England discovered that they could replace skilled with unskilled labor by mechanizing. The whole history of the Industrial Revolution is dominated by this strategy.

Here is how the nineteenth-century "philosopher of manufactures" Andrew Ure described the goal in 1835:

> By the infirmity of human nature it happens, that the more skillful the workman, the more self-willed and intractable he is apt to become, and, of course, the less fit a component of a mechanical system, in which, by occasional irregularities, he may do great damage to the whole. The grand object therefore of the modern manufacturer is, through the union of capital and science, to reduce the task of his work-people to the exercise of vigilance and dexterity. (Ure, 1835: 18)

Is such a gloomy version of the future of education really plausible? Is it likely that "self-willed and intractable" professors will disappear as have weavers, shoemakers, and typesetters? Probably not, but whether technology is about to deskill the professoriate is less important than the fact that this idea occupies a key place in the imagination of many educational reformers.

The idea of replacing teachers by computers is an old one, but until recently few educational technologists and administrators were convinced. The ideal of automated education is no doubt still a minority view, but it has gained sufficient plausibility from advances in computing and the Internet to occupy a considerable space in public discourse. Other current buzz words such as "self-paced individualized instruction" feed into this trend. The essential idea is that in a future virtual university, accomplishment will no longer depend on contact hours, indeed, on contact with professors.

Much of today's reform rhetoric, with its appeals to the revolutionary potential of virtual universities and competency-based degrees, hints at the obsolescence of the traditional campus and its teaching methods, arousing suspicion among faculty that technology will be used against them. In the longer run, should teachers really be expelled from the classroom, we would truly enter a new era. One fundamental project of modern societies, the substitution of technical control for traditional methods and devices for social arrangements, here overflows the sphere of production to which it has been largely confined up to now and enters the realm of social reproduction. In this model the "disembedding" of the educational process, its disconnection from the local setting of the campus, is also its depersonalization. If human contacts are no longer central in so fundamental a growth process as education, then surely we are headed for a very different ideal of adulthood and a very different kind of modern society from the one we live in at present. But is this a necessary consequence of modernization?

Ironically, contemporary theory (if not practice) in the business world has left behind the industrial era's fascination with deskilling. Starting with Thomas Peters and Robert Waterman's 1982 best-seller *In Search of Excellence*, Frederick Taylor's old model of deskilled labor and hierarchical management was blamed for everything that ailed American business. Since then the lesson has been hammered home in dozens of similar books devoted to exploring a third way, an alternative to the old opposition of "man" versus "machine."

As discussed in chapter 4, Shoshanna Zuboff's contribution to this literature emphasizes the *complementarity* of human and computer capabilities. While humans are best at dealing with unexpected situations and responding to novelty, computers can organize the vast amount of data required by modern production. A similar complementarity is at work in education: the teacher manages the complex and unpredictable communication process of the classroom, while data is delivered in textbooks (and now by computers as well).

The specifics of the business literature do not always apply to colleges and universities, but Zuboff's emphasis on technological *choice* is relevant. Unfortunately, though, higher education has not quite gotten the message. Many college presidents continue to sell their constituents on the *inevitability* of computerization, as though the very existence of these new devices sets the reform agenda in some clear-cut and unambiguous way. And there still exists plenty of faculty opposition to the supposed *consequences* of the new media, as though their impact were predetermined (Feenberg, 1999; Farber, 1998).

Higher education has a $200 billion budget and employs and services many millions of people. The shape of the educational future is the shape of our society, and increasingly it is corporate rather than professional models that prevail. The erosion of traditional faculty status continues apace in innovative institutions serving adult learners, now half the students in higher education. Even the older universities that now teach a declining fraction of students employ more and more part-timers in the search for "flexibility." And it is becoming more difficult to resist arguments against tenure that carry conviction with the public if not with most members of the university community.

This explains why there is so much faculty resistance to new technology. Faculty detect continuity in administration enthusiasm for cost-cutting at the expense of traditional educational roles and values. Between 1970 and 1995, the number of full-time faculty increased by about half, while over the same period part-time faculty multiplied two and one half times. If the trend continues, part-timers will overtake full-time faculty on college campuses in several years. At community colleges, part-time faculty are already in the majority.

This worrying trend parallels the growth of the nontraditional or returning student population. These students require different course schedules than the traditional ones to which faculty are attached. Largely because of this, adult education has developed outside the standard academic departments and procedures under direct administrative control. As a result, a vast parallel system of higher education has emerged in which faculty have low status and less power. Since it serves adult learners—precisely the students most likely to be open to distance learning—this parallel system has a free hand to experiment even if traditional universities resist.

These trends set a precedent for administration strategies that, many fear, are moving from deprofessionalization to deskilling. The replacement of full-time by part-time faculty is merely the opening act in the plan to replace the faculty as such by CD-ROMs. A new economic model of education is being sold under the guise of a new technological model. This is the route to what David Noble calls "digital diploma mills." Understandably, this is not a route many faculty wish to travel.

The issue of educational technology must therefore be framed in a broader context because it is not primarily a technical issue. It reflects the changing relation of management and professionalism, which in turn concerns issues of career patterns, standardization, quality, and control. The resolution of these issues and the evolution of educational technology will go hand in hand. In short, there exists a great temptation to think of technology as a managerial tool for centralizing the university. Something like this may actually happen in the confusing environment created by technological change. Once in place, bad decisions will be locked in technically and difficult to reverse.

Informating Education

Technologies are not mere means to ends; they also shape worlds. What kind of world is instituted by the Internet? The basic fact about computer networks is scarcity of bandwidth. This limitation can be overcome now to the point where audio and video can be distributed on the Internet. That possibility inspires plans for automated education.

But writing is the oldest technology we have for dealing with a narrow bandwidth. Plato was no doubt right to complain that writing cannot reproduce the actual experience of living human interaction. On the other hand, we now have a rich experience of written dialogue online. And we have discovered in that context that writing is not just a poor substitute for speech and physical presence but another fundamental medium with its own properties and powers. It is not impersonal, as is sometimes supposed. We know how to present ourselves as persons through written correspondence. Nor is it harder to write about ideas than to talk about them; most people can formulate difficult ideas more easily in written form than in speech in front of an audience.

These considerations on writing hold the key to the informating of online education. The online environment is essentially a *written world* (Feenberg, 1989). In this section I will argue that electronic networks can be appropriated by educational institutions with this in mind, and not turned into automated teaching machines or poor copies of the face-to-face classroom that they cannot adequately reproduce.

Wherever education takes place, the basic medium must be carefully distinguished from the enhancements and their roles distributed correctly. Speech is the basic medium in the classroom, supplemented with labs, movies, slides, textbooks, computer demonstrations, and so on. Similar enhancements to written interaction are possible on networks. No doubt these enhancements will continue to improve and perhaps someday change the nature of online education. But for many years to come, writing will continue to be the basic medium of online expression, the skeleton around which other technologies and experiences must be organized to build a viable learning environment.

Confusing the medium with the supplementary enhancements leads to the pedagogical absurdity of teacherless education. To replace online written interaction with the enhancements makes no more sense than to replace the teacher in the face-to-face classroom with labs, movies, slides, textbooks, and computer demonstrations. That was tried long ago with educational television and computer-aided instruction without success.

Despite the promise of automation, the ideal of dialogue has inspired some educational technologists since the early 1980s, and considerable progress has been made in using online education to support new forms of interaction among teachers and students (Harasim et al., 1995: chap. 3; Berge, 1999). In 1981 I worked with the design team that created the first online educational program. This was the School of Management and Strategic Studies at the Western Behavioral Sciences Institute in La Jolla, California (Feenberg, 1993). Our goal was to enable busy executives to participate in a humanistic educational experience despite job demands that made it impossible for them to attend regular university classes. The only way to do this at that time was the old-fashioned correspondence course, the reputation of which had fallen so low in the United States we did not envisage it. Instead, we opted for computer networking, a still experimental technology available primarily in a few large computer companies and universities, and on small publicly accessible servers such as the Electronic Information Exchange System (EIES) at the New Jersey Institute of Technology. These were the obscure forerunners of the Internet as we know it today. We succeeded in placing our school on EIES, and for nearly ten years I helped with its operation, trained teachers, and myself taught courses in it.

When we started out, online education was essentially untried. The equipment was expensive and primitive. We used Apple IIEs with 48K of memory and 300-baud modems. (Multiply by 1,000 and 100, respectively, to get current averages.) The complexity of basic computer operations in those days was such that it took a full page of printed instructions just to connect. The only available electronic mediation was asynchronous computer conferencing, which allows private groups to form online and share messages. Current online educational software such as Blackboard or Web CT continues to perform many of the functions of these early conferencing programs.

None of us had ever been a student in an online class or seen one in operation, and we did not know the answers to the most elementary pedagogical questions, such as how to start a class, how long or short messages should be, and how often the teacher should sign on and respond to the students. We soon discovered that computer conferencing was not very useful for delivering lectures, and of course it could not support any graphical contents, even the simple drawings teachers like to scribble on the blackboard. After considerable trial and many errors, we discovered how to sustain a Socratic pedagogy based on virtual classroom discussion. The school soon grew to include over 150 students in twenty-six countries around the world and inspired other experiments in online education. The field grew slowly and quietly on this original dialogic basis throughout the 1980s and early 1990s.

Using email and computer conferencing, faculty in many American universities have for years now been reproducing the excitement of classroom discussion online. For the instantaneous back and forth of real-time discussion, a slower but still engaging day-to-day rhythm is substituted. With time to reflect and compose questions and answers, students who might never have participated in a face-to-face setting bring forward their ideas. The use of writing imposes a discipline and helps focus thinking. Faculty learn to grasp students' ideas at a much deeper level as they engage with them online. Innovative pedagogical techniques such as collaborative learning have been adapted to the Internet and new forms of interaction invented (Harasim et al., 1995: chap. 6). In successful experiments, small classes are the rule: twenty is a good working number. There is little doubt that competent teachers under these conditions are able to reproduce a true equivalent of classroom interaction.[3]

At the Western Behavioral Sciences Institute, the emphasis was on human communication. Our version of online education was conceived in a break with the correspondence-school model. We gave up the use of elaborate prepackaged materials in exchange for living interaction. That choice is no longer necessary. The Internet can now do more than merely improve the materials available in the traditional correspondence course; it can also add human contact to an educational model that has always been relatively impersonal. Using email and discussion forums, groups of students can be assembled in online communities where they can participate in classroom discussion with teachers on a regular basis. The gap between correspondence education and online learning as we implemented it twenty years ago can now be closed.

An automated system of online education does not take advantage of this new potential of the Internet but perpetuates the old correspondence-school model. It simply extends the economies of scale associated with the distribution of written materials into the wide range of media supported by the Internet (Agre, 1999). But the social condition for the cost savings achieved by correspondence schools, whether traditional or Web based, is the isolation of the student. On the other hand, a system that also includes live interaction does so at a price: a qualified teacher must be in attendance at every iteration of the course. Institutions may save money on building costs but not on educational labor, the single largest item in most university budgets.

What does this say about the ambition to replace campuses with virtual universities? Large markets for distance learning will undoubtedly emerge, and this will be a blessing for many students who cannot attend college classes. This trend has important implications not only for working adults in the advanced capitalist world but for residents of rural areas in poorer countries. But if higher education is cut loose from the traditional university and its values, the blessing will turn into a disaster. The best way to maintain the connection is through ensuring that distance learning is "delivered" not just by CD-ROMs, but by living teachers, qualified to teach and interested in doing so online.

Then prepackaged materials will be seen to replace not the teacher but the lecture and the textbook. Interaction with the professor will continue to be the centerpiece of education, no matter what the medium. And of course for most people that interaction will continue to take place on campus if they have the means and the mobility to attend a college.

Conclusion: The Future of Educational Technology

Today we are confronted with two very different directions of development for democratic societies, one of which defines citizenship in terms of the functions individuals serve in systems such as markets, workplaces, and administrations, while the other conceives of the individuals as bearers of a range of potentialities that surpass any particular functional realization. The definition of those potentialities occurs in aesthetic experimentation, ethical and political debate, and technical controversies. The first view characterizes modernity as we know it. The tendency of this modernity is to replace human communication wherever possible by technical or bureaucratic systems that enhance the power of the few in the name of efficiency. Education, from this point of view, should be narrowly specialized and tightly controlled, both in terms of costs and content. Automated systems in which communication is restricted to the delivery of data and programs could serve this project.

The second view holds out the possibility of an alternative modernity that realizes human potentials ignored or suppressed in the present society. Many of those potentials are specifically communicative and depend on the very practices being eliminated under the present dispensation. Furthermore, those potentials can express themselves only in a communicatively open environment. This vision implies a broad education for citizenship and personal development, as well as the acquisition of technical skills.

Educational technology will not determine which of these paths is followed. On the contrary, the politics of the educational community interacting with national political trends will steer the future development of the technology. And this is precisely why it is so very important for a wide range of actors to be included in technological design (Wilson, 1999). Students and faculty bring a number of considerations to the table, including the desire to create tools that support human interaction, a desire that has already manifested itself forcefully in the earlier evolution of the computer.

Systems designed by administrations working with corporate suppliers will be quite different. Automating the classroom feeds directly into a preference for video, which seems to offer the closest equivalent to "real life" and a lot more entertainment. We are not talking about the old-fashioned talking-head video broadcast on television networks, but a new kind of computer mediated video capable of much more elaborate presentations. This has implications for course design. Automated products will tend to be quite elaborate since they must rely entirely on the computer to dramatize their message and motivate the student. Courseware designers and producers will manage the work of star faculty who can offer polished performances in the new medium. Predictably, educational technology will evolve to Hollywood levels of complexity.

When they actually engage with the new teaching technology, faculty sense immediately that it is not mature. In the actual experience of online education, technology is not a predefined thing at all, but an environment, an empty space faculty must inhabit and enliven. They have a craft relation to the technologies rather than a development strategy. They try to get the feel of it and figure out how to animate it, to project their "voice" in it. In doing so they are acting out of an ancient tradition that assigns education to human relations rather than devices.

This difference is reflected in different technological emphases. While it would be nice to be a "star" professor in an automated virtual class, most faculty do not aspire to that exalted status. Live video, with its complicated and intimidating apparatus, holds little attraction for either teachers or students. Of course, this may change as high-speed access over the Internet becomes commonplace, but we are many years away from achieving this in campus settings, much less in the home. The graphical capabilities of computers are better compared to blackboards than to classrooms; they are supplements to, rather than replacements for, teaching.

These considerations govern the design of online courses animated by a live professor. They will generally be created under his or her control in relatively simple and flexible formats. No computer professionals need be involved. As in the conventional classroom, much of the interest will lie in the interaction among students and between students and teachers. As far as techniques of presentation are concerned, a certain healthy amateurism is to be expected. Prepackaged computer-based materials will not replace the teacher but supplement his or her efforts, much as do textbooks today. Software designers will pursue user-friendliness and simplicity to serve faculty needs.

Although neither video conferencing nor automated learning have caught on with faculty, there is a long history of interactive text based applications such as the experiment at the Western Behavioral Sciences Institute described earlier. These experiences go back to a time when there were no more elaborate alternatives; it is widely assumed that the introduction of image and sound renders earlier approaches obsolete. But perhaps that is a mistake. The latest equipment is not always the best for the task. Could it be that our earliest experiences with computer conferencing were not merely constrained by the primitive equipment then available but also revealed something important about electronically mediated education? I believe this to be the case. Even after all these years the exciting online pedagogical experiences still involve human interactions and for the most part these continue to be text based.

But here is the rub: interactive text-based applications lack the pizzazz of video alternatives and cannot promise automation, nor can they be packaged and sold. They do not conform to the fantasy of total central control over a flexible, disseminated system defying spatial and temporal boundaries. On the contrary, they are labor intensive and will probably not cut costs very much. Hence the lack of interest from corporations and administrators, and the gradual eclipse of these technological options in public discussion (if not on campus) by far more expensive ones. But unlike the fancy alternatives, interactive text-based systems actually accomplish legitimate pedagogical objectives faculty and students recognize and respect.

To resist the automating trend in education is not simply to wallow in an old-fashioned Mr. Chips sentimentality. Rather, it is a question of different civilizational projects with different institutional bases. The traditional conception of education must be preserved not out of uncritical worship of the past but for the sake of the future. I have tried to show here that the educational technology of an advanced society might be shaped by educational dialogue rather than the production-oriented logic of automation. Should a dialogic approach to online education prevail on a large enough scale, it could be a factor making for fundamental social change. This prospect is explored in all its utopian implications in the next chapter.

III

The Dialectics of Technology

Did communism fail because it defied the "technological imperatives" of the industrial system? Does that failure prove that socialism in any form is incompatible with modern production? The critical theory of technology challenges these widespread views and argues that technology does not determine a particular form of society. Technology is in large measure a cultural product, and thus any given technological order is a potential starting point for divergent developments depending on the cultural environment that shapes it.

This section applies this nondeterministic approach to two related problems. The first chapter constructs a model of the transition to socialism based on the leading role of culture in the process of technological development. Although it was created under the cultural and economic constraints of capitalism, industrial technology could in principle be bent to new ones in the course of a transition to socialism. After its transformation, it could then be routinely employed in the service of cultural values quite different from those that presided over its creation. From an economic standpoint, the dependence of technology on culture means that alternative rationalizations *are possible, each equally "efficient" in terms of achieving its own ends, but employing different configurations of means to do so.*

The concluding chapter reformulates the radical critique of technology and attempts to draw out its positive implications for the future. Presenting a reconstructive project is the best response to the charge that the critique is irrationalist or technophobic. Scientific-technical rationality is not an ahistorical monolith that must be defended or rejected as a whole but an evolving complex of attributes that can be configured in a variety of ways with diverse social implications. Alternative rationalizations depend on which among these attributes is emphasized. The choice of emphasis depends, in turn, on politics and culture. A holistic form of rationality compatible with socialist goals is among the possibilities.

6

Beyond the Dilemma of Development

The Dilemma of Development

The Thesis of Convergence

According to an ancient tradition of Western political theory, societies cannot achieve both civic virtue and material prosperity. For centuries the rise and fall of the Roman Republic served as a cautionary tale illustrating pessimistic maxims. "Roman liberty," said Saint-Just, "was drowned in gold and delights" (Saint-Just, 1963: 63). There is a flaw in human nature: released by riches from a common struggle with nature, men grow soft and lose the spirit of self-sacrifice required for life in a free society. This is the dilemma Mandeville mockingly formulated in his famous doggerel (Mandeville, 1970: 76):

> . . . Fools only strive
> To make a Great an honest Hive . . .
> Bare Vertue can't make Nations live
> In Splendour; they, that would revive
> A Golden Age, must be as free,
> For Acorns, as for Honesty.

I shall call this "the dilemma of development," the view that two of the highest values pursued in public and private life are mutually exclusive.

Since Max Weber, modern social theory keeps reformulating something very much like this traditional view. New reasons are advanced to show that the satisfaction of material needs is fundamentally incompatible with the progress of human freedom. Today, the argument goes, prosperity requires a scale of enterprise, a management of production and markets, and an application of scientific and technical knowledge so far beyond the comprehension and control of ordinary citizens as to render them mere cogs

133

in an alienated mechanism. In such recent reformulations of the dilemma of development, the emphasis is less on moral flaws in human nature than on the gap between the cognitive capacities of the individual and the complex problems of technological society. This condition, it is said, is a general one today, regardless of the prevailing political system, be it capitalist democracy or communism.

Reformulated in this manner, the dilemma of development points to a central contradiction in democratic political theory. The redefinition of the state in the modern era revolves around two complementary demands: egalitarianism and a new efficacy in the performance of state functions. Divine law and inherited right no longer justify the coercive power of the state, which must now be derived from the people through public debate and elections. At the same time, a more efficient state requires expert administration by qualified individuals chosen for their abilities independent of class origin. Birth is replaced by equal participation in decisions of state, and by merit in the efficient execution of policy.

The reconciliation of equality and efficiency in the democratic state is the modern utopia par excellence, nowhere so far fully realized. The difficulty lies in the *contradiction of expertise and participation,* the two foundations of the system. They are supposed to be reconciled in the subordination of administration to democratically established policies, but in fact the unequal distribution of administrative power turns out to be increasingly subversive of equal participation. Weber's sober formulation of the dilemma reveals the dystopian implications for modern societies.

Marx's work belongs to a different tradition that seeks to transcend the dilemma, reconciling freedom and prosperity. Marx rejected the assumption that there is only one model of progress, one path to abundance. He argued that alternatives emerge with the Industrial Revolution. Thereafter, radically different industrial futures are possible, depending on whether the dominant political option is capitalist or socialist. The dilemma of development is an effect of capitalism that socialism would overcome in a new form of industrial society.

As Marx presents it, socialism is a new *civilizational project* and as such not comparable to ordinary political movements that aim at changes within the framework of the existing civilization. Such changes are inherently limited by the requirements of the existing technical system. But socialism would be a new culture in which different values, patterns of life, and organizational principles would yield a coherent, fully integrated social system of a new type with its own technical system. The study of development should therefore address itself to the possibility of alternative paths of modernization with different consequences for human freedom.

This socialist conception breaks with the usual dualistic contrast between traditional and modern society. In place of the binary oppositions of models like Tönnies's, Weber's or Parsons's, Marx proposed a ternary system in which the third term represents a qualitatively different stage. *According to Marx, the passage from tradition to modernity can no longer be understood entirely on modern terms as the rationalization of society through the breakup of an original organic social totality into its reified fragments. The fragmentation of society invites synthesis at a higher level, an integration and concretization of the results of modernity in a new, mediated totality.* This socialist conception of progress opens the future, which is arbitrarily blocked by the assumption that there can be only one type of modern society.

Given Marx's reputation as a technological determinist, it is ironic that many of the strongest arguments advanced against the very possibility of socialism rest on a deterministic understanding of technology. The sharpest formulation of this view is to be found in theories of "convergence" of all modern societies. These theories project the dilemma of development on a planetary scale. According to modernization theory, for example, the spread of the Western model is a predictable consequence of technological development. Societies moving out of the "acorns and honesty" stage—like the People's Republic of China—will confront the dilemma of development in full force. To quote Marx himself, "De te fabula narratur": the advanced societies are a destiny for their poorer neighbors (Marx, 1906: 13).

Such views can be traced back to Weber's theory of rationalization and his image of the "iron cage" in which modern societies are trapped. As social forecasts, convergence theories attempt to identify the central causes of social change and to predict the consequences. The main arguments for convergence are sociological and economic ones, based on broadly conceived "imperatives of modernization," such as the increasing specialization and division of labor. In designating these trends as central, the intent is to subordinate other presumably secondary sources of change such as culture and politics.

Before the fall of communism appeared to verify convergence theory, its critics argued with some success that it was "ethnocentric." It is, on the face of it, implausible that differing cultural values should have no impact on patterns of development. Surely the response to modernization may influence its course. The argument seems especially applicable to societies which are self-consciously committed to the development of a new culture and a future utterly unlike the present such as the Soviet Union and, more recently, Islamic socialism in Iran. In the early 1970s, when communism looked like a permanent feature of the landscape, Robert C. Tucker therefore proposed that we take the

> culture transforming and culture building process as the *central content* of "development" in its communist forms. Instead of treating communism as a modernizing movement, we will see certain ingredients of what Westerners call "modernization" as present in the processes of directed cultural change observable in communist societies. We will, in short, take care not to assume that the communists are recapitulating our developmental history in their peculiar manner; our theoretical perspective itself will become culture conscious. (Tucker, 1973: 88, 186–187)

Arguments of this sort have returned in defense of cultural particularity against globalism. But persuasive as is the general point, the confinement of difference to culture tends to vitiate the argument. Even where social scientists reject a single-factor explanation of social change and assert the possibility of different paths of modernization, their vision of economic and technological advance is remarkably stereotyped. As a result, the range of variation permitted by these more pluralistic theories is still very narrow. After all, these theorists admit, whatever the political, legal, or cultural differences between nations, all must accommodate the selfsame technology. But the social impact of the technological subsystem of society grows constantly as the economy expands in the course of modernization. A "developed" society is one in which few major decisions can be made outside the framework of the technical and economic constraints of this subsystem.

Hence, the reservations about convergence turn out to have little content in practice: even if a society that professes original values retains its system of government and ideology as it advances, the kinds of goods it produces, the way it produces them, the forms of daily life that emerge around consumption of those goods, the educational requirements of the society, and the careers etched into its division of labor would all come to resemble Western models.[1]

Some students of development, anxious to find signs of true variety, rely on the example of those exceptional nations that have mobilized the strongest resistance to incorporation into world technoculture. But such movements as the Chinese Cultural Revolution or Islamic socialism involve costly trade-offs of economic efficiency for ideological values. Insofar as it is truly significant and not merely an ethnic *point d'honneur*, cultural specificity can be preserved only at a price so high few are likely to pay it for long. The return of China under Deng to the modernizing fold signaled a general pattern to which other rebel nations will likely conform given enough time to measure the cost of difference.

Today, while some of the most extreme claims that used to be made in the name of convergence theory are controversial, a mitigated version of it is part of the common sense of the social sciences. The case for convergence seems quite strong indeed when the modest claim is made that industrial societies using the same technologies will tend to grow more similar in the increasing number of domains where technical imperatives impinge on social life. Stated in this form, what I will call the *thesis of convergence* appears obvious, but I will show that its conception of technology carries a powerful ethnocentric charge. That ethnocentricity is reflected in the view that whatever the differences between nations, the dilemma of development is an inescapable structural constraint affecting them all.

This chapter argues that democratic socialism involves a process of civilizational change more complex than anything we would normally consider under the heading of politics. Instead of pursuing the usual political argument for socialism, I have attempted to identify possible starting points for such a process. The result is not a utopian description of a perfect society, but rather an integrated series of democratic reforms affecting politics, economics, culture, and ultimately the technology of modern societies.

On these terms, socialism is a trajectory of development fraught with ambiguity. Any society attempting to move toward socialism will have to make difficult cultural and technical choices that will decide its chances of initiating a true transitional process. These choices will appear irrational or voluntaristic to observers who hold deterministic assumptions. It will not be easy to detect the first signs of fundamental civilizational change should they appear.

A better understanding of the process will require innovative approaches that do not prejudge the question of transition or convergence. This is equally true for historical studies of those brief experiments with radical policies that have occurred in communist societies. To avoid dogmatically dismissing all deviations from what has been the main line of development, our model must integrate a critical theory of technology. Only such a model can distinguish between systemic tendencies toward convergence or transition.

Technological Determinism

It is no easy task to develop concepts that would allow one to anticipate and describe radical civilizational change as opposed to reforms under the horizon of the existing civilization. Such concepts necessarily transgress cultural limitations of the society in which they are formulated. These limitations appear in the everyday assumption that our own culture is "natural" and that all that differs from it is absurd or impossible. Cultural limitations are also enshrined in the social sciences in powerful methods that treat the specific dilemmas and paradoxes of life in the existing modern societies as unavoidable consequences of industrialism in general.

When "modernity" is defined theoretically, these societies enter a conceptual heaven where their particular traits acquire universality and necessity. The subsequent application of these uncritical generalizations bestows an illusory inevitability on the present and forecloses alternatives for the future. Any action that points beyond the horizon of this conception appears irrational and regressive. If in fact these concepts comprehend the limits and potentialities of modernity as such, socialism, as it has been defined here, is excluded a priori.

In this context, the argument for the existence of socialist "potentialities" becomes a major task of critical social theory. This argument must be advanced on epistemological grounds through criticism of social scientific categories, very much as Marx elaborated his economic theory in conflict with the political economy of his times. Critical social theory must work out a new approach to modernity that not only faces the facts but that also encompasses them in categories broad enough to reveal their historical contingency. In the remainder of this chapter, I will apply such an approach to the consideration of methodological problems in the understanding of socialism.

The dominant view of modernization is based on the deterministic assumption that technology has its own autonomous logic of development. According to this view, technology is an invariant element that, once introduced, bends the recipient social system to its imperatives. This has implications for the possibility of a transition to socialism, for it implies that every attempt to build a new type of modern society is a mere detour that must eventually rejoin the path of convergence. On this account, history is essentially over except for the shouting.

Determinism is based on the following two theses:[2]

1. The pattern of technical progress is fixed, moving along one and the same track in all societies. Although political, cultural, and other factors may influence the pace of change, they cannot alter the general line of development that reflects the autonomous logic of discovery.
2. Social organization must adapt to technical progress at each stage of development according to "imperative" requirements of

technology. This adaptation executes an underlying technical necessity.

Given these assumptions, all societies can be ordered along a single continuum, the more advanced exemplifying future stages of the less advanced. Culture plays no significant role in shaping the history of technological development but can only motivate or obstruct progress along a fixed track. Technology appears to be an application of the laws of nature to problems of production, as independent of human will as the movements of the heavenly bodies. Some of the aura of science can then be transferred back to the machines that depend on its principles. The iron necessity of natural law is read into the process of technological development and through it into society as a whole.

The conception of the mechanical subsystem of society as an independent force with a self-propelling dynamic reflects the structure of capitalist society. The capitalist division of labor accomplishes just this separation of the means of production from the producers, of machines from their human users. A definition of technology that abstracts the mechanical conditions of production from living labor and culture therefore resonates ethnocentrically with our experience under capitalism. Abstracted and hypostasized technology as an independent and determining factor reflects the categorial underpinnings of our own world. This accounts for the plausibility of the theory.

Even where no explicit convergence theory is formulated, determinism often lurks in the background, and under its influence the researcher assumes concepts of industrialization and modernity derived uncritically from advanced capitalism. The bias of modernization theory is revealed, for example, in the way it contrasts two of its chief operative terms: technology and ideology. The imperatives of technology form a "techno-logic," and the goals socialists attempt to impose upon the process of modernization can, by analogy, be described as a corresponding "ideo-logic." Techno-logic has an influence that ideo-logic lacks and is always presented as something "real," substantial, objective, almost spontaneous in character, like a natural process. Ideo-logic is a matter of human will. It is "voluntaristic" and lacks ultimate force in contact with techno-logic.

This invidious comparison of terms is supported by a characteristic methodological procedure: whenever ideo-logic contributes to economic development, it is said to coincide momentarily with the imperatives of modernization at that stage. Hence, in the long run ideo-logic can accomplish nothing original but is destined to be outmoded by the very process of development it furthers. On the other hand, any socioeconomic change that does not accord with the standard pattern of modernization is attributed to the influence of ideo-logic, described as irrational, and dismissed as a passing aberration imposed by misguided political leaders. The impotence of ideo-logic is thus a matter of definition. Its efficacy only appears independently where it is doomed to fail because it stands in the way of progress.[3]

William Dunn formulated this position in terms of Amitai Etzioni's concept of "dual compliance." He saw communist societies caught in the crossfire of conflicting commitments to efficiency and revolutionary values (Dunn, 1974: 5[4]). The pursuit of an "ideo-logical" end such as egalitarianism has economic costs, while the pursuit of economic efficiency has, correspondingly, "social" costs in terms of the sacrifice of egalitarianism to productivity. Communist politics are therefore characterized by fluctuating emphases as one or the other goal temporarily gains the upper hand. They exhibit essentially Western patterns of modernization during cyclical emphases on efficiency, patterns that are unaffected by the time lost to technological progress while revolutionary values are emphasized.

According to this view, societies are free to resist the implicit logic of technological development in order to preserve indigenous ideological or national values, but they do so at a definite economic price. The voluntaristic imposition of values incompatible with technological imperatives involves a tradeoff of moral for material goods. Although this theory admits the possibility of small national variations, it continues to affirm the existence of a unique path of development along which societies may either limp or race, depending on the single-mindedness of their commitment to "efficiency." A socialist civilization, with its own distinctive culture and standard of wealth, is excluded in principle by the arbitrary identification of efficiency with the technical code of capitalism.

Determinism is not the monopoly of the critics of socialism. Some Western radicals concede that a socialist production system would be less "efficient" than capitalism. Socialism, they argue, would lower labor productivity in favor of increased returns of "soft" variables, such as job satisfaction, equality, and environmental protection. They thus implicitly affirm technological determinism and its associated dual compliance model of the relation of values to the economy (Bahro, 1984).

This view is most closely associated with the Green movements today, but it has a venerable history. William Morris first contrasted "useful work" with "useless toil" and called for a revival of craft labor as the only means of restoring workers' skills and recapturing the virtues of traditional community (Morris, 1973). A much more elaborate argument along the same lines underlies Lewis Mumford's approach to the history of technology. Mumford hopes "to persuade those who are concerned with maintaining democratic institutions to see that their constructive efforts must include technology itself" (Mumford, 1964: 7). He contrasts small-scale "democratic technics" with large-scale "authoritarian technics" going all the way back to ancient Egypt. Today, Morris and Mumford would no doubt be advocates of "alternative technology." Amory Lovins's distinction between "soft" and "hard" technologies corresponds to the polarities they identify while bringing their approach up to date (Lovins, 1977).

Theories of alternative technology attempt to construct a new technical code to guide the design of future technology. If one believes that technical development is socially determined, this is a plausible undertaking. However, there is an important ambiguity in many of these writings: it is often unclear whether industrial technology can be reconstructed to achieve their goals, or whether, like Morris, they reject it in favor of a return to simpler craft technology. Does the social determination of technology concern alternatives *within* industrialism or the choice *between* industry and craft?

This is a difference with enormous implications. The idea that industrial technology is irredeemable is essentially determinist. To claim that society must choose between industry and craft is to concede that the existing industrial system is the only possible one. Clearly, this is entirely different from arguing for the reconstruction of the industrial system through the incorporation of new values into industrial design.[4]

The risk of confusion is evident in Robin Clarke's list of utopian characteristics of soft technology. The list includes dozens of pairs of hard and soft attributes, including some, like the following, that could guide either the reconstruction of industry or a return to craft.

  1. ecologically unsound/ecologically sound
  10. alienation from nature/integration with nature
  21. centralist/decentralist
  24. technological accidents frequent and serious/technological accidents few and unimportant.

But alongside these ecumenical objectives, Clarke lists such things as:

  6. mass production/craft industry
  9. city emphasis/village emphasis
  13. world-wide trade/local bartering
  19. capital intensive/labour intensive.[5]

These attributes determine a strategy of deindustrialization that is incompatible with reconstruction.

Efficiency is not the enemy even from an environmental point of view. A better society need not be inefficient and poor. That position concedes too much to the dominant ideology. Means-ends rationality is no doubt an unsurpassable dimension of modernity, but it will have quite different results in cultures that measure success differently, define the legitimate domain of optimization differently, and have different ends in view. There thus is no reason of principle why one would have to retreat economically in order to achieve ecological and democratic objectives. At least it would make sense to explore the limits of industrial reconstruction before dispersing to labor-intensive village communities!

Profit is the most important measure of efficiency under capitalism. Because profit is realized on the sale of commodities, not on public and nonmarket goods, the extension of capitalist economic rationality may diminish the availability of these other goods without the costs appearing on any socially legitimated ledger. The GNP may rise as welfare declines without anyone but the immediate victims being the wiser. In their rush to catch up with capitalism, communist societies adopted fairly crude concepts of economic growth as their main measure of success. With only such measures to guide them, and no democratic checks on official abuses, it is not surprising that their record was (and in China still is) even worse than that of capitalism in domains such as environmental protection.

A socialist society dedicated not to simple economic growth but to the actualization of human capacities could employ more direct and varied measures of material well-being than these simple quantitative ones, As I will show later in this chapter, it could evolve an economic culture that encompassed goals systematically undervalued in the existing modern societies, such as education, environmental quality, and satisfaction at work. Such a society might also find it easier to bound the economy by other logics, for example, those of human relations, protection of the disabled, children's welfare, and so on. Despite these differences, the pursuit of efficiency entails sacrifices, but—and this is the crucial point—the system differences result in different sacrifices being made.

The dominant economic culture encourages trading off such "soft" goals as occupational safety or endangered species for "hard" cash. But these goals are not incompatible with the use of technology to achieve prosperity. Nor are they objectively less vital or desirable than profits or consumer goods. Clean air appears as a political issue only because it is a post hoc expense in cities designed around highly polluting private transportation, the only kind of transportation on which a profit can be made. A different form of urban design based on mass transit and mixed use might treat air quality as just another technical problem, no different in principle from dozens of other similar problems solved in running an efficient transportation system.

Goals that now appear as ideals or values would thus take on quite a different form in a society that embodied them in its technical code. In such a society no sacrifice of productivity would be involved in serving these ends, even if the predicted drop in the volume of consumer goods should in fact occur. This is no merely verbal point: the so-called soft variables would be pursued spontaneously by the individuals as a positive component of their own welfare and would not have to be imposed on them by artificial incentives or political coercion in opposition to their own perceived interests.

Deterministic theories share implausible assumptions about technological development that contradict the historical evidence. These are, first, the notion that technological development occurs along a single fixed track according to immanent technical criteria of progress, and, second, that social institutions must adapt to technological development. In reality, technology is not rigid but is routinely adapted to changing conditions. Sometimes it adapts to new scarcities or discoveries, and sometimes to the emergence of new cultural values. In any case, new constraints are not necessarily obstacles to efficiency but often stimulate technological change. Thus, technology does not pose an insuperable obstacle to the pursuit of "humanistic" values. There is no reason why it could not be reconstructed to conform to the values of a socialist society.

Technological development is a scene of social struggle in which various competing groups attempt to advance their interests and their corresponding civilizational projects. Many technically feasible outcomes are possible and not just the one imposed by the victors in the struggle. Critical theory of technology generalizes from such struggles to a position that contradicts determinism on each of its two theses. The nondeterministic position asserts that:

1. Technological development is overdetermined by both technical and social criteria of progress, and can therefore branch in any of several different directions depending on the prevailing hegemony.
2. While social institutions adapt to technological development, the process of adaptation is reciprocal, and technology changes in response to the conditions in which it finds itself as much as it influences them.

These propositions are based on the notion that technical objects are also social objects, as I argued in chapter 3. Only at the point of intersection of technical and social determinations is this or that concrete technology identified in its specificity and selected from among the wide range of possibilities supported by the available technical resources. On these assumptions, the technology of the existing industrial society must be described as a particular case of industrialism, relative to the dominant culture of capitalism rather than as a universal paradigm. This cultural qualification explains why it is impossible to generalize a priori from the existing modern society to conclusions valid for all such societies. The content and meaning of industrialism is not exhausted by our experience of it since technology contains potentialities that might yet be actualized in a different cultural context.

Ethics and Economics

This approach departs from traditional Marxism, with its deterministic belief in the preestablished harmony of economic growth and socialist politics. Does this new position represent a regression to a moralizing "ethical socialism" of the sort Marx rejected so scornfully? And if so, should that concern us today?

Marx's historicist critique of "abstract ethics" contrasts starkly with influential approaches such as Habermas's "quasitranscendental" grounding of democratic values. The Marxian view appears to confound "ought" with "is," but it also has the merit of providing a direction to action. Transcendental appeals do not offer much guidance once we move below the level of the most abstract principles of democratic discourse to the substantive issues that are of concern to individuals actually exercising their rights in the democratic process. Can philosophy lay down the ground rules and then withdraw from the debate? Marx was suspicious of the attempt to occupy a position above the fray. He attempted to find a way of linking the ideal with historically plausible transformations of the real. This is an attempt that can still interest us if we discard the deterministic framework in which he sometimes articulated it.

Marx was strongly influenced by Hegel's critique of Kantian ethical "formalism." Hegel rejected the idea that values subsist in an ideal sphere cut off from factual reality. He argued that all societies realize values in the everyday arrangements regarded as "facts" of social life by their members. Hegel judged values to be more or less "abstract" or "concrete" to the degree to which they achieved institutionalization. Thus, the family or state is more concrete than the as yet unmet demands of an emerging social group, and the latter are more concrete than a personal ideal that has no substantial reality whatsoever.

From this standpoint, Marx conceives of ethical values as, at worst, mere ideological veils for exploitation; at best, they represent utopian demands that cannot yet appear as the interests of any significant social group. Since on this account ethical values are by definition impractical, talk of socialist "ideals" would imply that capitalism is the only system capable of dealing with the *material* issues. As we have seen, this is how socialism is viewed by modernization theory, which considers it an ideology against which wealth must be traded off. Marx's concept of social revolution is intended to respond to this kind of objection, but he never actually worked out the details.

Marx regards socialism as a potentiality of capitalism, a radical social advance made possible by the achievements of the existing society. Marx often interprets the idea of potentiality deterministically, but a nondeterministic critical theory can retain his attempt to base ideas about the future on analysis of the present rather than on abstract ethical imperatives. Interests rather than moral values continue to be seen as the basis of historical change; however, to the extent that these interests are equivocal, they do not determine a single future but open up alternative historical trajectories.

The shift from deterministic laws to civilizational change implies a logic of contingency that must be expressed in a language different from that of traditional Marxism. For example, according to this approach socialism is *desirable* and *possible* rather than the necessary next stage of history. Marx's assumption that industrial technology *imperatively requires* socialist administration is replaced by the concept of *ambivalence*, which refers to the possibility of using the capitalist inheritance to build a socialist society by realizing its repressed technical potential. Similarly, the cultural concept of *economic code* must be substituted for the objectivistic assumption that classes have univocal, determined *interests* (Guillaume, 1975: 64). In sum, the same tendencies that, in traditional Marxism, are supposed to lead to the *inevitable* collapse of capitalism, now define the horizon of its progressive *potentialities*.

With the concept of potentiality, one can walk the fine line between idealist and reductionist accounts of the relation of ethics to economics. Idealism threatens tyrannical imposition of policies that have no roots in popular consciousness. Reductionism treats ethics as mere ideology and fails to grasp the contingency of interests on culture, which, as a valuative framework, is itself subject to rational judgment. Hence, reductionism fails to appreciate the role of ethical critique in challenging the established conception of interests in terms of a different understanding of human life.

Critical theory should neither dictate policy on ethical grounds, nor dismiss transcending reflection as utopian. Its mission today is to conceptualize the processes by which potentialities that still appear in ethical form can eventually be realized in an effective consciousness of self-interest and transform technical codes. Economic progress from one stage to the next occurs where repressed technical potential is released by fundamental cultural and social change. In economic terms, unrealized potentialities appear as vast *suboptimizations*, systematic underemployment of major resources, *as judged from the standpoint of the next stage*. These suboptimizations are due to the restrictions placed on technical and human development by the dominant economic culture. Only a new culture that shifts patterns of investment and consumption can shatter the economic premises of the existing civilization and yield a better way of life.

Because civilizational change effectively redefines what it is to be human, it has consequences for both ethical and economic advance. Thus, in the late nineteenth century, a rather narrow and socially restricted conception of humanity was replaced by a much broader one. We value human life, and especially the lives of working people, more than did our predecessors.[6] In the early days of abolitionism and labor regulation, all the economic arguments were on the side of opponents of the new view, which appeared to be "a false principle of humanity, which in the end is certain to defeat itself" (*Hansard's Debates*, 1844: lxxiii, 1123). It was not an economist but the novelists Charles Dickens and Harriet Beecher Stowe who played a major role in the moral evolution of English-speaking people by helping middle-class readers achieve a fuller affective identification with the lowest members of their societies. The result was unexpected: the evolution of moral sentiments, by altering the definition of human *being*, opened up new ways of *having*, and our society is the richer for it.

Social potentialities are raised to consciousness in both an economic and an ethical form, neither of which can be reduced to the other because they are different aspects of a single process. That process, civilizational change, establishes a new way of life with both ethical and economic implications (Gramsci, 1959: 140). Where the struggle for new ideals succeeds in restructuring society around a new culture, it will not be perceived as trading off wealth against virtue but as realizing the economic potentialities implied by its ethical claims. In poor countries, for example, movements to lower infant mortality, protect women's rights, and eliminate illiteracy are not merely moralistic. To these demands corresponds an economic strategy based on investing in human resources. Similarly, in rich countries environmentalists resist the suggestion that environmental protection is an idealistic obstacle to prosperity and attempt to redefine social wealth in terms that are more inclusive than the dominant view. Socialism would emerge from a whole series of coordinated changes of this type. The *lability of economic culture* explains how social movements are able to link the ideals and the interests of the underlying population in an innovative standard of welfare.

This approach to the concept of progress opens up a nondeterministic way of thinking about the connection between economic and cultural change. The generalized concept of suboptimization explains how powerful ideological motivations can anticipate a new economic order and aid in bringing it into being, even if it be through means that would be evaluated as uneconomic on the terms of the existing system.

The Transition to Socialism Revisited

Indices of the Transition

Over the last few decades socialist theory has responded to an accumulation of political disappointments by emphasizing its democratic heritage.[7] As we will see, that emphasis is not misplaced, but it confirms the tendency to understand radical change in essentially political terms. In describing socialism as the realization of suppressed technical potentialities, I have attempted to shift the emphasis to show that it is not so much a *political* as a *civilizational* alternative. The process of bootstrapping from one civilization to another is qualitatively different from politics, however radical. Because he understood this distinction, Marx did not treat socialism as a policy but instead asserted the existence of a historical "process" leading from capitalism to socialism. In fact, at one time Marx claimed that his most important discovery was the idea of a transition to socialism.[8]

In deterministic formulations, this process is described as "lawful." But what is the law of the transition? Paul Sweezey denies its existence: "The assumption, more often implied than spelled out, is that once socialism . . . has been firmly established, *its own inner dynamic will automatically propel it forward on the next leg of the journey to communism.* . . . No one, however, has succeeded in explaining what the 'law of motion' of socialism . . . is supposed to be" (Sweezey and Bettelheim, 1971: 125). Indeed, the notion that public ownership and planning would unleash an autonomous socialist dynamic was tested and decisively refuted in the Soviet Union.

It is long since time to drop the traditional Marxist reference to laws of history. Insofar as the idea of socialism has any meaning today, it must refer to a model of the dynamics of a possible civilizational change. Reconceptualized in this nondeterministic fashion, the transition is a civilizational project realized through a *trajectory of development* that imposes a global pattern of culture based on new values (Marcuse, 1964: 219ff.). Capitalism supports just such a civilizational project, and the Marxian model of socialist transition can be employed to define the logic of a corresponding socialist project. Unlike a utopia, which plays the role of unattainable "ideal" in opposition to the sorry state of social "reality," a dynamic transitional model can be used to develop concrete proposals for change and to test the claims and counterclaims of the theses of convergence and transition. However, it is not easy to apply this model, as we have seen in the case of communist societies. Societies are not immediately transformed by events such as revolutions, but sometimes evolve toward new forms in the spaces opened by these events. The transition is necessarily ambiguous precisely to the extent that it comes to terms with the sort of practical problems from which one cheerfully abstracts in theory. The question is whether convergent features take their place in a larger transitional process, or whether, on the contrary, those features merely contribute to creating or perpetuating the dominant model of industrial civilization. We need to determine what constitutes an indication of a divergent path and how its importance is to be weighed relative to the convergent features of a society.

The transition to socialism can be identified by the presence of phenomena that, taken separately, appear economically irrational or administratively ineffective from the standpoint of capitalist technological rationality, but that together initiate a process of civilizational change. Any phenomenon that can be better explained in the framework of a socialist strategy of development than in the corresponding capitalist framework can be considered a significant *index of the transition*. The theory of the transition identifies these phenomena as traces of an emerging cultural pattern. Hence, Marx and Engels define the transition in terms of measures which "appear economically insufficient and untenable, but which, in the course of the movement, outstrip themselves, necessitate further inroads upon the old social order, and are unavoidable as a means of entirely revolutionizing the mode of production" (Marx and Engels, 1979: 30).

A contemporary list of measures capable of setting in motion such a process would include extensive (if not universal) public ownership, the democratization of management, the spread of lifetime learning beyond the immediate needs of the economy, and the transformation of techniques and professional training to incorporate an ever wider range of human needs into the technical code. These indices of the transition will be analyzed in more detail later. They can be used to evaluate societies in terms of the extent to which they have moved off the capitalist track.

As a civilizational change, socialism is a coherent transformation in the very foundations of the social order. It aims to achieve a significant rise in the cultural level of the labor force and of all other subordinate social groups and a consequent change in the human type of the members of industrial society. It is not easy to reconstruct Marx's theory of the path to this result, but I will argue that it consists in three transitional processes: *socialization, democratization,* and *innovation:*[9]

1. The socialization of the means of production, accompanied by the early substitution of planning for markets in the allocation of industrial and cultural capital and other large-scale productive forces, and eventually, at a later stage, the disappearance of the market.
2. The radical democratization of society through an end to the vast economic, social, and political inequalities characteristic of class societies.
3. A new pattern of technological progress yielding innovations that overcome the sharp division of mental and manual labor characteristic of capitalism.

Any concept of socialism based on these premises can be called Marxian in inspiration. By the same token, the reconceptualization of socialism on the basis of the first or second component alone leads to a variety of non-Marxian positions. The Soviet model would have to be counted among these latter given its narrow emphasis on planning at the expense of democracy and technological change. Similarly, a position such as that of Habermas, which captures the democratic dimension of socialism but not its critique of technology, appears to fall outside the Marxian framework.

Marx's unified conception of socialism has by now been split into its component parts by history and analysis. His faith in planning has been mitigated by historical experience. Popular democratic movements in communist countries, like the emergence of new forms of technical politics in the West, also testify to the breakdown of the original Marxian synthesis.

Contemporary social theories that share certain Marxist premises but recognize the fragmentation of socialism are sometimes called post-Marxist. Such theories attempt to recover the democratic dimension of socialism against the exclusively economistic Soviet model.[10] This chapter presupposes this general critique and applies a similar approach in the technological domain. In what follows, I attempt an innovative formulation of the concept of socialism, taking into account the original Marxian notion but modifying it in accordance with historical experience and theoretical advances.

The reformulation hinges on the cultural and technological conditions for the requalification of the labor force. It is here that the Marxian conception of socialism becomes more than a political alternative and points toward fundamental civilizational change. But, where traditional Marxism assumed that workers would be guided by objectively ascertainable interests in transforming technology, I will argue that *democratic control of technically mediated institutions is a condition for generating an interest in a new direction of technological progress.* In other words, democracy itself is a "productive force" of a new type, shaping innovation in a future socialist society.[11]

These reflections are strictly conditional. It is impossible to predict the future, but one can attempt to outline a coherent path of development that would lead to a properly socialist outcome in favorable circumstances. The discussion is thus addressed not to the probability of that outcome but to its possibility. As I argued in the beginning of this chapter, establishing that possibility is not just an act of political faith but also has a heuristic function: it is one way of breaking the illusion of necessity in which the everyday world is cloaked.

Socialization

Traditionally, the theory of socialization emphasized nationalization of privately owned productive resources. Too little attention was paid to the distinctive character of public ownership in a socialist society. This mistake in emphasis is related to the deterministic bias of Marxism, which rooted nationalization in the short-term interests of the working class and founded immense hopes for long-term social and cultural change on this relatively simple act of state. Marxists thought that public ownership and central planning would have an impact comparable to that of the French Revolution, but in reality, they remain merely political and administrative choices that fail to transform culture as promised.

Marx's hypothetical construction of the interests of workers and his predictions about the future have been criticized and defended ad nauseum. Rather than continuing that rather fruitless debate, I will reformulate the concept of "proletarian interests" as the ideal-type of a *socialist economic code,* and then show how this approach aids in conceptualizing and studying the transition to socialism.

My goal is to identify the underlying technical logic of a civilizational transformation. As a civilizational project, socialism must involve changes as fundamental as those which gave rise to citizenship through the abolition of estates, or the invention of modern childhood through the gradual limitation of the labor market. I will argue that an expanded role for knowledge, skill, and democratic participation rather than state control of industry defines a comparably significant difference between socialism and all present-day modern societies, including communist ones. Marx's *Grundrisse* provides a basis for working out this idea, which, with a certain amount of imaginative interpretation, can be substituted for the usual economistic account.

In this text, workers are said to have an interest in work that draws on a wide range of abilities. This interest is supposed to determine a socialist process of rationalization and innovation. Out of that process will come a whole new technology in which work will be "life's prime want" instead of a burdensome obligation (Marx, 1972: 388). This goal will be achieved when labor "is of a scientific and at the same time general character, not merely human exertion as a specifically harnessed natural force, but exertion as subject, which appears in the production process not in a merely natural, spontaneous form, but as an activity regulating all the forces of nature" (Marx, 1973: 612).

The transition to this higher type of industrial society involves a deep change in economic culture. Capitalist society, Marx argues, distributes wealth in the form of ever more varied commodities, but the commodity form is only a limited reflection of the actual enrichment of the consumers' needs and faculties. "Real" wealth is the actualization of human capacities, mediated by material goods to be sure, but not identical with them. Marx writes,

> In fact, however, when the limited bourgeois form is stripped away, what is wealth other than the universality of individual needs, capacities, pleasures, productive forces, etc., created through universal exchange? The full development of human mastery over the forces of nature, those of so-called nature as well as of humanity's own nature? The absolute working-out of his creative potentialities, with no presupposition other than the previous historic development, which makes this totality of development, i.e., the development of all human powers as such the end in itself, not as measured on a *predetermined* yardstick? Where he does not reproduce himself in one specificity, but produces his totality? Strives not to remain something he has become, but is in the absolute movement of becoming? (Marx, 1973: 488)

The extension of transport and communications is a good example of Marx's new standard of wealth. Peasants confined mentally and physically to the small villages of their ancestors are "poor" by this standard, compared with modern individuals situated at the nexus of cosmopolitan interactions. Whether or not one shares Marx's disdain for rural life, the economic implications of his argument are clear. Once wealth is identified with the developed powers of the individual, there is a sense in which training and education, variety of experience and occupation, become a higher type of good. A socialist society, in the sense given that notion here, will value the enlargement of human experience and individuality as an end in itself, without subordinating these forms of wealth to the pursuit of a profit on the sale of the commodities associated with their acquisition.

Does this argument make economic sense? After all, overinvestment in human resources is as wasteful as any other misallocation despite our favorable prejudice toward education. The idea that education should be pursued for its own sake seems not much more likely to work than other similar exhortations to moral self-improvement.

But this objection depends on the culturally relative application of the distinction between *investment* and *welfare*. We signify the goals of production ethnocentrically in terms of capitalist concepts of wealth, that is to say, primarily as privately consumed commodities. In this framework, education is an investment rather than a positive component of individual welfare. The scarcity of knowledge and skill is a direct result of this economic code, which regulates the supply of knowledge by market demand and which rewards deskilling with a share of the savings realized by the replacement of skilled with unskilled labor.

Following Marx's argument in the *Grundrisse*, we could construct an ideal type of a socialist economic code in which educational activities that capitalist society considers as investments and evaluates in terms of productive efficiency would be placed in the category of consumption and evaluated as contributions to welfare. There is some precedent for this approach in the theory of the consumer value of educational services according to which education enhances the value of future consumption by refining appreciation (Becker, 1975: 69). Although this is a narrow foundation, the theory can be generalized to serve our purposes.

Why would this change in the social definition of wealth occur under socialism? Marx argues that the industrial economy not only produces a huge variety of commodities but also creates opportunities to apply the expanded powers of the individual in production (Marx, 1906: I, 533–534). This suggests economic reasons for developing human capacities. In this dynamic model the consumption of "real" wealth contributes to its production. Activities that increase workers' skill and intelligence increase the value of their labor power. Meanwhile, work itself becomes one important arena in which the individuals develop their powers.

But work remains work, however fulfilling. Thus, even under socialism workers will strive to reduce labor time while simultaneously increasing their leisure, much of which would be used for learning. And the more workers employ their leisure to learn, the more productive their labor and consequently the shorter the workday. "The saving of labour time (is) equal to an increase of free time, i.e., time for the full development of the individual, which in turn reacts back upon the productive power of labour as itself the greatest productive power" (Marx, 1973: 711–712). Socialist "interests" and the corresponding patterns of consumption develop the "wealth" of the individual personality and the productivity of labor in a self-reinforcing cycle.

Of all Marx's utopian ideas, this one seems to me the most interesting and fruitful. Here the economic circle is squared by the creation of an industrial *perpetuum mobile* that feeds off the very resources it consumes. The socialist labor process will be based on a synergism of the demand for skilled labor and the growth of human powers in leisure. A primary leisure activity pursued for its own sake increases the value of labor and so can be freely converted into an economic input. In the domain of human resources, consumption and investment become two sides of the same coin as an economic cost, education and training, becomes a benefit for the individuals.[12]

The higher levels of knowledge and skill achieved in this labor process will enhance efficiency, motivate the transformation of technology, and reconcile broader participation with the technical requirements of an industrial society. In this new system, there is no necessary trade-off between democracy and prosperity. Both these goals are achieved by integrating technical and economic codes around a much fuller development of the individual than is possible today.

Democratization

Can we bring this utopia down to earth to inform our analysis of the present and our speculations about the future? To give content to this notion, we must turn to a different domain of problems, the democratization of technically mediated institutions. Whatever else is involved in socialization, the discussion in chapter 2 shows the importance of the devolution of a considerable portion of management power to employees. But given the disqualifying effects of the capitalist division of labor, can they organize the firm? I think we can answer this question with a qualified "yes." Employees need not all be experts to play a role in corporate governance, but they must at least have capacities equivalent to those that enable investors to handle their investments and work together in selecting managers. Absent these capacities, socialization either remains purely formal or leads to disastrous mistakes.

Clearly, education is essential to democratization. Social ownership must extend beyond machines, buildings, and land to include the monopolized knowledge required for the management of industry. The democratic redistribution of culture thus becomes a function of the socialization process. But the *socialization of cultural capital* cannot be accomplished at the stroke of a pen; it implies a fundamental change in the institution of knowledge in view of achieving two objectives:[13]

1. To qualify the entire labor force, and not just a small elite, to participate effectively in management and politics.
2. To supply the volume of intellectual resources required to take advantage of technological options that rely on skill and intelligence more heavily than does the capitalist labor process.

Rudolph Bahro explains these goals, writing that socialist society should

> *produce quite intentionally a surplus of education* which is so great, both quantitatively and qualitatively, that it cannot possibly be trapped in the existing structures of work and leisure time, so that the contradictions of these structures comes to a head and their revolutionary transformation becomes indispensable. The emancipatory potential that is gathered in this way, and finds itself under too great a pressure in the confines of the existing conditions, has no other way out than by attacking the traditional division of labour in the reproduction process. (Bahro, 1978: 408)

The *Grundrisse*'s implicit educational theory appears to dovetail neatly with these considerations. But Marx does not address the issues Bahro raises. Instead, he offers a deterministic account of the redefinition of welfare as self-actualization and defers basic change until a remote, technologically advanced future. But as our discussion of computers has shown, even the most advanced technology does not automatically democratize society.

To free Marx's theory of its deterministic cast, it is necessary to identify a practical context in which education would have some purpose more compelling than the sheer enjoyment of learning. The democratic dimension of socialism offers such a context and purpose. Even though low skill levels would be associated with the inherited labor process for a long time, the politics of self-management on workplaces and in communities would provide a scene for the application of broadened cultural capacities. Higher levels of education would make possible the democratization not only of work but of other spheres of activity such as medicine and urban planning. Issues such as environmental protection could be addressed far more effectively where the public could be expected to understand them. The consumer value of education would be realized at first in relation to these public functions. Education would "pay off" there, if not economically, at least in terms of increased influence and better outcomes.

The scope and importance of education would broaden accordingly, and in this context the acquisition of knowledge and skill would no longer appear as a subtraction from individual welfare but as a component of it. Education would be *uncoupled* from society's economic needs and from individuals' investment strategies; it would become the driving force in social and technological change. Industrial society would bootstrap out of the knowledge deficit to a condition in which more and more individuals possessed the cultural qualifications needed to fulfill expanded social responsibilities.

Eventually, educational advance would make possible a leap to a higher level of labor productivity. The initial "overinvestment" in education would lead to the introduction of new technologies and work methods adapted to a highly educated labor force. Not technology but democratic social change would lead the transitional process, with technological progress an outcome rather than a cause of the establishment of new social relations. Thus *democracy appears as an economic and technological requirement of the transition to socialism.*

The socialization of culture defines a possible trajectory of development toward a new form of industrial civilization in which cultural competence and social responsibility are much more widely distributed than today. Although that project contrasts sharply with our expectations in the advanced capitalist world, it has partial precedents in Japan, the Soviet Union, and several other societies that responded to the challenge of modernization with enormous educational efforts both at the social and the individual level (Bailes, 1978).

It is true that the arc of cultural advance has nowhere been prolonged to the point where it generated major technological alternatives, but that possibility casts a critical shadow over current arrangements and refutes technocratic complacency and resignation. Those who would seek an easier path to a more participatory society must explain how that goal can be achieved on the basis of the level of culture inscribed in the existing division of labor.

Innovation

The cultural and political changes discussed earlier would create a new type of social environment for technological development. Skilled labor would be far more abundant than in a capitalist economy at a similar level of development. The supply would be limited primarily by the social cost (i.e., the cost of classrooms and teachers), once private costs had been reduced or disappeared through generalized educational consumption. Under these conditions, *highly qualified human resources would not be scarce but would be widely available as a nearly "free" good* on which the economy could draw at will.

In addition, patterns of innovation would change as democratic management increased margin of maneuver, enabling employees to alter the "rules of the game" in their favor. With the new management system would come new criteria for judging proposed innovations. The capitalist technical code, adjusted to the need to maximize profit and control the workforce, would be replaced by a different code that would take into account a wider range of variables. As Carol Gould writes, in comparison with capitalist managers, "members of a worker self-managed firm would be prone to be more sensitive to the impact that the use of given technologies would have on their conditions of work and the quality of work life. They might well also be responsive to issues of consumer need and environmental effect, since they are themselves also consumers and residents of the local area" (Gould, 1988: 277).

An economy developing under these conditions would favor new solutions to technical problems. In some cases, skill-intensive technologies might be adopted that would be discarded in a capitalist society with an economizing approach to knowledge. In other cases, work conditions and environmental protection might be enhanced by innovations that would be rejected in economies oriented toward short-term growth or profits. Different patterns of consumption and leisure pursuits would occupy a labor force that had a good education and performed interesting work, and the political process would no doubt take on a qualitatively different character. In short, this would be a socialist system of production in which technological change was governed by new principles.

There is a commonplace objection to this argument: government, it is often said, suppresses the individual freedom required for innovation. This view is popularly represented by the romantic myth of the innovator as an isolated genius at odds with ignorant bureaucrats. Is it true that any extension of social control will kill the goose that lays the golden eggs of progress? Is this perhaps what happened in the communist world?

While the myth is certainly overdrawn, the communist record in this domain lends it a kind of backhanded confirmation. Innovation in the Soviet Union was hampered by a variety of problems such as an excessive emphasis on technical professionalism, the isolation of research institutes from production, and the lack of advertising as a spur to demand for new products. As one would expect, the greatest obstacle was indeed bureaucratic lethargy and Soviet managers' aversion to risk.[14]

But all these problems appear to be due more to the obsession with central control than to public ownership as such. One does not hear of cases where innovations were suppressed out of concern for workplace democracy, ecology, or other social objectives. If socialism is tested by this experience, that is only because the absence of property rights made it possible to erect the obsession with control into an imposing barrier to change of any sort, an unfortunate outcome that would have been much more difficult to achieve under capitalism.

Still, the communist experience with innovation is not entirely negative. At various times, the Soviet Union and China favored worker involvement in technical change both to improve efficiency and to advance, or at least to prefigure, the eventual abolition of the division of mental and manual labor (Lee, 1977). For example, the Soviets established a system for encouraging workers to make the small technical improvements called "rationalizations." Workers were offered a means of claiming authorship and receiving bonuses for useful ideas. To promote worker participation in innovation, "complex brigades" of workers, engineers, and others were assembled to draft blueprints, test solutions, and refine original ideas. Several mass organizations mobilized large voluntary support networks to help worker-innovators overcome the bureaucratic obstacles to success.

Workers' contributions to rationalization and innovation were always overshadowed by engineering professionalism in the Soviet Union, not surprisingly in view of the Bolshevik faith in the saving power of technology. However, the Chinese case was quite different. Although they began by imitating the Soviet system, the Chinese soon became dissatisfied with it. In the Great Leap Forward and the Cultural Revolution, workers were freed from technical supervision to transform their firms under Party leadership. The Chinese version of "complex brigades" differed from the Russian one in terms of the balance of power between blue and white collars, a difference symbolized by the requirement that all members engage in manual labor. As Renssalaer Lee remarked in an article published during the Cultural Revolution: "The function of 'politics' in Communist China is largely to distribute opportunities of generating technological and cultural change. This redistribution occurs at the expense of professional elites and results in a close integration of change-producing actions with participation in labor" (Lee, 1973: 323).

We are now better able to judge these experiments than when Mao was still alive. It appears that often what was presented as a struggle for workers' control was actually a mere faction fight within the Communist Party. It is therefore difficult to know whether the policy failed because it was hopelessly voluntaristic or because of political mistakes. In any case, the overall results were disastrous, destroying valuable machinery and demoting or demoralizing skilled managers, teachers, engineers, and technicians. There is a warning here against populist anti-intellectualism. Nevertheless, there is something right about the idea of mobilizing the full resources of ordinary people in the technical process, not in opposition to the technical intelligentsia as in China but in the context of a wide consensus embracing managers, technical specialists, and workers. Perhaps someday this idea will receive a worthier test.

Although these examples are in no sense models, they show the interest in mass technical creativity in communist countries and point up the possibility of organizational experimentation even in the framework of a planned economy. There are interesting similarities between these experiments and attempts to promote innovation in certain large, high-technology capitalist firms. These firms cannot afford bureaucratic stagnation and have made radical departures from classical organizational models to promote technical creativity. Small teams combining a variety of skills are encouraged to work in an almost parasitic relation to the corporation, drawing on its resources for an unusually autonomous activity of research and development (Kidder, 1981; Pinchot, 1985).

Such teams bear a certain resemblance to another type of entrepreneurial activity carried out with great success in the bowels of a vast government bureaucracy, namely, scientific research. Most of the funding necessary for research is provided by governments through grants to universities. Individual faculty members, usually representing teams of researchers, compete for funding on the basis of carefully prepared proposals and a record of past accomplishments. While not without flaws, the system favors innovation. Yet until quite recently, scientific entrepreneurs were rarely engaged in capitalist competition on the open market. Their achievements cannot be credited to capitalism but fall squarely within the much maligned public sector. In sum, technical innovation in any advanced economy depends on institutional innovations that circumvent bureaucracy and privilege originality and creativity.

Socialism and the Middle Strata

Discussion of these issues was surprisingly subdued as communist nations struggled in the late 1980s to build more democratic and efficient economic systems (Goldman, 1987: 240). The dismantling of bureaucratic dictatorship and its clumsy planning machinery requires greater reliance on markets, either through privatization or through the creation of self-managing firms. Self-management is not without its problems, but the lack of enthusiasm for it among communist loyalists was perhaps due less to the unhappy Yugoslavian precedent than to the fact that they felt more at home with hierarchical control, regardless of who is at the helm, than with socialist ideals.[15] And they hoped to land on their feet, still in charge but now with the chance to get rich. Not the apparatus but workers themselves would have had to initiate democratic experiments if these were to occur at all. Unfortunately, workers were disarmed as a pressure group by popular revulsion from generations of abuse of power perpetrated in their name.

There are, furthermore, unsolved problems in the theory of the self-managed firm. For example, whatever the legal structure of enterprise, the socialist workforce must rely on professional and managerial personnel with considerable operational autonomy for a prolonged period, no doubt measured in generations rather than years or decades as Lenin had hoped. How much real change can be expected with the same social groups in charge? An elected management might be more responsive merely to workers' demands for health and safety on the job and job security. Indeed self-management might turn out to have few practical consequences because a technocratic consensus united workers and managers around the reproduction of the capitalist technical code.

Thus, formal democratization of the firm is a necessary but not a sufficient condition for a transition to socialism. The democratic tasks of the transition go beyond formal measures to include *recomposing formerly divided mental and manual labor in order to reduce the operational autonomy of leadership and reincorporate the alienated functions of management back into the collective laborer.*[16] Managers' actual authority must be accommodated to the gradual enlargement of workers' margin of maneuver. This *deep democratization* implies significant changes in the structure and knowledge base of the various technical and administrative specializations.[17] Furthermore, in advanced societies, where so many relationships outside the sphere of production are technically mediated, self-management in the workplace is only one dimension of a general attack on technocratic hegemony. The rules and roles governing the exercise of authority must be altered to promote greater autonomy not only in industry but in agent-client relations outside production as well.[18] In fact, democratization of industry might well follow rather than lead administrative changes in a variety of fields such as government services, science-based technical systems, medical practice, mass media production, teaching, and so on.

How plausible is this strategy for recomposing the unity of the collective laborer? In the introduction, I mentioned the importance of a culture of responsibility, without which those on the bottom of the system are unlikely to demand changes in the distribution of power. To be effective, this demand must meet a sympathetic response from a significant fraction of the technical elites to which it is addressed. Nothing can be done without their help, and it cannot be enlisted by violence or administrative fiat. But would technically qualified personnel participate in a process that diminished their operational autonomy?

One is tempted to answer this question a priori in the negative. After all, the Russian Revolution faced massive resistance on the part of technical and cultural elites. A few intellectuals and technical professionals supported the revolution as individuals, but such defections from the bourgeoisie remained a minor breach in the otherwise solid wall of hostility. Judging from the historical experience of radical professionalism in the new Left, conditions appear to have changed in technologically advanced societies. In the 1960s and '70s, many members of the middle strata contested their social roles in societies bent on exploitation and war. These movements went well beyond the philanthropic gesture of a few revolutionary intellectuals.

In fact the most powerful revolutionary movement to occur so far in an advanced society was characterized by intense "fraternization" between workers and sympathetic members of the bureaucracies, professions, and corporate administrations. During the French May Events of 1968 these latter proposed quite elaborate plans for reform of management and government agencies (Feenberg, 1999: chap. 2; Feenberg and Freedman, 2001). Thus, the idea of an alliance to reorganize the collective laborer is not merely idle speculation but resonates with an important historical experience.

To go beyond such anecdotal evidence would take a theory of the middle strata.[19] Such theories usually assume that classes have clearly defined interests independent of their political relations.[20] Judging from the May Events and other similar experiences, this assumption does not hold for the middle strata: in a revolutionary situation they enter into an internal crisis and lose confidence in their technocratic identity. There is an obvious reason for this instability that is obscured by traditional class theory: the middle strata are defined by their *place in organization* rather than by an economic function. The fragility of their social identity is due to the instrumental character of the organizations that support it. In the modern world, these owe their existence to their legitimacy as determined by legal or economic criteria that can change at a moment's notice.

Members of the middle strata have been hired, usually after acquiring appropriate educational credentials, to carry out an action based on specific technical codes. Unlike the other classes of modern society, which arise from an "organic" economic process, the middle strata acquire their class identity through a process of selection, rooted in an expert relationship to a body of knowledge. This is the origin of the "professionalist" ideology according to which they are the "agents" of "clients" in whose interests they act and for whom they perform services these latter cannot perform for themselves.

The middle strata serve the needs of the community within the limits imposed by the established hegemony. Like the technical code on which it is based, their action exhibits the double aspects of power/knowledge discussed in chapter 3. Where social struggle is weak or ideologically inarticulate, a technocratic self-understanding arises from the misperception of this tensionful limitation. But, when the "clients" rise in struggle, as in the May Events, the bureaucracy's legitimacy is challenged on a global scale. Its selection, its conception of service, its claim to represent the public interest are all shaken, and its self-image shattered. The repressive aspect of its work, as that work is organized and shaped from above, becomes clear in the light of resistance from below. Splits and conflicts paralyze it and block its functioning.

When the people appear "in person," they become the source of an alternative legitimacy different from the one granted hitherto by capitalist or communist elites in their name. The bureaucracy is no longer an interest in its own right engaged in maximizing its operational autonomy at the expense of the population, but becomes instead a scene of struggle on which popular interests are represented. The "people" are a recourse and an ally through which at least a major portion of the middle strata can be reconstituted and their "selection" reconfirmed under a different hegemony for different social purposes. The culmination of such a reconstitution would be the elaboration of new practices and technical codes representing a wider range of interests and aimed at reducing the operational autonomy of professional leadership. The concluding chapter of this book explores the philosophical implications of this new conception of socialism.

7

The Critical Theory of Technology

The Critique of Scientific-Technical Rationality

Modernity and Critique

Modernity is the affirmation of autonomy against every traditional or social authority (Pippin, 1991). Modern societies organize apparently neutral mediations such as markets, elections, administrations, and technical systems for the expression of an unlimited variety of contingent interests and visions of life that cannot and need not be justified, reconciled, or ranked. This system does not favor this or that substantive value but maximizes autonomy in general, promising liberation of the human essence from fixed definitions. Rationality enters this scheme only at the level of means, both the means individuals employ to achieve particular ends and the means instituted by society to mediate their relations. These means fall under formal norms of efficiency and equity.

Capitalist democracy is the most successful modern political institution. As a specific instance of modernity, capitalism is subject to critique either as all too modern or as not modern enough. The first type of critique is usually conservative. Heidegger, for example, condemns modern society as nihilistic and attempts to conceive a philosophical alternative to autonomy. Traditionalist reactions to modernity are of course commonplace today under the guise of ethnic or national identity. More interesting for our argument are those progressive critiques of capitalism which address it as a failed instance of modernity. Such arguments generally contrast the ideal of autonomy with capitalist realities, identify interests capitalism is structurally blocked from serving, or denounce the substantive goals it imposes in the course of structuring social life around neutral mediations.

The progressive critical strategy can be pursued in the two rather different ways we encountered in chapter 2. One approach argues that capitalism interferes with the neutral media—markets, elections, administrations, and technical systems—through which modern individuals pursue their interests. This is the logic of suspicion, the demystifying attack on vested interests that manipulate the public from behind the scenes. The product and process critique of technology is of this type. The other style of critique argues that "the medium is the message," that the media distort the contents they express. For example, not every good can find a place on the market. Markets are not therefore neutral arbiters of the community's values but prejudice choice wherever they are instituted. The question is not just who profits but what way of life is determined by the market. Since it appears to be essentially transparent and universal, however imperfect particular practical realizations may be, the critique must undermine the standard of rationality that defines it. The design critique of technology and the related theory of the technical code follow this general approach in the technical domain.

The critique of rationality also characterizes critical theory from its origins in Hegel and Marx, down through the early Marxist Lukács, Ernst Bloch, and the Frankfurt School. Today, some feminists and ecologists find resources in this tradition that they seem to be practically alone in continuing. Yet far more work of this type is needed in a society in which scientific-technical rationality has become the principal legitimating discourse. This chapter attempts to contribute to such a revival of radical social critique.

This critique usually contains at least an implicit reference to what Bloch called "Left Aristotelianism."[1] In one late essay, Bloch defines the agenda of a critical theory of scientific-technical rationality in terms of the still viable heritage of premodern, qualitative images of nature (Bloch, 1988: 59). Conceding that nature has the reified dimension attributed to it by modern science, Bloch argues that a modern holistic ontology must relativize that dimension with respect to other dimensions science ignores. These other dimensions are manifested in ecological crisis which, like economic crisis, demonstrates the limits of scientific-technical rationality (Bloch, 1988: 67). Bloch offers here a typical Hegelian-Marxist critique of the formalistic character of modern reason that fails adequately to grasp its "content" (nature).

But today, Bloch's formulation appears excessively optimistic. It is not the heritage of the premodern conception of nature that needs saving but the heritage of classical Critical Theory itself. The waves appear to be rapidly closing over that tradition under the combined attack of Habermas and postmodernism. What both have in common, despite their many obvious differences, is a rejection of that tradition's dialectical concept of reason, which is now identified with a nostalgic organicism that seeks a utopia in the past, in nature, in the immediate (Jay, 1984: chap. 15, epilogue). On this account, Critical Theory would be a regression behind the level of rationality achieved by modernity rather than a transcendence of its capitalist forms. A vigorous modernity or postmodernity, as the case may be, looks forward without illusion and affirms a culture based on fragmentation in which wholeness is at best a regulative ideal for the conversation of fractured identities.

One might object to the polemical exaggeration in these characterizations of Critical Theory. There is a certain arrogance in assuming that such profound students of Hegel as Lukács or Marcuse were mere romantics haunted by Rousseauian reveries. But the argument can be advanced more rapidly by accepting at the outset the necessary choice forced on us by the polemic against dialectics. It is true that these critical theorists retain a romantic reference to an original immediacy as a symbol of the dialectical reunification of what analysis has fragmented. They thus attempt to place romanticism within a more or less Hegelian framework rather than rejecting it outright. It is difficult to accurately characterize a position that hovers "dialectically" between alternatives it hopes to redeem rather than select. Is it possible to reformulate the critique without playing on these ambiguities, without opening a flank to attack by today's sober censors of intellectual nostalgia?

The task is complicated by a second problem. Because natural science and technology share a fundamentally similar form of rationality, Critical Theory tends to identify them. The critique of what has come to be called "technoscience" unveils the secret complicity between the apparently innocent activity of the researcher and the horrifying military applications. Science is undoubtedly influenced by society in all sorts of ways and can no more claim to be socially neutral than can technology. But despite their growing interconnections, science and technology are very different institutions (Goldman, 1990). The difference shows up in the reform programs that sound plausible in the two cases: political reform for technology and reform from within for science. Yet if technoscience is a single phenomenon, on what basis can one make this strategic distinction? In fact, critical theorists tend to waver uncomfortably between a utopian politics of technoscience (Marcuse) and acceptance of the neutrality of technoscience in its proper sphere (Habermas). Both positions are mistaken, but until we discriminate conceptually between science and technology, we will be unable to put forward a credible case for a critique and transformation of modern forms of rationality. Indeed, we will be easy targets for the charge of irrationalism.

The rest of this chapter attempts to resolve these problems. I first reconstruct several of the core arguments of the Critical Theory tradition and discuss similar arguments in contemporary feminism. In the second half of the chapter, I develop the critique of technology in a new way that avoids romantic subtexts and opens positive perspectives on the future. Along the way, I attempt to clarify the issues raised above and to show that Critical Theory reconceptualizes reason rather than rejecting it.

Reason and Domination

Critical Theory attacks capitalism by attacking its forms of rationality. The approach appears strangely circuitous. Why not solve the problem of poverty through redistribution? Why drag in a critique of the rationality of the market? Similarly, if one is opposed to deskilling, why not use regulation to protect the skill content of jobs, much as one now protects endangered species? Why complicate the issue with a critique of scientific-technical rationality? No such critique was required to introduce affirmative action, food stamps, and welfare. In Weberian terms, the argument would be that reforms motivated by substantively rational ends can soften the hard edges of a formally rationalized society. These proposals place us on the familiar terrain of dual compliance explored in chapter 6.

Such *moral reformism* has the advantage of assuming the self-evidences of the age. The formal mediations introduced by capitalism are not challenged, but their effects are compensated. Technical reason is not criticized but subordinated to humanistic objectives. The gradual moralization of social life can create a better world, trading off certain economic for human values. What is wrong with this approach?

In fact, modern critical theory grows out of the work of two thinkers who rejected it, Marx and Weber. They formulated some of the earliest social theories of formal rational systems such as markets and technology. These theories emphasize the self-expanding character of formal mediation. The dynamic of rationalization inherent in the system conflicts with substantive correctives. Since these correctives are by nature formally irrational, they create social tensions likely to be resolved at a later stage through the sacrifice of "ideals" for practical efficiency. Hence the political oscillations of the welfare state, caught in unresolvable goal conflicts. Both Marx and Weber are therefore skeptical of moralistic reformism, although they draw very different political conclusions.

Marx attempts to establish a coherent strategy of civilizational change based on a critique of the class bias of capitalist rationality. He analyzes the mechanisms by which market rationality reproduces the class structure and reinforces capitalist hegemony. In identifying these limits of capitalist rationality, Marx situates himself beyond them in a higher dialectical rationality. Socialism is then described as a new form of rational order rather than as a regression to premodern conditions or an irrational and inefficient excrescence on the market.

Marx's general approach was anticipated by Hegel. In Hegel, dialectical *reason* overcomes the tendency of analytic *understanding* to split objects up into abstractly separated parts. Hegel does not regress to the immediate givenness of the objects of the understanding but believes that reason can recapture totality at a higher level through mediating the fragmented parts. Hegel thus proposes moving forward from fragmentation to totality rather than backward to an original unity. But Marx's version of dialectics falls short because he fails to explain the dialectical rationality of the planned society he wants to substitute for capitalism.

Weber rejects dialectics and does not propose an alternative to capitalism. Although aware of its social bias, Weber has no philosophical critique of formal rationality; for him, as for most modern social theory, the rise to power of specific social strata in the course of rationalization is ultimately no more than an unavoidable side effect of progress. Thus, he overlooks the connection between the limitations of formal rationality and the problems of capitalism and bureaucracy.[2]

Lukács's early theory of reification first makes that connection explicit and sketches a theory of dialectical rationality. Lukács introduces the term "reification" to describe Marx's "fetishism" and Weber's "rationalization." He argues that the structure of both market and bureaucracy is essentially related to the structure of formal rationality, and brings to light the congruence of modes of thought and action that rest on the fragmentation of society, analytic thinking, technology, and the autonomization of production units under the control of private owners. Lukács thus explains the preestablished harmony between a particular organization of society and a historically concrete form of rationality, unifying in the same concept social facts that remain separate for Marx and Weber. Where Marx had foreseen a recovery of wholeness at the economic level, Lukács offers a similar argument at the level of culture, attacking capitalist fragmentation not from the standpoint of premodern organicism but in terms of a dialectical concept of the mediated totality (Feenberg, 1986: chap. 3).

Lukács's concept of totality is much contested, and I will not attempt to explain it in any detail here. His theory is intended to show how, starting out from the specific degradation of its life and work under the reign of the law of value, the proletariat can break with capitalist forms of thought and action and realize the potentialities for a very different type of society contained and repressed in capitalism. Lukács argues that the standpoint of the proletariat is not merely immanent to capitalism but opens up a broader view of the most fundamental limitations of that system. Lukács calls that broader view, in which capitalism is relativized with respect to its own potentialities, the "totality." Totality is thus not a synoptic view or a conceptual myth as critics contend but the basis of an immanent critique.

In Lukács, formal rationality is the basis of capitalist culture, and dialectical reason, by contrast, supports a socialist society. Thus, the same relation holds between formal rationality and capitalism as between dialectics and socialism. And, just as socialism does not reject the capitalist heritage but employs it as an ambivalent basis of development, so dialectics encompasses formal rationality in a larger framework that determines its limits and significance. This approach goes beyond dual compliance to suggest the possibility of founding socialism as an alternative civilization, as coherent and rational in its own way as capitalism.

But unfortunately, Lukács fails to pursue the discussion to its logical conclusion. He starts out by challenging the social generalization of natural scientific forms of thought in the rationalization process, an influential line of argument down to Habermas. This is a strange phenomenon on the face of it: all earlier cultures are based on substantive worldviews rather than formal rational principles, which, where they exist at all, are confined to very narrow social functions. But although Lukács dramatizes the strangeness of modern culture, he does not advance far beyond Weber in explaining the curious role of formal rationality of the scientific-technical type, nor does he have much by way of an account of how dialectical rationality transcends it in founding a socialist civilization. These limitations, which appear at first to be merely theoretical, turn out to have important consequences for social analysis as natural science and technology define the framework of capitalist civilization after World War II.

Marcuse goes beyond Lukács and attempts to explain the growing political role of science and technology in advanced capitalism. Continuing along the path opened in Adorno and Horkheimer's *Dialectic of Enlightenment*, he aims at nothing less than a general theory of the link between formalism and class domination throughout history, and on that basis he anticipates the main outlines of a new society, including its scientific and technical practice (Adorno and Horkheimer, 1972; Marcuse, 1964).

Like Lukács, Marcuse considers the universality of bias in the rationalization process to be a *problem* and not simply an accident of world-historical scope. He writes:

Scientific-technical rationality and manipulation are welded together into new forms of social control. Can one rest content with the assumption that this unscientific outcome is the result of a specific societal *application* of science? I think that the general direction in which it came to be applied was inherent in pure science even where no practical purposes were intended, and that the point can be identified where theoretical Reason turns into social practice. (Marcuse, 1964: 146)

We can rephrase Marcuse's point by asking what it means that formal systems are generally available for applications biased to favor domination. Is there something about their very structure that opens them to such applications? What happened "originally" in the initial construction of the formal mode of abstraction that rendered it pliable in this particular way?

It is difficult to follow Marcuse's argument to this point because we do not normally think of such formal systems as mathematics or technology as essentially implicated in their own applications. Rather, they appear neutral in themselves. Of course, one can make a bad use of them just as one might pick up a rock and throw it at a passerby. It would be comical to suggest that the rock is "biased" a priori toward such uses, that its hardness is the essential precondition by which it lends itself to violence. Marcuse's very question reverses our normal assumptions and connects formal neutrality and domination as moments in a dialectical totality. This is perhaps admissible to the extent that formal systems, unlike rocks, are human inventions created for a purpose in specific social contexts.

Marcuse's treatment of this problem depends on his dialectical ontology, which, in turn, presupposes the distinction between "substantive" and "logico-mathematical" or "formal" universals (Marcuse, 1964: chap. 5). This distinction separates a holistic approach to human and natural systems from the mechanistic breakdown of these systems into their reified parts.[3] Substantive universals are essences constructed through an abstractive process that brings to the fore the internal coherence and potentialities of their objects. These objects are not isolated and self-subsistent things but contextually dependent "wholes" developing in essential interaction with an environment. Formal thinking, on the contrary, abstracts from the whole not toward its potentialities but rather toward its "form." By "form," Marcuse intends abstract properties that are isolated from each other and from the inner order of the objects from which they are abstracted. These properties include colors, shapes, number, and so on.

Formal universals decontextualize their objects in both time and space, evacuating their "content" and abstracting from their developmental dynamics. Instead of transcending the given toward its essential potentialities, this type of universality classifies or quantifies objects in terms of the function they can be made to serve in an instrumental system imposed on them from without. Although apparently neutral and value free, in suppressing the dimensions of contextual relatedness and potentiality, the *decontextualizing practice* of formal abstraction transforms its objects into mere means, an operation that prejudices their status as much as any valuative choice.

Here is the core of Marcuse's argument. Formal universals are indeed "value-free" in the sense that they do not prescribe the ends of the objects they conceive as means; however, they are value-laden in systematically overlooking the difference between the extrinsic values of an instrumental subject and the intrinsic telos of an independent, self-developing object. Insofar as formal thinking considers its objects only in terms of their utility, it treats their potentialities as no different from the outcome of a technical manipulation. The essential difference between self-development and control is obscured, and a founding bias is thereby introduced. The very conception of value from which formal universals are "free" is itself a product of the abstractive process in which formalism obscures the nature of potentiality. Despite, or rather because of, its neutrality as between potentialities and utilitarian values, formal reason is biased toward the actual, what is already realized and available for technical control.

Methodologically, this bias appears in the inability to grasp history and social contexts as the scene of development. Formal abstraction works with the immediate appearance of its artificially isolated object. It accepts this appearance as truth and in so doing comes under the horizon of the existing reified society and its modes of practice. The range of manipulation opened by formal abstraction is the uncritically accepted horizon of domination under which its objects lie. These objects can be used, but not transformed, adapted to the dominant social purposes, but not transcended toward the realization of their potentialities in the context of a better society.

This is why formal systems are intrinsically available as a power base. In cutting the essential connections between objects and their history and contexts, formal abstraction ignores the inner tensions in reality that open possibilities of progressive development. Instead, objects are conceptualized as fixed and frozen, unchanging in themselves but available for manipulation from above.

This construction of objectivity comes back to haunt formal thinking in the biased application of its products. Repressive applications arise as soon as its abstractions are reintegrated to a real world of historical contingencies. Then it becomes clear that "formalization and functionalization are, *prior* to all application, the 'pure form' of a concrete societal practice" (Marcuse, 1964: 157).

The hypothetical system of forms and functions becomes dependent on another system—a preestablished universe of ends, in which and *for* which it develops. What appeared extraneous, foreign to the theoretical project, shows forth as part of its very structure (method and concepts); pure objectivity reveals itself as object *for* a *subjectivity* which provides the Telos, the ends. In the construction of the technological reality, there is no such thing as a purely rational scientific order; the process of technological rationality is a political process. (Marcuse, 1964: 168)

According to Marcuse, such formal abstraction is the technical "a priori" of modern capitalist society and its communist imitators.

Toward a Successor Technoscience?

Marcuse's theory of potentiality implies a participatory epistemology and a holistic ontology. The potentialities of objects come into focus in active involvement with them as wholes, rather than through calculative contemplation of their manipulable components: "creative receptivity versus repressive productivity" (Marcuse, 1974: II, 286). Marcuse conceives this receptivity under the categories of the erotic and the aesthetic, which he generalizes beyond the spheres of sexuality and art to include a dereified relationship to nature. Nature is not merely an object of technical conquest but can be an active partner of human beings. We should stand in "a 'human relation' to matter . . . [which] is part of the *life* environment and thus assumes traits of a living object" (Marcuse, 1972: 65).

These ideas have an affinity with certain strands of feminist theory, and in the early 1970s Marcuse formulated his concept of socialism in feminist terms. In his view, capitalist patriarchy shelters women to some degree from the full force of reification by confining them to subordinate roles in the home. In the struggle between "eros and aggression," women are inclined to the former as a consequence of the very oppression they suffer. Marcusean socialism would generalize the "female" traits of "tenderness, receptivity, sensuousness" in creating a society freed of male domination (Marcuse, 1972: 74–78). A new science would emerge from these changes, incorporating human values into its very structure.

This convergence of Critical Theory and feminism is less surprising than it may seem at first. From Aristotle to Hegel to the Frankfurt School, holistic ontologies have offered a powerful alternative to the mechanistic worldview. Feminists who privilege modes of knowing based on involvement and receptivity find resources in this tradition (Bordo, 1987: 103–105). Their gendered epistemologies have inspired a whole contemporary literature that has striking similarities to certain positions of the Frankfurt School. As Sandra Harding writes,

> The feminist standpoint epistemologies ground a distinctive feminist science in a theory of gendered activity and social experience. They simultaneously privilege women or feminists (the accounts vary) epistemically and yet also claim to overcome the dichotomizing that is characteristic of the Enlightenment/bourgeois world view and its science. It is useful to think of the standpoint epistemologies, like the appeals to feminist empiricism, as "successor science" projects: in significant ways, they aim to reconstruct the original goals of modern science. (Harding, 1986: 142)

Marcuse's critique of the repressive implications of modern scientific-technical thinking also culminates in a successor science project. He rejects scientific pretensions to value neutrality and argues for science "becoming political" in order to recognize the suppressed dimensions of inner and outer nature (Marcuse, 1964: 233–234). Similarly, Harding summarizes one feminist account as demanding "an epistemology which holds that appeals to the subjective are legitimate, that intellectual and emotional domains must be united, that the domination of reductionism and linearity must be replaced by the harmony of holism and complexity" (Harding, 1986: 144).

The idea of an alternative science parallels at a more fundamental level the similar notion of an alternative technology. If, like machines, facts and theories are social constructions, how can they be innocent and neutral? Once social criticism shows how deeply these supposedly autonomous fields have been marked by politics, they can be treated as ambivalent institutions subject to reconstruction in the context of a new hegemony (Marcuse, 1964: 233–234).

This parallel raises a delicate question. What is the role of politics in the transformation of technoscience? Despite ritual disclaimers, the critique of scientific-technical rationality appears to lead straight to political control of research not just through familiar external manipulations such as grants, but far more profoundly at the level of fundamental epistemological choices. After all, if science is completely colonized by a false rationality, then it is difficult to see how it could reform itself (even with a boost from a reformed NSF). Indeed, why should its fate differ fundamentally from that of other oppressive superstructures such as law? Earlier chapters in this book have in fact discussed the transformation of technology as a political affair, and unless one distinguishes science from technology, it, too, would seem to fall under an external practical critique.

But there are warning signs posted along this path. Shortly after the Russian Revolution, an organization called Proletcult argued for the substitution of a new proletarian culture for the reactionary inheritance of bourgeois technology, science, and even language (Claudin-Urondo, 1975: 47–60). Up to this point Marxists had generally considered these phenomena as nonideological. The exemption of science from political critique was a foundational assumption of orthodox Marxism. Following Engels, most Marxists connected the genesis of modern science with early bourgeois society, while insisting that this historical background in no way diminished the universality of modern scientific achievements. Proletcult resolved this split between genesis and validity, treating science as Marxism had always treated the superstructures. The embarrassing residue of transhistorical truth was eliminated from the system.

Although both Lenin and Stalin opposed this view in theory, Lysenko was able to introduce political criteria into the actual institutions of Russian science. His genetic theories won state support while most of his scientific adversaries were executed. The catastrophic failure of this experiment in "proletarian" thought continues to inspire widespread fear of any ideology critique of natural science (Graham, 1998).

Even those unaware of this history are likely to be affected by it, so deeply did it discredit the project of politicizing science. For the most part, current social criticism of science responds to this dangerous precedent by arguing against political interference and instead calls for the "reclamation from within of science" (Keller, 1985: 178). Civilizational change would eventually promote scientific change without the risk of further Lysenko affairs. Not political power but scientists' own evolving categories and perceptions in a radically new social environment would inspire new types of questions and new theories generated spontaneously in the course of research by scientists themselves. As Marcuse writes, scientific "hypotheses, without losing their rational character, would develop in an essentially different experimental context (that of a pacified world); consequently, science would arrive at essentially different concepts of nature and establish essentially different facts" (Marcuse, 1964: 166–167).

This view of scientific progress and its likely course makes sense, however, noninterventionism is incompatible with the statement of clear guidelines for a successor science. One must choose between affirming the self-reconstructive powers of science, which will surely yield an unexpected outcome, or devising an extrinsic program anticipating a future state of science that would have to be implemented politically. The first alternative allows us only to contest premature totalizations, such as reductionist paradigms in sociobiology or "neurophilosophy"; it does not dictate theoretical developments. Social critique of science cannot contain the future, but only hold it open.

These qualifications raise questions about the extrinsic ontological and epistemological criteria used to evaluate current science. What, one might ask, guarantees that in a "pacified" world, a holistic science would discover ways to overcome the split between value and fact, emotion and reason, part and whole? How can we foresee today the general outline of the results of future research? Perhaps scientific method will change far less than we imagine and instead new theories will address the problems that concern us today. What is more, holism itself is politically controversial. There is no lack of evidence that it can be accommodated to repressive ends (Haraway, 1989: 256). Thus, Donna Haraway writes, "Evaluations and critiques cannot leap over the crafted standards for producing credible accounts in the natural sciences because neither the critiques nor the objects of their discourse have any place to stand 'outside' to legitimate such an arrogant overview. To insist on value and story-ladenness at the heart of the production of scientific knowledge is not equivalent to standing nowhere talking about nothing but one's biases—quite the opposite" (Haraway, 1989: 13).

Haraway's doubts about the successor science project are reasonable, and one does not appear to pay a high political price for the caution she recommends. But similar doubts might be raised about politically motivated reform in every sphere. For example, one might argue that technological change cannot be anticipated from outside the engineering profession, legal change from outside the legal profession, and so on. That would result in the dismissal of political criteria for sociotechnical transformation that have emerged laboriously from generations of struggle and analysis.

There is another way to look at the difficulty. The holistic critique of modern science is perhaps misdirected. Alienated objectivism has an obvious *venue* in our experience other than natural science, with which few people have any direct contact. Rather, the living source of the critique is our participation in technically mediated social institutions. The operational autonomy these institutions support founds an epistemological standpoint that is congruent with the detached analytic standpoint of science but that has neither scientific purpose nor institutional context. It is as though the discursive framework of scientific rationality had escaped the confines of inquiry to become a cultural principle and a basis of social organization. This is in fact the original insight of Lukács's theory of reification: "What is important is to recognize clearly that all human relations (viewed as the objects of social activity) assume increasingly the objective forms of the abstract elements of the conceptual systems of natural science and of the abstract substrata of the laws of nature. And also, the subject of this 'action' likewise assumes increasingly the attitude of the pure observer of these—artificially abstract—processes, the attitude of the experimenter" (Lukács, 1971: 131).[4]

Unlike the successor science project, *technological holism* cannot be accused of extrinsic political interference because, as I argued in chapter 3, ordinary people are intrinsic participants in technical processes. They can transform technology through enlarging the margin of maneuver they already enjoy in the technical networks in which they are enrolled. The extrapolation of the logic of that transformation to the domain of the sciences is a different story. The point is not that science is purer than technology but that social contradictions traverse science differently. Because science does not form the life-world of ordinary people, but only affects them through technology, it remains a specialized activity. The holistic criteria of change relevant to the critique of technology do not therefore apply to science, or at any rate not in the same way.[5]

Distinguishing between the critique of natural science and the critique of technology has both strategic and theoretical consequences. The idea of a successor technoscience combines a plausible approach to technological change with speculative and politically charged proposals for scientific change. The entire enterprise risks foundering because of the connection. Conservative objections to technological critique can shelter behind the self-righteous defense of scientific freedom. The only effective response is to clearly separate a nonteleological critique of science from the teleological critique of technology based on notions of human, social, and natural potential.

These strategic considerations raise a larger problem. Richard Bernstein argues that to define "true human potentiality" we must be prepared to defend the supposedly outdated ontologies of Aristotle and Hegel. He points out, "This is not a rarefied philosophical or intellectual problem when we remind ourselves that however much we condemn totalitarianism and fascism as 'untrue' and 'evil,' they are *also* realizations of human potentialities" (Bernstein, 1988: 24). In Bernstein's view, one can oppose totalitarianism and fascism from the standpoint of a modern formal concept of freedom, but the old teleological approach is no longer intellectually respectable.

This argument challenges Critical Theory either to find a nonontological formulation of the notion of potentiality or to come forward openly in defense of a holistic ontology of some sort. In the following I attempt to carry out the first program; however, I can conceive of no way of including science as well as technology in this project. A holistic conception of nature as such is by definition a speculative ontological project until such time as science, on its own terms, gives a scientific content to the notion.

Ontological holism is of course an interesting notion, but the critique of technological rationality does not require it. A nonontological formulation of a critical theory of technology is possible on terms that leave natural science out of account. I believe this is the best way to counter the undifferentiated defense of technoscience in the writings of the many philosophers and social theorists who see a threat to rationality as a whole in any critique of technology.

Instrumentalization Theory

Two Types of Instrumentalization

The holistic technology critique I propose depends on an analytic distinction between what I call the primary and secondary instrumentalizations.[6] The primary instrumentalization is the technical orientation toward reality that Heidegger identified as the technological "mode of revealing." However, as we have seen, the technical involves not just an orientation but also action in the world, and that action is socially conditioned through and through. Hence the need for a theory of secondary instrumentalizations through which the skeletal primary instrumentalization takes on body and weight in actual devices and systems in a social context.

An analogy with literature explains how these two levels together form a single "essence of technology." Literature depends on an imaginative orientation toward reality. Yet it is obvious that a definition of literature that included only that orientation would be incomplete. What about genres such as the novel or tragedy? What about composition and performance? Markets and careers? Surely all this belongs to literature too. The essence of literature must include a reference to imagination, to be sure, but it must include a lot more besides, and this carries us into social territory we must explore if we really want to understand it.

Technology is similar. A complete definition must show how the orientation toward reality characteristic of technology is combined with the realization of technology in the social world. A very simple example can illustrate this point.

Carpentry involves perceiving wood as a resource and grasping the affordances it offers. In phenomenological language, we could say that the world reveals itself to the carpenter as such a resource, as such affordances. Without this primary instrumentalization of wood, no one would have thought to make a saw, but a saw is not just an "application" of a technical orientation toward wood. Rather, it is a concrete object produced in a specific society according to a social logic. Even such basic facts about saw design as whether it will cut on the push or the pull are socially relative. To understand the form of the saw, its manufacture, its symbolic status, and so on, we need more than a theory of technical orientation. Furthermore, a theory of technical orientation will not tell us what becomes of persons whose lives are dedicated to working wood, how that activity will shape their hands, their reflexes, their language and personality so that it will make sense to call someone a carpenter. All these are secondary instrumentalizations, inseparable from the essence of technology.

My intent in analyzing technology at these two levels is to combine essentialist insights into the technical orientation toward the world with critical and constructivist insights into the social nature of technology. I will show that what are usually presented as competing theories are in fact analytically distinguishable levels in a complex object.

For example, Marcuse's critical account focuses on the primary instrumentalization of the object of technical practice. In the next section, I will break this conception down into the various moments through which the object is isolated and exposed to external manipulation. As discussed in chapter 3, these moments are the basis for formal bias which works with the technical elements released from the instrumentalized objects.

But as they develop, technologies reappropriate aspects of contextual relatedness and self-development from which abstraction was originally made in establishing the technical object relation. It is only because technology has these integrative potentialities that it can be enlisted to repair the damage it does, for example, by redesigning technical processes to take into account their effects on workers, users, and the environment. The description of "informating" technology in chapters 4 and 5 attempts to conceptualize such potentialities of the computer, and a later section of this chapter discusses the theoretical implications of integrative technical development.

On the basis of this concept of integration, I argue that technique is dialectical. A full definition of it must include a secondary instrumentalization that works with dimensions of the object denied at the primary level. This dialectical account of technology breaks with the overly negative evaluation of technology in the Frankfurt School. On the other hand, it continues Critical Theory's search for a positive moment in Enlightenment that compensates for the disaster of modernity. That moment surfaces in concepts like Adorno's "mindfulness of nature" or Marcuse's notion of "potentiality." Instrumentalization theory identifies resources in the technical sphere through which it can be realized in a redeemed modernity.

The complementarity of primary and secondary instrumentalization is a normal aspect of the technical sphere. Secondary instrumentalizations lie at the intersection of technical action and the other action systems with which technique is inextricably linked insofar as it is a social enterprise. The dialectics of technology is thus not a mysterious "new concept of reason" but an ordinary aspect of the technical sphere, familiar to all who work with machines if not to all who write about them.

But capitalism has a unique relation to these aspects of technique. Because its hegemony rests on formal bias, it strives to reduce technique to the primary level of decontextualization, calculation, and control. The definition of "technique" is narrowed as much as possible to the primary instrumentalization, and other aspects of technique are considered nontechnical. Suppressed are the integrative potentialities of technique that compensate for some of the negative effects of the primary instrumentalization.

The dialectic of technology is short-circuited under capitalism in one especially important domain: the technical control of the labor force. Special obstacles to secondary instrumentalization are encountered wherever integrative technical change would threaten that control. These obstacles are not merely ideological but are incorporated into technical codes that determine formally biased designs. As we have seen, the integration of skill and intelligence into production is often arrested by the fear that the firm will become dependent on its workers. The larger context of work, which includes these suppressed potentialities, is uncovered in a critique of the formal bias of existing designs. The critical theory of technology exposes the obstacles to the release of technology's integrative potential and thus serves as the link between political and technical discourse.

The Dialectic of Technology

In traditional societies, technique is always embedded in a larger framework of social relations. Not only does technical practice serve extratechnical values—it does that in all societies, including capitalist ones—but more than that, it is contextualized by practices that define its place in an encompassing nontechnical action system. One finds remnants of such a structure today in child rearing and artistic production. The parent who employs modern medicine, the artist who welds a sculpture or uses videotape, integrate these technologies into a larger framework of nurturing or aesthetic practices. Although the actors may rationalize the technologies they employ, the larger system in which these technologies are embedded resists rationalization and does not fall under the norm of efficiency (Feenberg, 1995: chap. 7).

Capitalist labor organization is no longer embedded in the various social subsystems it serves, controlled by nontechnical forms of action such as religious or paternal moral authority. Capitalism liberates technique from such internal controls and organizes work and an ever enlarging share of the rest of the social system in pursuit of efficiency and power. Thus even though technique in itself has many similar traits in precapitalist and capitalist societies, only in the latter is it a universal human destiny (Habermas, 1970: 94–98).

This destiny can be summarized as four reifying moments of technical practice that have always characterized the object relation in the small technical enclaves of social life but that embrace society as a whole for the first time under capitalism. To each of these reifying moments, there corresponds a compensating integrative moment that, as we will see, is severely restricted as it is accommodated to capitalism.

1. *Decontextualization and Systematization:* the separation of the technical object from its immediate context, and a corresponding systematization through which the decontextualized objects are connected with each other, with human users, and nature to form devices and technical organizations.

2. *Reductionism and Mediation:* the separation of primary from secondary qualities, that is, the reduction of objects to their useful aspects, and a corresponding mediation of technical devices by aesthetic and ethical qualities that are incorporated into their design.

3. *Autonomization and Vocation:* the separation of subject from object, that is, the protection of the autonomized technical actor from the immediate consequences of its actions, and a corresponding vocational investment of the actor who is shaped as a person with an occupation by the technical actions in which he or she engages.

4. *Positioning and Initiative:* the subject situates or positions itself strategically to navigate among its objects and control them, and a corresponding sphere of initiative in which those of the "objects" which are in fact subordinated human beings, workers and consumers, enjoy a certain tactical free play.

Capitalism applies the four primary moments most broadly, while partially suppressing secondary moments of the technical relation. The remainder of this section will show how these characteristics of technical action apply to both the collective laborer and to nature as the object of production under capitalism.

DECONTEXTUALIZATION AND SYSTEMATIZATION. Capitalist technology is based on the *reified decontextualization* of the objects it constructs. It is because basic technical elements are abstracted from all particular contexts that they can be combined in devices and reinserted into any context whatsoever to further a hegemonic interest. Capitalism emerges from the generalization of this feature of technology at the expense of labor and the natural environment. Communist societies imitated these aspects of the capitalist inheritance and so offered no alternative in this respect.[7]

The construction of abstract labor power under capitalism is unique in achieving a properly technical decontextualization of human capacities. All earlier societies employed human labor in the context of the social conditions of its reproduction, such as the family and community. The creative powers of labor were developed through vocations such as crafts transmitted from one generation to the next. Thus, however impoverished and exploited, the worker always remained the organizer of technical action, not its object.

Under capitalism, on the contrary, the hand, back, and elbow are required to release their schemas of action on exactly the same terms as tree trunks, fire, or oil. To get at these technical potentials, workers must be split off from institutions such as community and family and reduced to pure instrumentalities. Workers on the assembly line are not essentially members of a community, nor are they merely a source of muscle power as a slave might be: insofar as possible, they are components of the machinery. In chapter 5, we saw how the computer can be used to extend this logic to education, reducing human inputs to mechanical routines. The reifying extraction of technical elements thus harmonizes with the requirements of the capitalist division of labor, as they are both based on decontextualizing practice.

Decontextualization is of course only the starting point in technical development since the decontextualized elements must be combined with each other to be useful. The resulting device must then be related to other devices and to its natural environment. "Systematization" is the secondary instrumentalization in which these connections are established. The process of systematization has the potential for overcoming the mutilating effects of decontextualization where technical design addresses a sufficiently wide range of contexts. Capitalism does greatly enlarge that range insofar as devices form each others' contexts, integrating enormous numbers of them in tightly coupled networks. This gives rise to what I call "system-centered design," the typical design strategy of modern societies.[8] However, where the well-being of workers and nature are concerned, it limits those contexts as much as possible for the sake of control and profits. A socialist technology would not impose such limits on systematization but would reach out to embrace the widest range of contexts in all areas.

REDUCTIONISM AND MEDIATION.   Technical means are "abstracted" by reducing complex totalities to those of their elements through which they are exposed to control from above. I will call these controlling elements "primary qualities," not in Locke's epistemological sense but in terms of their essential place in particular technical projects. "Secondary qualities" include everything else about the object, everything that is unimportant to the technical project in which it is enrolled. To the extent that all of reality comes under the sign of technique, the real is progressively reduced to primary qualities.

For example, a valley chosen as a roadbed presents itself to technical reason as a certain concatenation of (primary) geographical and geological qualities subject to manipulation in the interest of transport. Other secondary qualities, such as the valley's plant and animal life or its historical and aesthetic associations, can be overlooked in reconstructing it. A reduction of this sort is unfortunate in the case of a green valley, but it is tragic in the case of a human being. The essential object of capitalist action is the worker. Since he is located "above" the social subsystems he commands, the manager cannot rely on means that emerge spontaneously within those subsystems, such as the moral or sentimental social controls of the family. Formal abstraction, which produces technical knowledge by decontextualizing its objects and reducing them to their primary qualities, supplies means to this decontextualized subject as well.

The reduction of the technical object to primary qualities is compensated to some extent in all societies by aesthetic and ethical investments that enrich it once again and adapt it to its environment. All traditional craftsmen apply ethical or religious rules in the course of their work in order to adjust their technical interventions to the requirements of meaning and social stability. They also produce and ornament simultaneously in order to reinsert the object extracted from nature into its new social context. This "mediation-centered design" process disappears in modern societies.[9] They are unique in distinguishing production from aesthetics and ethical regulation. They are heedless of the social insertion of their objects, substitute packaging for an inherent aesthetic elaboration, and are indifferent to the unintended consequences of technology for human beings and nature. Various system crises result from this artificial separation of technique, ethics, and aesthetics.

AUTONOMIZATION AND VOCATION.   These reflections on capitalism as a quasitechnical system suggest a metaphoric application to society of Newton's third law: "For every action there is an equal and opposite reaction." In mechanics, actor and object belong to the same system and so every effect is simultaneously a cause, every object simultaneously a subject. In technical action, however, the subject is unaffected by the object on which it acts, thus forming an exception to Newton's law. Technical action autonomizes the subject through dissipating or deferring feedback from the object of action to the actor.[10] This autonomization of the subject has momentous social implications under capitalism, where subject (manager) and object (worker) are both human beings.

Ordinary human relations have a "Newtonian" character. Every action one friend, lover, or family member directs toward another provokes a comparable reaction that promptly affects the initiator of the exchange. The human relations involved in the organization of traditional work are similar. For example, the father, as leader of the familial work group, is exposed by his treatment of his dependent coworkers to consequences fully in proportion to his effects on them. If he drives his "workers" too hard, he suffers in his family, which must aid them to recover. Here action is caught up in a short feedback loop, returning promptly to the acting subject in an "equal and opposite reaction."

The case is different in the technical sphere. The driver of an automobile accelerates to high speeds while experiencing only a slight pressure and small vibrations; the marksman shoots and experiences only a small force transmitted to his shoulder by the stock of the gun. By the same token, management controls workers while minimizing and channeling resistance so far as possible. The absolute disproportion between the "reaction" experienced by the actor and the effect of his action distinguishes these activities as technical. The feedback loop is extended here as far as possible to isolate the subject from the effects of his or her action. Extrapolating this disposition to the limit, one arrives at the ideal of the god, external to the system on which it operates and omnipotent in relation to it.

In fact, of course, human beings are not gods but finite beings. As such, they are part of every system on which they act. The strategic manipulation of people appears to require independence on the part of the actor and passivity on the part of the human object on which he acts. But in fact this polarity is an illusion masking reciprocal interactions. One cannot affect other people without approaching them and becoming in some measure vulnerable to them. *The nearest approximation to being truly "above" the social system to which the actor belongs is for that system itself to reproduce the actor's operational autonomy within it.* This is the nature of capitalist leadership. The capitalist's operational autonomy provides opportunities to place workers in a dependent position where they need precisely the sort of leadership the capitalist supplies. The capitalist enterprise consists in such loops of circular causality through which the enterprise reproduces itself in response to internal tensions and encounters with the outside world.[11]

Once established in this way, the collective laborer can be organized only through external coordination, which gradually comes to seem like just one of the many technical conditions of cooperative production. So normal does it become to exercise control from above that management functions are transferred first from owners to hired executives and eventually, under state socialism, to civil servants, without fundamentally altering the labor process.

In precapitalist societies the autonomization of the technical subject with respect to its objects is overcome in the acquisition of a craft, a vocation. Here what I have called the "Newtonian" character of action, the reciprocity of the relation of subject to object, is recovered in a technical context at a higher level. In vocation, the subject is no longer isolated from objects but is transformed by its own technical relation to them. This relation exceeds passive contemplation or external manipulation and involves the worker as bodily subject and member of a community. It is precisely this quality of traditional technical practice that is eliminated in deskilling and that must be recaptured in a modern context to create a socialist technology. The example of online education discussed in chapter 5 illustrates the contrast. A vocation centered design process would preserve faculty skills by supporting their application in the online environment.

POSITIONING AND INITIATIVE.   In a sense all technique is navigation. Just as the sailor uses the "law" of the winds to reach a destination and the trader anticipates the movements of the market and rides them to success, so too the technical subject falls in with the object's own tendencies to extract a desired outcome. By positioning itself strategically with respect to its objects, the technical subject turns their inherent properties to account. Lukács calls this a "contemplative" form of practice because it changes the "form" of its objects but not their nature (Feenberg, 2000).

The capitalist, like the bureaucrat who inherits his powers in state socialist societies, has established an interiority from which to *act on* social reality, rather than *acting out of* a reality in which he is essentially engaged. Situated in this ideal social locus "above" social processes, he "positions" himself advantageously with respect to the "things" into which his world is fragmented, including the human communities in which he works and lives. Capitalist practice thus has a strategic aspect: it is based not on a substantive role *within* a given social group but rather on an external relationship to groups in general. The operational autonomy the capitalist enjoys once he enters a social system is the trace of his quasi-externality. Operational autonomy is the occupation of a strategic position with respect to a reified reality.

Capitalist management and product design aims to limit and channel the little initiative that remains to workers and consumers. Their margin of maneuver is reduced to occasional tactical gestures. But the enlargement of margin of maneuver in a socialist trajectory of development would lead to voluntary cooperation in the coordination of effort. It seems appropriate to call this praxis "collegial" since individuals participate in it only insofar as they share responsibility for an institution. In precapitalist societies, such cooperation was often regulated by tradition or paternal authority exercised within moral limits that represented interests of the work group and the craft. In modern societies collegiality is an alternative to traditional bureaucracy with widespread, if imperfect, applications in the organization of professionals such as teachers and doctors. Reformed and generalized, it has the potential for reducing alienation through substituting conscious cooperation for control from above.

Technological Holism

Recontextualizing Practice

The hegemony of capital does not rest on a particular technique of social control but more fundamentally on the technical reconstruction of the entire field of social relations within which it operates. The power of the businessman or bureaucrat is already present in the fragmentation of the various social spheres of production, management and labor, family and home life, economics and politics, and so on. The fragmented individuals and institutions can be organized only by agents who dominate them from above.

The secondary instrumentalizations support the reintegration of object with context, primary with secondary qualities, subject with object, and leadership with group. In today's industrial societies, technical practice supports these progressive forms of integration only to the extent that political protest or competitive pressures impose them, but under socialism, technique could incorporate integrative principles and procedures in its basic modus operandi. This new form of technical practice would be characterized by the movement *through reification to reintegration*. It would be adapted to the requirements of a socialist society much as contemporary technique is adapted to the requirements of capitalism.

Since decontextualization predestines technology to serve capitalist power, socialism must recover some of those contextual elements lost in the narrowing of technology to class-specific applications. This requires a *recontextualizing practice* oriented toward a wide range of interests that capitalism represents only partially, interests that reflect human and natural potentialities capitalism ignores or suppresses.

These interests correspond to the lost contexts from which technology is abstracted and the "secondary qualities" of its objects, the sacrificed dimensions of society and nature that bear the burden of technical action. In an earlier period, the socialist movement brought the existence of such interests to light through labor's resistance to total instrumentalization by capital. More recently, feminism and ecology have familiarized us with other suppressed dimensions.

A socialist technical code would be oriented toward the reintegration of the contexts and secondary qualities of both the subjects and objects of capitalist technique. These include ecological, medical, aesthetic, urbanistic, and work-democratic considerations that capitalist and communist societies encounter as "problems," "externalities," and "crises." Health and environmental considerations, the enrichment of work and industrial democracy, must all be internalized as *engineering* objectives. This can be accomplished by multiplying the technical systems that are brought to bear on design to take into account more and more of the essential features of the object of the technology, the needs of operators, consumers, and clients, and the requirements of the environment.

There are probably limits to how far one can go in this direction in the existing industrial civilization. The point is not that capitalism is incapable of dealing with many of its current problems through reactive crisis avoidance.[12] It does usually meet crises with solutions of some sort. But the solutions are often so flawed that they provoke public resistance, as in the case of costly environmental regulation. Deeper problems, such as the pernicious dependence on the automobile, cannot even be posed in the framework of the system.

The need for a general overhaul of technology is ever more apparent, and that overhaul is incompatible with the continued existence of a system of control from above based on social fragmentation. So long as environmental hazards or job dissatisfaction appear as "externalities" they cannot be fundamentally overcome. In this respect, the capitalist or communist bureaucrat cannot claim to be the neutral agent of society's choices because the system that places him or her in a position to represent society has immense substantive consequences.

The underlying problem is the reified separation of labor, consumption, and social decision-making in all modern industrial societies. Given the authoritarian structure of the industrial enterprise, labor has no direct influence on the design of technology but instead manifests its wishes in union strife. Because they do not participate in the original networks of design choice, workers' interests can only be incorporated later through a posteriori regulations that sometimes appear to conflict with the direction of technical progress. But labor is not so much opposed to the advance of technology as to a system in which it is the object rather than the subject of progress.[13] In another social system where it had more influence at an earlier stage in design, it could return to the technical elements and recombine them in conformity with the requirements of a different technical code.

A similar observation applies to environmental problems. These problems appear as such to individuals in social roles remote from industrial decision-making. The very same person who, as a decision maker, accepts the environmentally destructive implications of the dominant technical code flees privately with his family to distant suburbs to find a safe haven from the consequences of decisions such as his. The political protest against pollution returns to haunt the design process in the form of external regulation once flawed technologies have been unleashed on society.

Soviet-style planning offered no improvement over capitalist regulation (O'Connor, 1989). Soviet production depended on transferred technology designed according to capitalist technical codes. No socialist innovation process addressed the inherent flaws of this technology, and a management system based on production quotas left the imported technological base essentially intact. Regulation and planning are thus not so much alternatives to reification as ways of achieving a partial recognition of the totality under the horizon of reification, that is to say, in a social order based on mastery through fragmentation.

The external character of regulation in both capitalist and communist economies introduces inefficiencies into the operation of industrial processes. The problem is not the expense of serving needs such as health, safety, clean air and water, aesthetic goals, and full employment. There is nothing inherently inefficient about such expenditures so long as a proportionate benefit is received. Rather, the essential problem lies in the cascading impacts of the various ex post facto "fixes" imposed on technologies, the workplace, and the environment.

Because technology is designed in abstraction from these so-called soft values, including them at a later stage has highly visible costs. These costs appear to represent essential trade-offs inscribed in the very nature of industrial society when in reality they are side effects of a reified design process. The design of the automobile engine, for example, is complicated by the addition of inelegant pollution control devices, such as catalytic converters. The design of cities is compromised, in turn, by attempts to adapt them to ever more automobiles, and so on. It would be easy to multiply such examples of the social construction of the dilemma of environmental values versus technical efficiency.

The process in which capitalism assembled a collective laborer and supplied it with tools was essentially fragmenting. The mark of that origin can be removed through a new process of sociotechnical integration. The technical heritage must be *overcome* insofar as it reflects the social requirements of capitalism. The many connections that industrial societies today treat as external must be internalized as technology is reproduced under the aegis of a new dereifying technical code. This is why the integration of the social and technical subsectors requires more than a central plan: it will take technical progress to reform the technology inherited from capitalism.

Concretization

That progress can be theorized in terms of Gilbert Simondon's concept of the "concretization" of technology (Simondon, 1958: chap. 1). Concretization is the discovery of synergisms between technologies and their various environments. Recall that Simondon situates technologies along a continuum that runs from less to more structurally integrated designs. He describes loose designs, in which each part performs a separate function, as "abstract." In the course of technical progress, parts are redesigned to perform multiple functions and structural interactions take on functional roles. These integrative changes yield a more "concrete" technical object that is in fact a system rather than a bunch of externally related elements. For example, a typical concretization occurs in engine design when the surfaces used for the dissipation of heat are merged with those used to reinforce the engine case: two separate structures and their distinct functions are combined in a single structure with two functions.

Simondon argues that technical objects are adapted to their multiple milieus by concretizing advances. Technologies must be compatible with the major constraints of their technical and natural environments: a car's metal skin must protect it from the weather while also reducing air drag to increase effective power; the base of a light bulb must seal it for operation within a certain range of temperatures and pressures while also fitting in standard sockets. All developed technologies exhibit more or less elegant condensations aimed at achieving compatibilities of this sort.

The most sophisticated technologies employ synergies between their various milieus to create a semiartificial environment that supports their own functioning. Simondon calls the combined technical and natural conditions these technologies generate an "associated milieu." It forms a niche with which the technology is in continual recursive causal interaction. The associated milieu

> is that by which the technical object conditions itself in its functioning. This milieu is not manufactured, or at least not totally manufactured; it is a certain order of natural elements surrounding the technical object and linked to a certain order of elements constituting the technical object. The associated milieu mediates the relation between the manufactured technical elements and the natural elements within which the technical object functions. (Simondon, 1958: 57, my trans.)

This higher level of "organic" concreteness is achieved where the technology itself generates the environmental conditions to which it is adapted, as when the heat generated by a motor supplies a favorable operating environment. Energy-efficient housing design offers another example of a technical system that is not simply compatible with environmental constraints but that internalizes them, making them in some sense part of the "machinery." In this case, factors that are only externally and accidentally related in most homes, such as the direction of sunlight and the distribution of glass surfaces, are purposefully combined to achieve a desired effect. The niche in which the house operates is constituted by its angle with respect to the sun.

Human beings are also an operating environment. The craftsman is actually the most important associated milieu of traditional tools, which are adapted primarily to their human users. Although modern machines are organized as technical "individuals" and do not depend on human operators to the same degree, it is still possible to adapt them to an environment of intelligence and skill. As we saw, this was the argument of Shoshana Zuboff and Larry Hirschhorn, discussed in chapter 4. But the capitalist technical code militates against solutions to technical problems that place workers once again at the center of the technical system.

The idea of a "concrete technology," which includes nature in its very structure, contradicts the commonplace notion that technical progress "conquers" nature. In Simondon's theory the most advanced forms of progress create complex synergies of technical and natural forces. Such synergies are achieved by creative acts of invention that transcend apparent constraints or trade-offs and generate a relatively autonomous system out of elements that at first seem opposed or disconnected. *The passage from abstract technical beginnings to concrete outcomes is a general integrative tendency of technological development* that overcomes the reified heritage of capitalist industrialism.

The theory of concretization shows how technical progress might be able to address contemporary social problems through advances that incorporate the wider contexts of human and environmental needs into the structure of machines. While there is no strictly technological imperative dictating such an approach, strategies of concretization could embrace these contexts as they do others in the course of technical development. Where these contexts include environmental considerations, the technology is reintegrated or adapted to nature; where they include the capacities of the human operators, the technology progresses beyond deskilling to become the basis for vocational self-development.

The argument shows that socialist demands for environmentally sound technology and humane, democratic, and safe work are not extrinsic to the logic of technology but respond to the inner tendency of technical development to construct synergistic totalities of natural, human, and technical elements. Nor would the incorporation of socialist requirements into the structure of technology diminish productive efficiency so long as it was achieved through further concretization rather than through multiplying external controls in ever more abstract designs.

All modern industrial societies stand today at the crossroads, facing two different directions of technical development. They can either intensify the exploitation of human beings and nature, or they can take a new path in which the integrative tendencies of technology support emancipatory applications. This choice is essentially political. The first path yields a formally biased system that consistently reinforces elite power. The second path requires a concretizing application of technical principles, taking into account the many larger contexts on which technology has impacts. These contexts reflect potentialities—values—that can be realized only through a new organization of society.

Forward to Nature

Some environmentalists argue that the problems caused by modern technology can be solved only by returning to more primitive conditions. This position belongs to a long tradition of antitechnological critique that denounces the alienation of modern society from nature. The "nature" in question is the immediacy from which the objects of technical practice are originally decontextualized, including naturelike elements of culture such as the family. But the price of a return to immediate "naturalness" is the reduction of individuals to mere functions of the whole, absorbed in service to its goals. Such a return to nature would be a reactionary retreat behind the level of emancipation achieved by modernity.

Is there a way of restoring the broken unity of society and nature while avoiding the moral cost of romantic retreat? Or are we destined to oscillate forever between the poles of primitive and modern, solidarity and individuality, domination by nature and domination of nature? This is the ultimate question that a critical theory of technology must address. I have shown that an implausible return to nature is not the only alternative to contemporary industrial society.

Although a new civilization cannot be extracted out of nostalgia for the old, nostalgia is a significant symbolic articulation of interests that are ignored today. These interests point not backward but *forward to nature*, toward a *totality* consciously composed in terms of a wide range of human needs and concerns. This conception of totality as the goal of a process of mediation rather than as an organic presupposition suggests a reply to some common objections to radical arguments for social reconstruction.

We cannot recover what reification has lost by regressing to pretechnological conditions, to some prior unity irrelevant to the contemporary world. The solution is neither a romantic return to the primitive, qualitative, and natural, nor a speculative leap into a "new age" and a whole "new technology." On the contrary, the critical concept of totality aids in identifying the *contingency* of the existing technological system, the points at which it can be invested with new values and bent to new purposes. Those points are to be found where the fragmentation of the established system maintains an alienated power.

The reified systems constructed by capitalist technology must be resituated in the larger contexts from which they are abstracted *today*, not in the past. A partial return to craft labor might be desirable, but it is no solution to the alienation of industrial labor; a further technical advance is needed to reduce alienation through empowering the kind of workers employed in today's society. The horse and plow are not the "context" to which modern agriculture needs to be related but rather the actual environmental and health considerations from which it is abstracted in being constituted as a technological enterprise according to the prevailing technical codes.

We take the reification of technology for granted today, but the present system is completely artificial. Never before have human beings organized their practice in fragments and left the integration of the bits and pieces to chance. The technical environment of capitalism is essentially fragile, constantly at risk from externalities and conflicts, and unable to adjust to the ecological and social problems it causes. As industry becomes ever more powerful, the fragility of the system as a whole increases despite our best efforts to regulate sanity into an insane process of development.

In the past, tradition and custom accomplished a many-sided integration of society and nature. Premodern societies had an organic quality like all other living things on the surface of the earth. Unlike our Promethean assaults on nature, their technologies, however primitive, *conquered time* by constantly reproducing a viable relationship between society and nature.[14] This is the one "conquest" our vaunted technology seems unable to achieve. We must recover the lost art of survival formerly contained in tradition and custom.

That goal cannot be achieved by a regression to traditional forms of personal identity, however comforting these may be in an anomic society. What is required, rather, is a rational recognition of the natural and human constraints on technical development. Such recognition should not be confused with passive submission to external necessity. That confusion arises from the capitalist fixation on the paradigm of primary instrumentalization in terms of which the objects of technique appear simply as raw materials in service to extrinsic goals. Synergisms by which the environment can be enlisted in the structure of appropriate technology are overlooked. These are captured at the level of secondary instrumentalization, which determines a different paradigm of technical practice.

This conception of practice conforms with our current understanding of biological adaptation. From an evolutionary standpoint, living things relate to their environment actively as well as passively, selecting out that dimension of the world around them to which they adapt. This process of selection is of course unconscious, but it is formally quite similar to the way in which a human society might choose to treat the variety of natural limits it confronts.

In adapting, living things engage in concretizing strategies not so different from the technical developments discussed here. They, too, incorporate environmental constraints into their structure, something that human societies must also learn to do through redesigning technology in more concrete forms.[15] No social system can be natural, but a socialist society would have at least some of the essential interdependence with its environment that characterizes organic beings. It would therefore represent an advance to a higher level of integration between humanity and nature (Moscovici, 1968: 562).

Nature as a context of development is not a final purpose but a dialectical limitation that invites transcendence through adaptation. To conceptualize a totality once again, we need not know in advance precisely in what way human beings will confront the limitations they meet. We need only gain insight into the *form of the process* of mediation. As the structure of a new social practice, this mediating activity opens infinite possibilities rather than foreclosing the future in some preconceived utopia. Adaptation maintains the formal character of the modern concept of freedom and therefore does not reduce individuals to mere functions of society. Freedom lies in this lack of determinacy.

Notes

1. INTRODUCTION

1. See, for an example, Rescher (1969). Emmanuel Mesthene (1970: 48–57) suggests that rather than limiting technology, values will change to take advantage of the new opportunities it creates.

2. For a review of this trend, see Winner (1977). I discuss Heidegger at length in Feenberg (1999: chap. 8).

3. Qualifying Heidegger and Ellul as "fatalistic" seems reasonable despite the protests of their advocates. How else can one describe a view that says, "We can at most only wake the readiness for the expectation [of God]?" (Heidegger, 1977b: 18). Ellul's defenders present him as delivering essentially the same message. See Christians (1981: 153).

4. For another statement of the radical version of the two-sector thesis, see Gorz (1980b) and Gorz (1988).

5. For more on the subject of Japanese modernity, see Feenberg (1995: chaps. 8 and 9.) There I reconsider this negative judgment. In the final analysis, the issue remains open.

6. The most powerful statement of this position prior to the publication of *One-Dimensional Man* (1964) was Adorno and Horkheimer's *Dialectic of Enlightenment* (1972).

7. For an account of the 1960s at its most radical, see Feenberg and Freedman (2001). Recent demonstrations against the WTO and the IMF show that the spirit of resistance is not entirely dead.

8. Borgmann (1984) offers a persuasive account of these structures.

9. Latour describes something similar as the "delegation" of norms to devices (Latour, 1992).

10. For a review of the Marxist theory of the labor process, see Thompson (1983).

11. See the discussion of contingent development in MacKenzie (1984). For an economic argument for contingency, see Arthur (1989).

12. For a defense of market socialism, see Schweikart (1993). For the other side of the argument, see Stiglitz (1994).

191

13. Much is at stake in balancing job mobility and the community values that lead people to cling desperately to their role in a particular workplace. The costs of an extreme emphasis on either value are enormous. The American system of total mobility and consequent insecurity is profoundly unsatisfactory judging by the problems of anomie, substance abuse, and crime associated with it. The European alternative protects community to a far greater extent but at the expense of unacceptably high unemployment rates. Neither system is stable in the long run. Creative solutions are needed whatever the economic system of the future.

14. The words "Critical Theory" will be capitalized in reference to the classic Frankfurt School, lowercase when used generically to refer to any approach that offers a roughly comparable social critique of rationality.

2. TECHNOLOGY AND TRANSITION

1. This aspect of Marx's work is of course no longer ignored. It is remarkable that not only Bell but several generations of "orthodox" Marxists could fail to understand the importance of the 200-page discussion of these matters in part 4 of volume 1 of *Capital.* For more on this subject, see Rattansi (1982).

2. See Hans Jonas's (1984: 186) choice of the following significant subtitle for a discussion of Marx: "'Reconstruction of the Planet Earth' through Untrammeled Technology."

3. Marx at first assumed that capitalism could satisfy workers' vital needs for food and shelter only inadequately and episodically. Insofar as the capitalist organization of labor is also incompatible with workers' interest in self-actualization, their vital needs will be satisfied only where the obstacles to their human development are removed. The later theory of "relative immiseration" recognized the possibility of a rising income floor without facing the implications of this reformulation for a deterministic conception of socialism. The claim that the impoverishment of the working class is relative is only a negative way of stating that under capitalism workers' lot gradually improves. If that is so, socialism is not the only adequate representation of workers' interests; they can also "get ahead" under capitalism (Przeworski, 1985: 237ff.).

4. Marx (1963: 161–162). For a good account of Marx's early political theory, see Avineri (1968). On the relation of reason and need in the early Marx, see Feenberg (1986: chap. 2).

5. For more on the question of management and expertise in the Soviet Union, see Azrael (1966) and Bailes (1978). The Soviet view is explained in Gvishiani (1972).

6. Engels writes that the worker of the past "doffed his cap to the rich, to the priest and to the officials of the state and inwardly was altogether a slave. It is precisely modern large-scale industry which has turned the worker, formerly chained to the land, into a completely propertyless proletarian, liberated from all traditional fetters, *a free outlaw*. . . . This is the 'intellectual emancipation' of the lower classes" (1970: 22–23).

7. Lenin explained the Russian system as "state capitalism under proletarian dictatorship," a "special stage of the social revolution" not anticipated by socialist theory (Lenin, 1967b: II, 678–679).

3. THE BIAS OF TECHNOLOGY

1. For useful discussions of relevant issues in Weber, see McIntosh (1983) and Schluchter (1979). On the terms "substantive" and "formal" rationality, see Weber (1964: 35–40).

2. One of his longer discussions of technology (but as knowledge) is contained in Foucault (1997: 159ff.).

3. See Deleuze (1986). For Marcuse's critique of the notion that class agents control and challenge the system, see Marcuse (1964: 31–33).

4. Despite the ritual claims for Foucault's uniqueness, this theory signifies Marcuse's rejection of Reichian style Freudo-Marxism and the introduction of a new approach to domination as the mobilization of socially constructed identities. For a typical dismissal of Marcuse, see Rajchman (1985: 83–84). Marcuse would have been surprised to learn of the existence of the "Reich-Marcuse model." In conversation, he enjoyed pointing out the good health of capitalism in the age of sexual liberation, in diametrical opposition to Reich's predictions.

5. Cf. Dews (1987: 161ff.). Deleuze's question recalls Balzac's proud assertion "Je fais partie de l'opposition qui s'appelle la vie" (quoted in Picon, 1956: 114).

6. Conservative opponents of radical change would certainly agree!

7. Marcuse's preface to *One-Dimensional Man* (1964) is a masterpiece of wavering on these issues. See especially p. xv.

8. This problem is discussed at length in the later chapters of Dews (1987).

9. For more on the cultural application of the semiotic concept of code, see Barthes (1969: 94 ff.).

10. Barthes makes a similar point, writing that "Langue/Parole" must be supplemented in the technical domain by a "troisième élément, pré-signifiant, matière ou substance, et qui serait le support (nécessaire) de la signification" (1969: 105).

11. For a theory of technology based on a similar distinction, see Simondon (1958: chap. 1).

12. My account of the bias of formalism in terms of the "fit" of apparently neutral constructions in concrete historical situations is similar to some of Latour's formulations. See, for example, his account of map making (1987: 215ff.).

13. To my knowledge, the first recorded statement of the theory that neutrality is itself a kind of bias appears in Plato's *Gorgias*. There Callicles rejects the laws on the grounds that their neutrality, which takes the form of equal treatment of the strong and weak, responds to special interests of the weak. Callicles argues, "I can quite imagine that the manufacturers of laws and conventions are the weak, the majority, in fact. It is for themselves and their own advantage that they make their laws and distribute their praises and their censures. It is to frighten men who are stronger and able to

enforce superiority that they keep declaring . . . that injustice consists in seeking to get the better of one's neighbor. They are quite content, I suppose, to be on equal terms with others since they are themselves inferior" (Plato, 1952: 51).

14. This approach calls to mind Jon Elster's Marxist version of game theory. His theory of "rational expectations" resembles the theories discussed in this section in recognizing the relative freedom acting subjects enjoy within the framework of any gamelike system. That even dominated groups have choices is a necessary consequence of organizing human activities around rules. However, Elster conceives the social game as a contest for power and income. He treats the technical framework as a mere backdrop, but I argue that it is far more than that, that it is in fact the main stakes in the struggle over civilizational models. For a presentation of Elster's views and responses by critics, see "Marxism, Functionalism, Game Theory: A Debate," in *Theory and Society*, vol. 11, no. 4 (July 1982). I have discussed the comparison between technology and games in Feenberg (1995: chap. 9).

15. De Certeau and Elias do not address the question of the motives and specific objectives of change, nor will I here. These motives include fulfilling work and wider social participation. They have been sketched in the first two chapters of this book and will be taken up in more detail in the last two chapters in the context of the theory of socialist culture. Here the issue is not why society should be changed, but whether and how it can be changed where the will to change is present.

16. This view of technical activity is supported by a number of recent contributions to the understanding of the relation of rules and plans to performance. For example, Lucy Suchman's theory of computer interface design emphasizes the complex ways in which the implicit plans of action embodied in devices are instrumentalized and modified by actors in the course of action. Users are not so much controlled by machines as mobilized by them in relatively unpredictable ways. But neither Suchman nor her sources consider the paradigmatic case for modern industrial society in which plans are established by an elite in order to reproduce its power through the actions of its subordinates. See Suchman (1987: 185ff.).

4. POSTINDUSTRIAL DISCOURSES

1. Diebold (1952); Vonnegut (1967).

2. There are a few passages in the *Grundrisse* where Marx anticipated automation as we understand the term, but these merely extrapolate to the limit tendencies he identified in industrial society from the very beginning.

3. Such ideas were not unique to Marx. See, for example, the astonishingly prescient passage by Anthime Corbon, vice-president of the Constituent Assembly of 1848, cited by Georges Friedman on the title page of *Le travail en miettes* (1964).

4. Concrete case studies that generally confirm Hirschhorn and Zuboff's approach are contained in Wilkinson (1983). Cf. Mary Weir (1977).

5. For a variety of early views on this subject, see Haugeland (1980). For a recent attempt to understand the state of the field and to reform it, see Agre (1997).

6. The point seems obvious today, but it was a quite eccentric view of the computer world until the recent fascination with the Internet. For an early defense of the communicative potential of computer networks, see Hiltz and Turoff (1976).

7. For the early discussions on self-organization, see Yovits and Cameron (1960) and Von Foerster (1962).

8. See also one of the starting points in the debate, Dreyfus and Dreyfus (1986).

9. This aspect of Heidegger's theory is curiously anticipated by Marx's critique of economic fetishism and its role in obscuring the activity of the producer. Marx writes, "It is generally by their imperfections as products, that the means of production in any process assert themselves in their character as products. A blunt knife or weak thread forcibly remind us of Mr. A., the cutler, or Mr. B., the spinner. In the finished product the labour by means of which it has acquired its useful qualities is not palpable, has apparently vanished" (Marx, 1906: I, 203).

10. For another formulation of this approach, see Suchman (1987).

11. The history of communications media is particularly rich in illustrations of this thesis. See de Sola Pool, (1977: chaps. 1, 2, and 4); and Fischer (1988). The French videotext network underwent an evolution in some ways similar to that of the early telephone. See Marchand (1987) and Feenberg (1995: chap. 7).

12. For a feminist critique of Cartesianism with certain similarities to this approach, see Bordo (1987).

5. THE FACTORY OR THE CITY

This chapter draws on recent work I have done in the field of online education. It was not included in the original edition of *Critical Theory of Technology*. It stands here as an application of the interpretation of the computer in the previous chapter.

1. For accounts of the centrality of the city to modern life, see Sennet (1978) and Berman (1988).

2. For discussions of the technical code of the Internet, see Flanigan et al. (2000) and Bakardjieva and Feenberg (2001).

3. For an up-to-date review of the issues by a select faculty group at the University of Illinois, see *Teaching at an Internet Distance* (2000).

6. BEYOND THE DILEMMA OF DEVELOPMENT

1. For a review of these theories, see Meyer (1970). Daniel Bell writes, "While the phrase 'technological imperatives' is too rigid and deterministic, in all industrial societies there are certain common constraints which tend to shape similar actions and force the use of common techniques. For all theorists of industrial society (and to this extent Marx as well) the locus (or primary institution) of the society is the industrial enterprise and the axis of the society is the social hierarchy which derives from the organization of labor around machine production. From this point of view there are some common characteristics for all industrial societies: the tech-

nology is everywhere the same; the kind of technical and engineering knowledge (and the schooling to provide these) is the same; classification of jobs and skills is roughly the same. More broadly, one finds that the proportion of technical occupations increases in each society relative to other categories; that the spread of wages is roughly the same (so are the prestige hierarchies); and that management is primarily a technical skill" (Bell, 1973: 75).

2. "To be a technological determinist is obviously to believe that in some sense technical change *causes* social change, indeed that it is the most important cause of social change. But to give full weight to the first term in expressions such as a '*prime mover*' and '*independent* variable,' it would also have to be believed that technical change is itself uncaused, at least by social factors" (MacKenzie, 1984: 25(3), 474).

3. This procedure is widespread. I first noticed it in an otherwise interesting article by Richard Baum (1975) from which I borrow the terms "techno-" and "ideo-logic."

4. In sharpening the issue in this way, I am no doubt overlooking the many intermediary positions that suggest, for example, dual economies in which industrial and craft labor exist side by side. And it is important to note that environmentalism is by no means generally antitechnological. However, these positions are often confused with each other. A clarification of their differences is best achieved by confronting pure formulations.

5. For the full list and much relevant comment, see Dickson (1975: 103–104). For a further discussion of the ambiguities of environmental politics, see Feenberg (1999: chap. 3). For the argument against Murray Bookchin's version of the position criticized here, see Light (1998).

6. See Sen (1976–1977: 6: 337). Sen's principle of "metaranking" of preference orders could be applied to the problem of civilizational comparisons.

7. For wide-ranging surveys of the contemporary discussion of socialism and democracy, see Cunningham (1987) and Gould (1988).

8. "What I did that was new was to prove: 1) that the existence of classes is only bound up with particular, historical phases in the development of production, 2) that the class struggle necessarily leads to the dictatorship of the proletariat, 3) that this dictatorship itself only constitutes the transition to the abolition of all classes and to a classless society" (From a letter of Marx to Weydemeyer dated March 5, 1852, in Lenin, 1967a: II, 291). "Communism is for us not a *state of affairs* still to be established, not an *ideal* to which reality [will] have to adjust. We call communism the *real* movement which abolishes the present state of affairs. The conditions of this movement result from premises now in existence" (Easton and Guddat, 1967: 426).

9. The two most important texts for understanding the Marxian theory of the transition are "The Critique of the Gotha Program" and "The Civil War in France." See Marx (1972: 383–398, 526–576). For a review of the theory, see Stephens (1979: chap. 1).

10. For examples, see Laclau and Mouffe (1985); Boggs (1986).

11. This is the argument with respect to capitalism of Dokes and Rosier (1988: 291–294).

12. Educational programs that required full-time attendance would still have significant costs to the individuals; but part-time adult education, pursued as a leisure activity, would fall in a different category and might make a large (free) contribution to the economy. For the distinction between these different costs, see Becker (1975: 194–195).

13. On the political implications of the concept of cultural capital, see Gouldner (1979) and Bahro (1978: 278).

14. For discussions of the problems of innovation in communist societies, see Burks (1970) and Berliner (1988). For a classic discussion of the wide variety of contexts of innovation see Jewkes, Sawers, and Stillerman (1959).

15. Since Yugoslavian workers did not own shares in their firms, they took advantage of easy credit rather than improving efficiency, badly indebting the economy. While this is undoubtedly a serious problem, it is difficult to believe that technical solutions cannot be found through appropriate credit regulation and incentive systems such as tying pensions to the income of firms. Dangerously loose credit policies are not specific to socialism, as the American Savings and Loan crisis amply demonstrated.

16. There is a large literature on the concept of democratic management. See, for examples, Blumberg (1976); Lindenfeld and Rothschild-Whitt (1982); and Rosanvallon (1976). For recent philosophical defenses of self-managing socialism, see Gould (1988: chaps. 4 and 9) and Schweikert (1993).

17. A recent book by Judith Green (1999) takes up this term independent of my approach.

18. Arguments for this conclusion are offered in articles by Gorz, Maccio, and Il Manifesto in Gorz (1978).

19. For a collection surveying the debate on the class status of the middle strata, see Walker (1979).

20. For an interesting exception, see E. O. Wright (1978).

7. THE CRITICAL THEORY OF TECHNOLOGY

1. I am grateful to John Ely for pointing out this connection. For accounts of the tension in Marxism between naturalistic holism and theory of the social construction of nature, see Ely (1988), Ely (1989), and Vogel (1995).

2. See Schluchter (1979: 57, 117–118).

3. The contribution of the Frankfurt School to the age-old debate on the problem of universals deserves a study. I would guess that such a study would find considerable agreement, if not a doctrine. For example, Marcuse's position and Adorno's have more in common than is usually recognized. Michael Ryan points out that in contrast to Marcuse, who claims that universals like "freedom" contain more con-

tent than is ever realized in particular institutions, Adorno claims that it is the particular that contains an excess of content with respect to the universal (Ryan 1982: 73). But the universal at issue is different. The surplus to which Adorno refers is precisely the basis on which Marcuse refuses to identify limited realizations of freedom with the universal (Marcuse, 1964: 105–106).

4. The passivity of the experimenter to which Lukács refers is only apparent: the experimenter actively constructs the observed object but, at least in Lukács's view, is not aware of having done so and interprets the experiment as the voice of nature. While Lukács does not criticize the epistemological consequences of this illusion in natural science, in the social arena it defines reification.

5. Is there still a distinction between science and technology? Not if you believe certain science studies scholars who talk about a single unified "technoscience." The concept of "scaling up" is supposed to get us from the laboratory to society. But that concept can mask the tremendously complex and differentiated processes involved in applying new scientific ideas to production. There is a significant gap here that justifies the distinction.

6. For a complementary exposition of instrumentalization theory, see Feenberg (1999: chap. 9).

7. For more on the relation of technical elements to social bias, see chapter 3.

8. I called this "system congruent design" in the conclusion to *Alternative Modernity* (Feenberg, 1995: 228).

9. I called this "expressive design" in the conclusion to *Alternative Modernity* (Feenberg, 1995: 225).

10. For the environmental consequences of autonomization, see O'Connor (1989) and Beck (1992).

11. This analysis can be clarified in terms of Jean-Pierre Dupuy's system theoretic interpretation of the concept of alienation. Dupuy defines "autonomy" as the ability of a system to reproduce certain stable characteristics under a variety of conditions. These stable characteristics can be considered "system effects," emergent behaviors proper to the system itself. Dupuy's analysis of panic illustrates this notion by showing that leadership in crowds is a system effect: the power that apparently flows down from the leader is in fact based on the relations governing the interactions of the mass. The leader is an "endogenous fixed point . . . produced by the crowd although the crowd believes itself to have been produced by it. Such a tangling of different levels is . . . a distinguishing feature of autonomous systems" (Dupuy, n.d.: 23).

12. The theory of reactive crisis avoidance as the general form of movement of the capitalist state can be extended to the domain of technology using Simondon's categories of concrete and abstract design. See Habermas (1975); Offe (1987); O'Connor (1984).

13. See "A Technology Bill of Rights," in Shaiken (1984). On the role of workers in innovation, see Wilkinson (1983: chap. 9).

14. It is true that some premodern societies destroyed their own natural environments, for example, through overgrazing. However, one can hardly compare

destructive processes that took many centuries to show their effects with modern environmental problems and the threat of nuclear weapons.

15. Levins and Lewontin (1985: 104). Merleau-Ponty (1963) expressed the idea clearly in an early book: "This signifies that the organism itself measures the action of things upon it and itself delimits its milieu by a circular process which is without analogy in the physical world."

References

Adorno, Theodor, and Max Horkheimer (1972). *Dialectic of Enlightenment.* Trans. J. Cummings. New York: Herder and Herder.

Agre, Philip (1997). *Computation and Human Experience.* Cambridge: Cambridge University Press.

—— (1998). "The Distances of Education: Defining the Role of Information Technology in the University." *Academe* (September).

Anderson, Thomas, ed. (1963). *Masters of Russian Marxism.* New York: Appleton, Century, Crofts.

Arthur, Brian (1989). "Competing Technologies, Increasing Returns, and Lock-In by Historical Events." *Economic Journal,* vol. 99.

Atlan, Henri (1979). *Entre le cristal et la fumée: Essai sur l'organisation du vivant.* Paris: Seuil.

Avineri, Shlomo (1968). *The Social and Political Thought of Karl Marx.* Cambridge: Cambridge University Press.

Azrael, Jeremy (1966). *Managerial Power and Soviet Politics.* Cambridge, Mass.: Harvard University Press.

Bahro, Rudolph (1978). *The Alternative in Eastern Europe.* Trans. D. Fernbach. London: New Left Books.

—— (1984). *From Red to Green.* London: Verso.

Bailes, Kendall (1978). *Technology and Society under Lenin and Stalin.* Princeton: Princeton University Press.

Bakardjieva, Maria, and Andrew Feenberg (2001). "Community Technology and Democratic Rationalization." *Information Society,* forthcoming.

Balibar, Etienne (1965). "Sur les concepts fondamentaux du matérialisme historique." In L. Althusser, E. Balibar, and R. Establet, eds., *Lire le Capital.* Paris: Maspero.

Barthes, Roland (1969). "Eléments de Sémiologie." In *Le degré zéro de l'écriture.* Paris: Gonthier.

Baudrillard, Jean (1968). *Le système des objets.* Paris: Gallimard.

Baum, Richard (1975). "Technology, Economic Organization, and Social Change: Maoism and the Chinese Revolution." In B. Staiger, ed., *China in the Seventies*. Wiesbaden: Otto Harrassowitz.

Bebel, August (1904). *Woman under Socialism*. Trans. D. de Leon. New York: New York Labor News.

Beck, Ulrich (1992). *Risk Society*. London: Sage.

Becker, Gary (1975). *Human Capital*. Chicago: University of Chicago Press.

Bell, Daniel (1962). *The End of Ideology: On the Exhaustion of Political Ideals in the Fifties*. New York: Free Press.

———— (1973). *The Coming of Post-Industrial Society*. New York: Basic Books.

Benjamin, Walter (1969). *Illuminations*. Trans. H. Zohn. New York: Shocken.

Berge, Zane (1999). "Interaction in Post-Secondary Web-Based Learning." *Educational Technology*, vol. 39, no. 1.

Berliner, Joseph (1988). *Soviet Industry from Stalin to Gorbachev*. Ithaca: Cornell University Press.

Berman, Marshall (1988). *All That Is Solid Melts into Air*. New York: Penguin.

Bernstein, Richard (1988). "Negativity: Theme and Variations." In R. Pippin, A. Feenberg, and C. Weber, eds., *Marcuse: Critical Theory and the Promise of Utopia*. South Hadley, Mass.: Bergin and Garvey.

Bloch, Ernst (1988). "Art and Society." In *The Utopian Function of Art and Literature*. Trans. J. Zipes and F. Mecklenburg. Cambridge, Mass.: MIT Press.

Blumberg, Paul (1976). *Industrial Democracy*. New York: Schocken.

Boggs, Carl (1986). *Social Movements and Political Power*. Philadelphia: Temple University Press.

Bordo, Susan (1987). *The Flight to Objectivity: Essays on Cartesianism and Culture*. Albany: SUNY Press.

Borgmann, Albert (1984). *Technology and the Character of Contemporary Life*. Chicago: University of Chicago Press.

Bourdieu, Pierre (1977). *Outline of a Theory of Practice*. Trans. R. Nice. New York: Cambridge University Press.

Bowles, Samuel, and Herbert Gintis (1976). *Schooling in Capitalist America*. New York: Basic Books.

Braverman, Harry (1974). *Labor and Monopoly Capital*. New York: Monthly Review.

Buckingham, Walter (1961). *Automation*. New York: Harper and Row.

Burks, R. V. (1970). "Technology and Political Change." In Chalmers Johnson, ed., *Change in Communist Systems*. Stanford: Stanford University Press.

Buroway, Michael (1979). *Manufacturing Consent*. Chicago: University of Chicago Press.

Callon, Michel (1986). "Some Elements of a Sociology of Translation: Domestication of the Scallops and the Fishermen of St. Brieuc Bay." In John Law, ed., *Power, Action, and Belief: A New Sociology of Knowledge?* London: Routledge and Kegan Paul.

de Certeau, Michel (1980). *L'invention du quotidien*. Paris: UGE.

Christians, Clifford (1981). "Ellul on Solution: An Alternative but No Prophecy." In C. Christians and J. M. Van Hook, eds., *Jacques Ellul: Interpretive Essays.* Urbana: University of Illinois Press.

Claudin-Urondo, Carmen (1975). *Lenine et la revolution culturelle.* Paris: Mouton.

Coopers & Lybrand (1997). "The Transformation of Higher Education in the Digital Age." Report based on the Learning Partnership Roundtable, Aspen Institute, Maryland, July 1997.

Cunningham, Frank (1987). "Democratic Theory and Socialism." Cambridge: Cambridge University Press.

Deleuze, Gilles (1986). *Foucault.* Trans. S. Hand. Minneapolis: University of Minnesota Press.

Dews, Peter (1987). *Logics of Disintegration.* London: Verso.

Dickson, David (1979). *The Politics of Alternative Technology.* New York: Universe Books.

Diebold, John (1952). *Automation.* New York: D. Van Nostrand.

Doekès, Pierre, and Bernard Rosier (1988). *L'histoire ambiguë: Croissance et développement en question.* Paris: Presses Universitaires de France.

Dreyfus, Hubert, and Paul Rabinow (1983). *Michel Foucault: Beyond Structuralism and Hermeneutics.* Chicago: University of Chicago Press.

Dunn, William N. (1974). "The Economics of Organizational Ideology: The Problem of Dual Compliance in the Worker-Managed Socialist Firm." *Journal of Comparative Administration,* vol. 5, no. 4.

Dupuy, Jean-Pierre (n.d.). "The Autonomy of Social Reality: On the Contribution of the Theory of Systems to the Theory of Society." Unpublished manuscript, p. 23.

——— (1982). *Ordres et desordres.* Paris: Seuil.

——— (1985). "Histoires de cybernetiques." *Cahiers du CREA,* no. 7.

Elias, Norbert (1978). *What Is Sociology?* New York: Columbia University Press.

Ellul, Jacques (1964). *The Technological Society.* Trans. J. Wilkinson. New York: Vintage.

Elster, Jon (1982). "Marxism, Functionalism, Game Theory: A Debate." *Theory and Society,* vol. 11, no. 4.

Ely, John (1988). "Lukács's Construction of Nature." *Capitalism, Nature, Socialism,* no. 1.

——— (1989). "Ernst Bloch and the Second Contradiction of Capitalism." *Capitalism, Nature, Socialism,* no. 2.

Engels, Frederick (1959). "On Authority." In L. Feuer, ed., *Marx and Engels: Basic Works on Politics and Philosophy.* New York: Anchor.

——— (1968). "Socialism: Utopian and Scientific." In Marx and Engels, *Selected Works.* Moscow: Progress Publishers.

——— (1970). *The Housing Question.* Moscow: Progress Publishers.

Farber, Jerry (1998). "The Third Circle: On Education and Distance Learning." *Sociological Perspectives,* vol. 41, no. 4.

Feenberg, Andrew (1970). "Technocracy and Rebellion." *Telos* (Summer).

———— (1986). *Lukács, Marx, and the Sources of Critical Theory*. New York: Oxford University Press.

———— (1988). "The Bias of Technology." In R. Pippin, A. Feenberg, and C. Webel, eds., *Marcuse: Critical Theory and the Promise of Utopia*, South Hadley, Mass.: Bergin and Garvey.

———— (1989). "The Written World." In A. Kaye and R. Mason, eds., *Mindweave: Communication, Computers, and Distance Education*. Oxford: Pergamon Press.

———— (1993). "Building a Global Network: The WBSI Experience." In L. Harasim, ed., *Global Networks: Computerizing the International Community*. Cambridge, Mass.: MIT Press.

———— (1995). *Alternative Modernity*. Berkeley: University of California Press.

———— (1999). "Reflections on the Distance Learning Controversy." *Canadian Journal of Distance Education*, vol. 24.

———— (2000). "A Fresh Look at Lukács: On Steven Vogel's *Against Nature*." *Rethinking Marxism*, vol. 11, no. 4.

Feenberg, Andrew, and Jim Freedman (2001). *When Poetry Ruled the Streets: The French May Events of 1968*. Albany: State University of New York Press.

Fischer, Claude (1988). "'Touch Someone': The Telephone Industry Discovers Sociability." *Technology and Culture*, vol. 29.

Flanagin, Andrew, Wendy Jo Maynard Farinola, and Miriam J. Metzger (2000). "The Technical Code of the Internet/World Wide Web." *Critical Studies in Media Communication*, vol. 17, no. 4.

Fleron, F., Jr. (1977). "Technology and Communist Culture: Bellagio, Italy, Aug. 22–28, 1975." *Technology and Culture*, vol. 18, no. 4.

————, ed. (1977). *Technology and Communist Culture: The Socio-Cultural Impact of Technology under Socialism*. New York: Praeger.

von Foerster, Heinz, ed. (1962). *Principles of Self-Organization*. New York: Pergamon.

Foltz, P. W. (1996). "Latent Semantic Analysis for Text-Based Research." *Behavior Research Methods, Instruments and Computers*, vol. 28, no. 2.

Foucault, Michel (1977). *Discipline and Punish*. Trans. A. Sheridan. New York: Pantheon.

———— (1980). *Power/Knowledge*. Trans. C. Gordon, L. Marshall, J. Mepham, and K. Soper. New York: Pantheon.

———— (1988a). *Politics, Philosophy, Culture*. Trans. A. Sheridan. New York: Routledge.

———— (1988b). *The Final Foucault*. Ed. J. Bernauer and D. Rasmussen. Cambridge, Mass.: MIT Press.

———— (1997). *Il faut défendre la société*. Paris: Gallimard/Seuil.

Fox Keller, Evelyn (1985). *Reflections on Gender and Science*. New Haven: Yale University Press.

Friedman, Georges (1964). *Le travail en miettes*. Paris: Gallimard.

Gendron, Bernard (1984). "Marx and the Technological Theory of History." *Philosophical Forum*, vol. 6, no. 4.

Goldman, Marshall (1987). *Gorbachev's Challenge*. New York: Norton.

Goldman, Steven (1990). "Philosophy, Engineering, and Western Culture." In Paul Durbin, ed., *Broad and Narrow Interpretations of Philosophy of Technology.* Dordrecht: Kluwer Academic Publishers.

Gorz, André, ed. (1980a). *The Division of Labor.* Sussex: Harvester.

—— (1980b). *Adieux au proletariat.* Paris: Galilée.

—— (1988). *Metamorphoses du travail quete du sens.* Paris: Galilée.

Gould, Carol (1988). *Rethinking Democracy.* Cambridge: Cambridge University Press.

Gouldner, Alvin (1979). *The Future of the Intellectuals and the Rise of the New Class.* New York: Seabury.

—— (1980). *The Two Marxisms: Contradictions and Anomalies in the Development of Theory.* New York: Seabury.

Graham, Loren (1998). *What We Have Learned About Science and Technology from the Russian Experience.* Stanford: Stanford University Press.

Gramsci, Antonio (1959). *The Modern Prince.* New York: International Publishers.

Green, Judith (1999). *Deep Democracy.* Lanham: Rowman and Littlefield.

Guillaume, Marc (1975). *Le capital et son double.* Paris: PUF.

Gvishiani, D. (1972). *Organization and Management.* Moscow: Progress.

Habermas, Jürgen (1970). *Toward a Rational Society.* Trans. J. Shapiro. Boston: Beacon.

—— (1975). *Legitimation Crisis.* Trans. T. McCarthy. Boston: Beacon.

Hansard's Debates, Third Series: Parliamentary Debates, 1830–1891, vol. 73, 1844 (Feb. 22–Apr. 22): 1088.

Harasim, Linda, S. R. Hiltz, L. Teles, and M. Turoff (1995). *Learning Networks: A Field Guide to Teaching and Learning Online.* Cambridge, Mass.: MIT Press.

Haraway, Donna (1989). *Primate Visions: Gender, Race, and Nature in the World of Modern Science.* New York: Routledge.

Harding, Sandra (1986). *The Science Question in Feminism.* Ithaca: Cornell University Press.

—— (1990). "Feminism, Science, and the Anti-Enlightenment Critiques." In L. Nicholson, ed., *Feminism/Postmodernism.* New York: Routledge.

Harootunian, H. D. (1989). "Visible Discourses/Invisible Ideologies." In Masao Miyoshi and H. D. Harootunian, eds., *Postmodernism and Japan.* Durham, N.C.: Duke University Press.

Haugeland, John, ed. (1980). *Mind Design: Philosophy, Psychology, Artificial Intelligence.* Cambridge, Mass.: MIT Press.

Heidegger, Martin (1977a). *The Question Concerning Technology.* Trans. W. Lovitt. New York: Harper and Row.

—— (1977b). "Only a God Can Save Us Now." Trans. D. Schendler. *Graduate Faculty Philosophy Journal,* vol. 6, no. 1.

—— (1998). "Traditional Language and Technological Language." Trans. W. Gregory. *Journal of Philosophical Research,* vol. 23.

Hiltz, Starr Roxanne, and Murray Turoff (1978). *The Network Nation: Human Communication via Computer.* Reading, Mass.: Addison-Wesley.

Hirschhorn, Larry (1984). *Beyond Mechanization: Work and Technology in a Post-industrial Age.* Cambridge, Mass.: MIT Press.

Hofstadter, Douglas (1979). *Gödel, Escher, Bach.* New York: Basic Books.

Ihde, Don (1990). *Technology and the Lifeworld.* Bloomington: Indiana University Press.

Jantsch, Erich, and Conrad Waddington (1976). *Evolution and Consciousness.* Reading, Mass.: Addison-Wesley.

Jay, Martin (1984). *Marxism and Totality: The Adventures of a Concept from Lukács to Habermas.* Berkeley: University of California Press.

Jewkes, John, David Sawers, and Richard Stillerman (1959). *The Sources of Invention.* New York: St. Martin's.

Johansen, Robert (1988). *Groupware: Computer Support for Business Teams.* New York: Free Press.

Jonas, Hans (1984). *The Imperative of Responsibility.* Chicago: University of Chicago Press.

Kearsley, G. (1993). "Intelligent Agents and Instructional Systems: Implications of a New Paradigm." *Journal of Artificial Intelligence and Education,* vol. 4, no. 4.

Kellner, Douglas, ed. (1971). *Karl Korsch: Revolutionary Theory.* Austin: University of Texas Press.

Kidder, Tracy (1981). *The Soul of a New Machine.* New York: Little, Brown.

Laclau, Ernesto, and Chantal Mouffe (1985). *Hegemony and Socialist Strategy.* London: Verso.

Lasch, Christopher (1979). *The Culture of Narcissism.* New York: Norton.

Latour, Bruno (1987). *Science in Action: How to Follow Scientists and Engineers through Society.* Cambridge, Mass.: Harvard University Press.

——— (1992). "Where Are the Missing Masses? The Sociology of a Few Mundane Artifacts." In W. Bijker and J. Law, eds., *Shaping Technology/Building Society: Studies in Sociotechnical Change.* Cambridge, Mass.: MIT Press.

——— (1999). *Politiques de la nature: Comment faire entrer la science en démocratie.* Paris: La Découverte.

Lee, Rensselaer W., III (1973). "The Politics of Technology in Communist China." *Comparative Politics,* vol. 5.

——— (1977). "Mass Innovation and Communist Culture: The Soviet and Chinese Cases." In F. Fleron, ed., *Technology and Communist Culture.* New York: Praeger.

Lenin, Vladimir (1967a). "The State and Revolution." In Lenin, *Selected Works.* New York: International Publishers.

——— (1967b). *Selected Works.* New York: International Publishers.

Levins, Richard, and Richard Lewontin (1985). *The Dialectical Biologist.* Cambridge, Mass.: Harvard University Press.

Light, Andrew, ed. (1998). *Social Ecology after Bookchin.* New York: Guilford.

Lindenfeld, Frank, and Joyce Rothschild-Whitt, eds. (1982). *Workplace Democracy and Social Change.* Boston: Porter Sargent.

Lovins, Amory (1977). *Soft Energy Paths: Toward a Durable Peace*. San Francisco: Friends of the Earth.

Lyotard, Jean François (1979). *La condition postmoderne*. Paris: Editions de Minuit.

—— (1984). *The Postmodern Condition: A Report on Knowledge*. Trans. G. Bennington and B. Massumi. Minneapolis: University of Minnesota Press.

MacKenzie, Donald (1984). "Marx and the Machine." *Technology and Culture*, vol. 25, no. 3.

Mandel, Ernest (1967). *La formation de la pensée economique de Karl Marx*. Paris: Maspero.

de Mandeville, Bernard (1970). *The Fable of the Bees*. Baltimore: Penguin.

Mannheim, Karl (1936). *Ideology and Utopia*. Trans. L. Wirth and E. Shils. New York: Harcourt Brace.

Marchand, Marie (1987). *La grande aventure du Minitel*. Paris: Larousse.

Marcuse, Herbert (1941). "Some Social Implications of Modern Technology. In *Philosophy and Science*, ix: 3.

—— (1964). *One-Dimensional Man*. Boston: Beacon.

—— (1968). "Industrialization and Capitalism in the Work of Max Weber." In *Negations*. Trans. J. Shapiro. Boston: Beacon.

—— (1969). *An Essay on Liberation*. Boston: Beacon.

—— (1972). "Nature and Revolution." In *Counter-revolution and Revolt*. Boston: Beacon.

—— (1974). "Marxism and Feminism." *Women's Studies*, vol. 2.

Marx, Karl (1906 reprint). *Capital*. Trans. E. Aveling. New York: Modern Library.

—— (1959 reprint). *Capi al*. Moscow: Progress Publishers.

—— (1967). "Critical Notes on 'The King of Prussia and Social Reform,'" in Loyd Easton and Kurt Guddat, eds., *Writings of the Young Marx on Philosophy and Society*. New York: Anchor.

—— (1969). "The Civil War in France." In Marx and Engels, *Selected Works*. New York: International Publishers.

—— (1973). *Grundrisse*. Baltimore: Penguin.

Marx, Karl, and Frederick Engels (1979). *The Communist Manifesto*. New York: International Publishers.

Maturana, Humberto, and Fransisco Varela (1987). *The Tree of Knowledge*. Boston: Shambhala.

McCarthy, Thomas (1981). *The Critical Theory of Jürgen Habermas*. Cambridge, Mass.: MIT Press.

McIntosh, Donald (1983). "Max Weber as a Critical Theorist." *Theory and Society*, vol. 12, no. 1.

McMurtry, John (1978). *The Structure of Marx's World-View*. Princeton: Princeton University Press.

Merchant, Carolyn (1980). *The Death of Nature: Women, Ecology, and the Scientific Revolution*. New York: Harper and Row.

Merleau-Ponty (1963). *The Structure of Behavior*. Trans. A. Fisher. Boston: Beacon.

Mesthene, Emmanuel (1970). *Technological Change*. New York: Signet.

Meyer, Alfred (1970). "Theories of Convergence." In C. Johnson, ed., *Change in Communist Systems.* Stanford: Stanford University Press.

Miller, Richard W. (1984). *Analyzing Marx: Morality, Power, and History.* Princeton: Princeton University Press.

Morris, William (1973). "Useful Work versus Useless Toil." In A. L. Norton, ed., *Political Writings of William Morris.* New York: International Publishers.

Moscovici, Serge (1968). *Essai sur l'histoire humaine de la nature.* Paris: Flammarion.

Mumford, Lewis (1964). "Authoritarian and Democratic Technics." *Technology and Culture,* vol. 5, no. 1.

Noble, David (1984). *Forces of Production.* New York: Oxford University Press.

———— (1997). "Digital Diploma Mills: The Automation of Higher Education." Posted online at http://classweb.moorhead.msus.edu/teach/noble.htm. Accessed April 2000.

O'Connor, James (1984). *The Meaning of Crisis.* Oxford: Basil Blackwell.

———— (1989). "Political Economy of Ecology of Socialism and Capitalism." *Capitalism, Nature, Socialism,* no. 3.

O'Connor, Martin (1989). "Codependency and Indeterminacy: A Critique of the Theory of Production." *Capitalism, Nature, Socialism,* no. 3.

Offe, Claus (1987). *Contradictions of the Welfare State.* Ed. J. Keane. Cambridge, Mass.: MIT Press.

Picon, Gaetan (1956). *Balzac par lui-même.* Paris: Seuil.

Pinch, Trevor, Thomas Hughes, and Wiebe Bijker (1989). *The Social Construction of Technological Systems.* Cambridge, Mass.: MIT Press.

Pinchot, Gifford, III (1985). *Intrapreneuring.* New York: Harper and Row.

Pippin, Robert (1991). *Modernism as a Philosophical Problem: On the Dissatisfactions of European High Culture.* New York: Basil Blackwell.

Plato (1952). *Gorgias.* New York: Bobbs-Merrill.

———— (1961). *Collected Dialogues.* New York: Pantheon.

Poulantzas, Nicos (1986). *Pouvoir politique et classes sociales.* Paris: Maspero.

Przeworski, Adam (1985). *Capitalism and Social Democracy.* Cambridge: Cambridge University Press.

Rajchman, John (1985). *Michel Foucault: The Freedom of Philosophy.* New York: Columbia University Press, 1985.

Rattansi, Ali (1982). *Marx and the Division of Labour.* London: Macmillan.

Rescher, Nicholas (1969). "What Is Value Change? A Framework for Research." In K. Baier and N. Rescher, eds., *Values and the Future.* New York: Free Press.

Rosanvallon, Pierre (1976). *L'age de l'autogestion.* Paris: Seuil.

Ryan, Michael (1982). *Marxism and Deconstruction: A Critical Appraisal.* Baltimore: Johns Hopkins University Press.

Rybczynski, Witold (1991). *Paper Heroes: Appropriate Technology: Panacea or Pipe Dream?* New York: Penguin.

de Saint-Just, Louis Antoine (1963). *L'esprit de la révolution.* Paris: UGE.

Schluchter, Wolfgang (1979). *The Rise of Western Rationalism: Max Weber's Developmental History.* Trans. G. Roth. Berkeley: University of California Press.

Schweickart, David (1993). *Against Capitalism.* Cambridge: Cambridge University Press.

Sen, Amartya (1976–1977). "Rational Fools: A Critique of the Behavioral Foundations of Economic Theory." *Philosophy and Public Affairs* 20, vol. 6.

Sennet, Richard (1978). *The Fall of Public Man.* New York: Vintage.

Shaiken, Harley (1984). *Work Transformed.* Lexington, Mass.: D. C. Heath.

Simondon, Gilbert (1958). *Du mode d'existence des objets techniques.* Paris: Aubier.

de Sola Pool, Ithiel, ed. (1977). *The Social Impact of the Telephone.* Cambridge, Mass.: MIT Press.

Stephens, John D. (1979). *The Transition from Capitalism to Socialism.* Urbana: University of Illinois Press.

Stiglitz, Joseph (1994). *Whither Socialism?* Cambridge, Mass.: MIT Press.

Suchman, Lucy (1987). *Plans and Situated Actions: The Problem of Human-Machine Communication.* Cambridge: Cambridge University Press.

Sweezey, Paul, and Charles Bettelheim (1971). *On the Transition to Socialism.* New York: Monthly Review Press.

Szelenyi, Ivan (1982). "The Intelligentsia in the Class Structure of State-Socialist Societies." *American Journal of Sociology,* vol. 88, supplement.

Tanizaki, Jun'Ichiro (1977). *In Praise of Shadows.* Trans. Harper and Seidensticker. New Haven, Conn.: Leete's Island Books.

Teaching at an Internet Distance: The Pedagogy of Online Teaching and Learning. The Report of a 1998–1999 University of Illinois Faculty Seminar (2000). Posted online at http://www.vpaa.uillinois.edu/tid/report/. Accessed May 2000.

Thompson, Paul (1983). *The Nature of Work.* London: Macmillan.

Tucker, Robert C., ed. (1972). *The Marx-Engels Reader.* New York: Norton.

——— (1973). "Culture, Political Culture, and Communist Society." *Political Science Quarterly,* vol. 88.

Turkle, Sherry (1984). *The Second Self.* New York: Simon and Schuster.

Ure, Andrew (1835). *The Philosophy of Manufactures.* London: Charles Knight.

Vajda, Mihaily (1981). *State and Socialism.* New York: St. Martin's.

Varela, Fransisco (1984). "The Creative Circle: Sketches on the Natural History of Circularity." In Paul Watzlawick, ed., *The Invented Reality.* New York: Norton.

Vogel, Steven (1995). *Against Nature: The Concept of Nature in Critical Theory.* Unpublished manuscript.

Vonnegut, Kurt (1967). *Player Piano.* New York: Avon.

Walker, Pat, ed. (1979). *Between Labor and Capital.* Boston: South End.

Weir, Mary (1977). "Are Computer Systems and Humanised Work Compatible?" In Richard Ottoway, ed., *Humanising the Workplace.* London: Croom Helm.

Wellmer, Albrecht (1974). *Critical Theory of Society.* Trans. J. Cumming. New York: Seabury.

Whiteside, John, and Dennis Wixon (1988). "Contextualism as a World View for the Reformation of Meetings." *CSCW 88: Proceedings of the Conference on Computer-Supported Cooperative Work.* Baltimore, Association for Computing Machinery, 1988.

Wiener, Norbert (1950). *The Human Use of Human Beings.* Boston: Houghton Mifflin.

Wilkinson, Barry (1983). *The Shopfloor Politics of New Technology.* London: Heineman Educational Books.

Wilson, Brent (1999). "Adoption of Learning Technologies: Toward New Frameworks for Understanding the Link between Design and Use." *Educational Technology,* vol. 39, no. 1.

Winner, Langdon (1977). *Autonomous Technology.* Cambridge, Mass.: MIT Press.

———— (1986). "Do Artifacts Have Politics?" In *The Whale and the Reactor.* Chicago: University of Chicago Press.

Winograd, Terry, and Fernando Flores (1987). *Understanding Computers and Cognition.* Reading, Mass.: Addison-Wesley.

Work in America: Report of Special Task Force to the Secretary of Health, Education, and Welfare (1973). Cambridge, Mass.: MIT Press.

Wright, Erik Olin (1979). *Class, Crisis, and the State.* London: Verso.

Yovits, Marshall, and Scott Cameron, eds. (1960). *Self-Organizing Systems.* Oxford: Pergamon.

Zuboff, Shoshana (1988). *In the Age of the Smart Machine.* New York: Basic.

Index

211

social role of, 40, 68, 75, 79–80
subjugated, 73, 85
Kuhn, Thomas, 68

Labor. *See also* Automation; Informating;
  Technology
  decontextualized, 178–179
  discipline, 44, 66
  division of, 42–44, 47–50, 60, 115, 153–154
  skill and, 17, 42–43, 123–124, 150–153,
    187–188
Labor process theory, 22, 41–43, 49
Latour, Bruno, 28–32, 81, 120
Lee, Rensselaer, 157
Lenin, V. I., 59, 172
Levin, Michael, xi
Liberalism, 112
Lovins, Amory, 141
Ludd, Ned, 45
Lukács, Georg, 13, 45, 112, 163–164, 166–
  167, 173, 182, 198 n. 4
Lyotard, François, 117–118
Lysenko, Trofim, 172

Machinery, 43, 45–46, 64, 98, 102, 109–110.
  See also Technology
Management, 16, 22, 93–96, 159–160, 180–
  183
Mandeville, Bernard de, 133
Mannheim, Karl, 4
Mao Tse Tung, 157
Marcuse, Herbert, 14, 33–34, 64–74, 167–
  171, 176
Margin of maneuver. *See also* Ambivalence;
  Resistance; Politics
  automation and, 96
  codes and, 100–101
  defined, 84–85
  democratization and, 92, 183
  innovation and, 92, 174
  and tactics, 85–87
Market, 24–26, 66, 162–163, 165–166. *See
  also* Bureaucracy
Marotto, Robert, xi
Marx, Karl. *See also* Education; Marxism;
  Socialism
  on alienation, 39–40, 42
  on ethics, 33, 143–144
  on interests, 145
  on rationality, 165–166
  on revolution, 54–57
  on socialism, vii, 50–52, 58–60, 134–135,
    147–148

on state, 56, 62
on technology, vii, 23–24, 45–48, 92
on the transition to socialism, 52–53, 57–
  58, 196 n. 8
on wealth, 151
Marxism. *See also* Communism; Marx,
  Karl; Socialism
  Bell on, 40–41, 51
  forces of production in, 44–45, 66–67
  labor process in, 42
  property in, 40
  technology in, 45–48
  traditional, 39–40, 47, 63, 150
  transition to socialism in, 51–54, 58–59
Materialism, 98
Maturana, Humberto, 102–105
May Events of 1968, 57, 160–161
Means and ends, 5, 53, 63, 162, 169–170.
  See also Ambivalence; Media theory;
  Neutrality
Media theory, 163
Mediation, technical, 23–24, 61, 65, 73, 86–
  88, 173
Merchant, Carolyn, 27
Microtechniques, 67–68, 71, 75
Middle strata, 159–161. *See also*
  Management
Minitel, 118–119
Modernity, 7, 11, 14, 110–112, 114, 128,
  135, 139, 162, 176
Modernization, 10–11, 135–136, 138–139
Morality. *See* Ethics
Morris, William, 140–141
Mumford, Lewis, 140–141

Nature. *See also* Holism
  conquest of, 13–14, 187
  potentialities and, 33, 163, 170, 173–174
  return to, 8, 188–189
  technique and, 179–180, 190
Need, 55, 57, 148, 184
Neo-connectionism, 101
Networking, 99–100
Neutrality. *See also* Value
  ambivalence and, 53
  as bias, 80–82, 168–169
  of knowledge, 68
  of mediations, 163
  and rationality, 66
  relative, 77–78
  of technology, v, 5–6, 82
  and values, v, 15, 81, 171
New Left, 42, 160

Rockmore, Thomas, xi
Romanticism, 164–165, 189
Russell, Bertrand, 103, 112
Russia. *See* Soviet Union

Saint-Just, Louis Antoine de, 112, 133
Schelling, F. W. J. von, 30
Science. *See also* Rationality
  class character of, 148
  holistic ontology and, 27–28, 163, 170–
    171, 174–175
  modern, 110–111
  and reification, 173
  successor, 171–174
  and technology, 139, 164, 173
Self-actualization. *See* Capacities;
  Potentiality
Self-management, 154, 158–159. *See also*
  Workers' councils
Self-organization, 55–56, 92, 102–103. *See*
  also Democracy; Self-reference
Self-reference, 102–103, 106, 111–113. *See*
  also Self-organization
Shaiken, Harley, 93
Simondon, Gilbert, 108, 186–187
Skill. *See* Labor
Slavery, 146
Socialism. *See also* Control; Education;
  Innovation; Marxism
  as civilization, 18, 134–135, 140, 147–
    150, 165–166
  critique of, 24–26
  defined, 4, 148–149
  and democracy, 52, 56, 149, 155, 159
  and nature, 14, 190
  "organizing activity" of, 55, 57, 87
  phases of, 39, 51, 59–60
  and planning, 24, 58
  possibility of, 50, 138, 140, 155
  as potentiality, 138, 145–146
  and state, 13, 56, 62
  and technology, vii, 13, 50, 143, 183–184,
    188
  transition to, 51–54, 61, 147–150
  and welfare state, 26–27
  working class and, 50
Social science, 68, 138
Society, precapitalist or traditional, 75, 177,
  183, 189–190
Soviet Union. *See also* Communism
  collapse of, vii–viii, 11–12, 60
  convergence of, 60

innovation in, 157
instrumentalism of, 11–12, 60
planning in, 25, 185
science in, 172
and state, 56, 59–60
technology in, 54
Stalin, viii, 25
State. *See also* Politics
  Marx on, 55–57, 61–62
  and socialism, 13, 61–62, 87
  welfare, 26–27
The State and Revolution, 59
Stiglitz, Joseph, 24–25
Stowe, Harriet Beecher, 146
Strategy and tactics, 16–17, 84–85, 87, 105,
  182. *See also* Operational autonomy;
  Margin of maneuver; Resistance
Structuralism, 84
Subject. *See also* Action; Interiority;
  Resistance
  finitude of, 110–112, 181
  Marx on, 54–55, 61
  of social change, 60, 63–64
  technical, 181–182
  technology studies and, 29–30
Suboptimization, 44, 94, 146–147
Substantive theory of technology. *See*
  Technology
Suchman, Lucy, 194 n. 16
System, 69–70, 186
Systematization, 178–180

Tanizaki, Jun'Ichiro, 11
Taylorism, 93–95
Technocracy, 161. *See also* Dystopia
Technology. *See also* Ambivalence;
  Concretization; Critical theory of
  technology; Democratization; Design;
  Instrumentalization; Marx, Karl;
  Neutrality; Operational autonomy;
  Science
  alternative, 141, 171
  autonomy of, 5, 14, 38–39
  bounding of, 8–13, 142–143
  and culture, 107–108, 142, 144
  imperatives of, 138–140, 195–196 n. 1
  instrumental theory of, 5–7, 63, 65
  "soft" and "hard," 141
  substantive theory of, 5, 7–9, 12–14, 74
  transfer of, 11
Techno-science, 72, 164, 174, 198 n. 5
Thomas, Paul, xi

Tönnies, Ferdinand, 135
Totality, 135, 166–167, 189–190. *See also*
  Concretization; Holism
Trade-offs
  and civilizational change, 18
  and determinism, 140
  and instrumental theory, 6
  and socialism, 142–143
  and technological design, 187
Tradition, 6–7, 11, 111, 135, 189–190
Transition to socialism. *See* Socialism
Trotsky, Leon, 58
Truth, 6, 68, 73
Tucker, Robert, 136

Underdetermination, 21
Understanding Computers and Cognition, 103
Universal, 33, 197–198 n. 3
Universality. *See also* Bias; Neutrality
  and bias, 66, 80
  of modernity, 138, 163
  of technology, 6, 11, 61
University. *See* Education
Ure, Andrew, 42, 122
Utopia, 4, 18, 96, 134, 153, 144–145, 190

Value. *See also* Code; Ideal; Technology;
  Trade-offs
  and culture, 9–10
  and fact, 18, 21, 31, 144
  freedom, 65, 68, 169
  Hegel and Marx on, 144
  ideological, 136, 139–140
  and socialism, 143, 188
  and technology, v, 64
Varela, Francisco, 103–104

Vocation, 178, 182
Voluntarism, 62, 139–140

Waterman, Robert, 123
Wealth, 134, 142, 146, 151–153
Weber, Max, 7, 60, 66, 77, 81, 133–134,
  165–167
Welfare. *See* Wealth
Wellmer, Albrecht, 47
Western Behavioral Sciences Institute, xi,
  125–127
Westernization. *See* Culture
Whitehead, Alfred North, 102
Wiener, Norbert, 110
Winner, Langdon, xi
Winograd, Terry, 104–107
Women, 29, 146
Work. *See* Labor
Workers' councils, 56–58, 87. *See also*
  Collegiality; Democratization;
  Expertise; Self-management
Working class. *See also* Automation; Class;
  Control; Labor
  interests of, 49–50, 150
  Marcuse on, 71
  Marxism and, 61, 192 nn. 3, 6
  in postindustrial society, 93–96
  and socialism, 50
  and technological design, 185
Work Transformed, 93
World, 19, 104–105
Writing and speech, 116, 124–125

Yugoslavia, vii, 197 n. 15

Zuboff, Shoshana, 94–96, 99, 106, 123